The Spanish-Americans
of New Mexico

A HERITAGE OF PRIDE

The Spanish-Americans of New Mexico

A HERITAGE OF PRIDE

Nancie L. González

Albuquerque
University of New Mexico Press

FOR

Ian and Kevin, my sons of Spanish, Anglo, and Indian descent

ACKNOWLEDGMENTS

Grateful acknowledgment is made to John Geffroy, William Harrison, and Maria Vincent, who ably assisted in the research for this book; to the many officials and citizens of the state of New Mexico who gave of their time and shared their knowledge and memories with me; and to my colleagues and students in social science who read and criticized various sections of the manuscript in its early stages and discussed untiringly many of the issues presented. Dr. Bert Zippel gave special assistance with statistical analyses and the construction of the tables in Chapter VII. I owe the development of the ideas in this book to the stimulation received through my association with all of these individuals.

The photographs were selected from the extensive and impressive collection of Professor Albert W. Vogel of the University of New Mexico, to whom grateful acknowledgment is made.

The original version of this book was prepared for the Mexican-American Study Project of the University of California, Los Angeles, of which Professor Leo Grebler is the director. I wish to express my gratitude to Professor Grebler for his guidance and encouragement.

Nancie González
Albuquerque, New Mexico

CONTENTS

Introduction ix

I Setting 5

II Language, Race, and Culture 15

III Early Settlement and Traditional Culture 33

IV Social System 58

    Kinship 59

    Community 63

    La Raza 70

    Social Class and the Legend of Cultural Differences 75

V Voluntary Associations 86

VI The Wages of Change 116

VII Effects of Urbanization 136

    Juvenile Delinquency 137

    Credit Unions 147

    Higher Education 149

    Representation in High-Status Professions 156

    Intermarriage with Anglos 165

    Changes in Religious Behavior 172

VIII The Continuing Scene: Activism in New Mexico, 1966– 1969 179

    The Alianza 180

	The Brown Berets	186
	Other Groups	189
IX	Summary and Conclusions	197
	Bibliography	215
	Index	237

MAP OF NEW MEXICO   pages 2 and 3

ILLUSTRATIONS   following page 80

TABLES

1 Membership in University of New Mexico Greek Social Clubs at Five-year Intervals, 1925–1965, by Ethnic Origin as Indicated by Surname   112

2 Frequency Distribution of Candidates for Degrees in Various Colleges of the University of New Mexico, June 1965, by Presumed Ethnic Origin, Based upon Surname   153

3 Numbers of All Persons and Those with Spanish Surnames in Selected Professions as Listed in Telephone Directories of Nine Major New Mexican Cities, 1966   159

4 Frequencies of Different Types of Ceremonies in Marriages Involving Hispanos Recorded on Mondays of Selected Years in Bernalillo County, New Mexico   167

5 Frequencies of Ethnic Endogamous and Mixed Marriages Recorded on Mondays of Selected Years in Bernalillo County, New Mexico   168

6 Frequencies of Ethnic Endogamous and Exogamous Marriages Recorded on Mondays of Selected Years in Bernalillo County, New Mexico   168

7 Comparison of Figures Concerning Intermarriage of Hispanos and Anglos at Roughly Ten-year Intervals from 1915–1964   170

INTRODUCTION

In recent years social scientists have become newly interested in the Spanish-speaking population of the United States. The 1960 *U.S. Census of Population* gives a figure of over 3.5 million persons of Spanish surname concentrated in the five southwestern states of Texas, New Mexico, Colorado, Arizona, and California alone. It has been estimated that the 1970 census will show from 9 to 10 million in the entire U.S.[1] Even though California has the largest number of persons with Spanish surnames, followed closely by Texas, the percentage of such persons in relation to the total state population is highest in New Mexico (28.3%). However, although the percentage of Americans of Spanish heritage in the other states mentioned increased during the decade 1950–1960, it declined in New Mexico. In fact, this percentage has been gradually declining in New Mexico ever since its conquest by the United States in 1846. As late as 1940, over half the population of this state was of Spanish descent.

These figures suggest that the social facts in regard to the Spanish-American population of New Mexico may be somewhat different from other areas in the United States with large-sized Spanish-surname populations. A closer look at the state confirms this impression, as will be shown in the succeeding chapters. Certainly in order to understand these facts, the history of the state must be taken into consideration, as well as the resulting rather unusual present-day cultural configuration. Native New Mexicans today, whether of Indian, Spanish, or Anglo descent, are quite properly proud of their state's unique heritage; and the stranger will soon be informed that New Mexico's Spanish-speaking population is, of course, completely different from all other Spanish-speaking groups in the United States and also distinct from that found in modern Mexico. The New Mexico-phile will be quick to point out that the local brand of Latin culture goes back directly to the original Spanish *conquistadores*. Some of the more fervent also claim that the really important Spanish-Americans are in fact direct descendants, with unbroken "pure" Spanish lineages, of these first settlers, who are usually assumed to have been purebred Spaniards. This idea, based upon some truth and much fiction, has today become part and parcel of what might be called "the New Mexico legend," which is, in turn, part of the total cultural pattern that distinguishes this state from all the others.[2]

This tendency toward romanticism is not of recent origin. New Mexico has inspired romantic and poetic responses from visitors of all backgrounds and cultures for over 400 years. Reports of the wonderful seven cities of Cibola excited the imaginations of the Spanish rulers in Spain and Mexico and led to the expeditions of Coronado, Chamuscado and Rodriguez, and Espejo between the years 1539–1583. Even though these explorers found no gold or jewels in the area, their reports—especially Espejo's report, which appears to have been greatly exaggerated— led to the conquest and settlement of the area in 1598 by Don Juan de Oñate and about five hundred followers. The Pueblo Revolt of 1680 led to widespread destruction of the settlements and forced all Spaniards in the area to retreat to the El Paso area (now Texas), but a successful reconquest was made in 1693.

Since that time the region has been continuously occupied by persons of European descent, living in close proximity to Indians of several cultural backgrounds and often intermingling socially, culturally, and racially with them.

It is perhaps due to the fact that New Mexico has retained and placed a high positive value upon the various historical cultural components that the state continues to impress many observers as being a romantic, exotic, rather mysterious and wondrous place. Epithets such as The Land of *Poco Tiempo,* The Land of Enchantment, Satan's Paradise—to name only a few of the better known—are commonplace. These refer not only to the physical topography of the state but also to the type of culture found there.

Ruth Laughlin Barker has referred to New Mexico as "a country within a country" (1931:307), a definition which may in part help to explain the reactions many have when first visiting the state. Although on the one hand New Mexico is firmly and strongly integrated with the nation as a whole, it yet presents some, often startling, differences from other areas of the United States. The facts that it was occupied by Spanish *conquistadores* before the first English settlement at Jamestown and that it did not become a part of the United States until 1846 are clearly of great importance. The stamp of Spanish culture was firmly impressed upon the land during the intervening two hundred-odd years. Such cultural items as language, foods, art motifs, religion, social institutions, and even world view are in many ways more akin to those found south of the border than to the culture derived largely from northern Europe to be found elsewhere in the United States. Indeed, John Burma has said, "New Mexico is, in many respects, an extension of Latin America into United States territory" (1954:4). Latin-American visitors to the area comment that they feel at home, and social scientists who have studied on both sides of the border recognize innumerable parallels, particularly between old Mexico and New Mexico.[3]

New Mexico is the only state in the union which may be said to be effectively bilingual. This has repercussions in the school system, advertising media, court system, entertainment world, etc. In many cities, towns, and villages, Spanish may be spoken on the streets and in other public places almost as often as English, if not more often. Spanish surnames and place names abound throughout the state; though they may frequently be mispronounced (by Spanish as well as English speakers), they are rarely misspelled and never elicit a raised eyebrow. Unfortunately, the Spanish language is not taught in the elementary years, and this has resulted in its becoming a "second-class" language, passed on only imperfectly through the oral tradition alone.

That certain other elements of Spanish culture also survive in what may seem to be unlikely places is indicated by the following brief note in the *Albuquerque Journal,* January 26, 1966:

> Santa Fe—Sen. Tibo Chavez, D.-Valencia, inquired Tuesday during a senate session what the senate rules had to say about a member eating tortillas in the chamber. He referred to Sen. Mathias Chacon, D.-Rio Arriba, who was taking a quick lunch during the discussion on senate reapportionment. Sen. W. C. Wheatley, D.-Union, president protem who was presiding, said the rules only required that eating of tortillas be done quietly.

New Mexico is also a different country in that it is relatively unknown and little understood in the eastern states. A favorite anecdote told by New Mexicans refers to the otherwise well-educated easterner who believes that hostile Indians still occasionally go on the warpath and that gunfighters commonly shoot it out on the streets of small frontier towns. Although these are, hopefully, exaggerations of the average easterner's ignorance, it is true that letters occasionally go astray because they are addressed to Mexico, instead of New Mexico, and that misconceptions do exist concerning the social, cultural, and political institutions of the state.[4] Here again, the romantic element creeps in, and it must be pointed out in all fairness that the New Mexican himself not only derives a great deal of glee from hearing such stories but actively encourages their persistence. It is also relevant that in recent years New Mexico has profited from the tourist industry, and it is obviously to the state's advantage to emphasize the cultural distinctions which it has to offer to the knowledgeable as well as to the relatively undiscriminating tourist.

The three components of the New Mexican culture and population are known locally as Indian, Spanish-American, and Anglo. The term "Indian" includes Pueblo, Navajo, and Apache —all distinct cultures—each one of which might be further subdivided on the basis of linguistic and other cultural criteria. "Spanish-American" is also a term which may subsume three somewhat different groups: the descendants of the Spanish Colonials; the Mexican-Americans, whose ancestors came more recently from Mexico; and the Mexican nationals, of whom there are relatively few at the present time. Finally, "Anglo" refers to anyone not belonging to either of the above groups and may even include European nationals and Negroes.[5] Elements of all three cultural components have been commercialized: the Indian dances, jewelry, blankets, and pottery; the sleepy little Spanish towns tucked away along the mountain streams, with their picturesque architecture and handicrafts; and the burial spot of Billy the Kid. But at the same time, there are excellent museums, archaeological sites, authentic Indian societies, Spanish-American peasant villages, and many viable and unique true art forms to interest the more serious student of culture. The institutions of higher learning in the state have long attracted musicians, writers, and other specialists interested in studying various aspects of this fascinating tri-cultural situation. The resulting literature is vast, although somewhat uneven in terms of subject covered and quality of presentation. Furthermore, much of it is in the form of unpublished theses and dissertations not readily available to the public.

The primary purpose of this book is to present an up-to-date synthetic account of the sociocultural system of the Spanish-Americans in the state of New Mexico. Historical as well as contemporary materials have been used to describe previously existing structures and to illustrate the processes of change. The background study consisted primarily of a systematic review of the existing literature dealing especially with the social, economic, and cultural characteristics of this population. Some original research of an exploratory nature was conducted concerning those topics which seemed to be lacking or under-represented in the available resources. An attempt will be made to describe this culture both as a functioning subsystem and in relation to the broader society of which it is an integral part. It is suggested that one of the important factors in explaining the persistence of Spanish (as well as Indian) culture traits and complexes in this area for so long after its conquest by an alien society has been the partial commitment of Anglos themselves to the values characteristic of these culture patterns. Another, perhaps equally important, factor has been the lack of industrial development in the state, and its consequent sparse population and continued commitment to a more rural-based economy. In a sense, it could be said that these factors permitted the persistence of the values which had served well in earlier times.

It is hoped that this study will furnish a basis and a stimulus for further research, and at the same time provide a context by means of which the New Mexican "Hispanos" may be compared with other segments of the total Spanish-speaking population of the United States. For, although the total configuration seems different in many ways, nevertheless, as will become apparent in the following chapters, there are many elements of the general situation which are comparable to those found elsewhere.

Notes

[1] H. Gallegos, director of the Southwest Council of La Raza, *Albuquerque Journal,* October 1, 1968. Barrett and Samora (1963:20) estimate that the population has been under-enumerated by about 10% because many do not have Spanish surnames yet identify themselves historically and culturally with the population.

[2] Edmonson (1957:16) has also written of what he calls "the social myth of the 'Spanish heritage.'"

[3] Burma (1954:4); De Anis (1942:73); Marden and Meyer (1962:140).

[4] A recent incident will illustrate this point. An Albuquerque matron wrote to the Scott Paper Company in Philadelphia requesting information about their new paper dresses. The company regretfully informed her that certain regulations prevented them from exporting this product to foreign countries. This exchange was reported in the local newspapers and caused quite a stir among residents, many of whom banded together to send letters of protest to the paper company, eliciting from them an immediate, embarrassed apology. (See *Albuquerque Tribune,* November 10, 14, 1966.)

[5] The total Negro population of New Mexico has always been rather small, and it has been only recently that members of this group have been noticeable as a minority faction. Occasionally Negroes will be lumped with Anglos as opposed to those of Spanish heritage in a somewhat joking fashion.

*The Spanish-Americans
of New Mexico*

A HERITAGE OF PRIDE

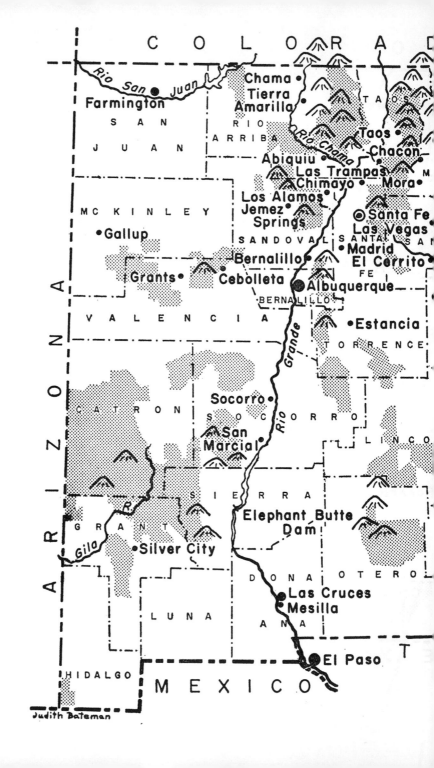

COLORADO

Rio San Juan

Farmington

SAN

JUAN

MCKINLEY

RIO
ARRIBA

Chama
Tierra
Amarilla

TAOS

Rio Chama

Taos
Chacon

Abiquiu
Las Trampas
Chimayo
Mora

Los Alamos
Jemez
Springs

Gallup

SANDOVAL

SANTA FE

Santa Fe
Las Vegas

Bernalillo
Cebolleta

Grants

VALENCIA

BERNALILLO

Madrid
El Cerrito

Albuquerque

Estancia

TORRENCE

ARIZONA

CATRON

SOCORRO

Socorro

San
Marcial

Rio
Grande

LINCO

SIERRA

Elephant Butte
Dam

GRANT

Gila R.

Silver City

OTERO

DONA

Las Cruces
Mesilla

LUNA

ANA

El Paso

HIDALGO

MEXICO

T

Judith Bateman

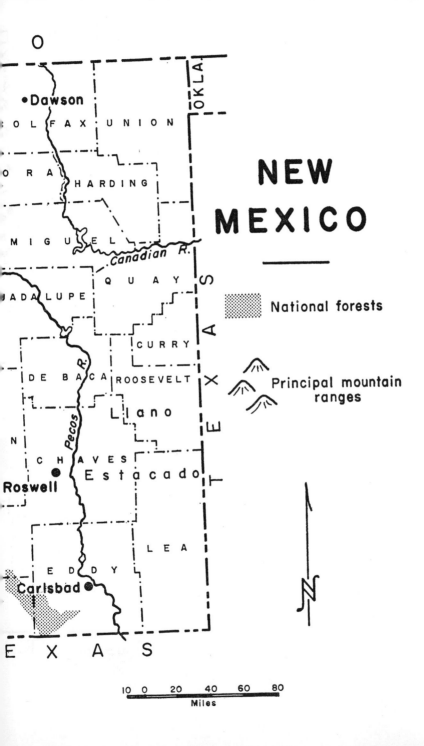

Chapter I

SETTING

From the vast sweeps of the White Sands in the southern central area, to the lofty reaches of the Sangre de Cristo range in the north, New Mexico presents a varied and often spectacular landscape, the particular features of which have played an important part in the history of the state. For the early Spaniards the southern desert regions, including the famed *Jornada del Muerto* (Journey of Death), were not highly attractive and were to be passed by as quickly as possible in the trek toward the more fertile mountain river valleys. The valley of the Rio Grande provided a natural highway and is still the route of U.S. 85 from El Paso, Texas, to Bernalillo, just north of Albuquerque.

In 1598 the earliest settlement, at San Juan, was close to the junction of the Rio Grande and the Rio Chama. Although it seems evident that the explorers before Oñate were looking primarily for mineral riches and not for agricultural land, nevertheless, by the time of Oñate's arrival in 1598 it was clear that, in order to survive, agricultural settlements must be made. The majority of persons in Oñate's company were brought for just that purpose. Unlike the Indians in the Valley of Mexico, the

Indians of New Mexico were sufficient neither in number nor productivity to support a nonagricultural Spanish population. Castañeda, reporting on the Coronado expedition of 1540–1542, stated:

> Granted that they did not find the riches of which they had been told, they found a place in which to search for them and the beginning of a good country to settle in, so as to go on further from there (Castañeda 1904:xxxiii).

The northern mountain valleys also provided the Spaniards a haven relatively safe from the depredations of the marauding non-Pueblo Indians, especially the Navajo, Apache, Ute, and Comanche on the east and west. During the seventeenth and eighteenth centuries the Spaniards gradually extended their settlements northward throughout a delta-shaped area with its apex at about Sante Fe. From that point the settlements spread out fanlike along the Chama to the northwest and along the Rio Grande to the northeast, as well as along the smaller tributary streams within this general area, and northward into the San Luis Valley of Colorado. During this period settlements like beads on a chain also were made southward along the Rio Grande to about Belen.[1]

Not until well into the nineteenth century were settlements regularly made outside this area; the Estancia Valley was settled in the 1820's, Socorro in 1816, Las Vegas and Mora in 1835, the Mesilla Valley in the 1840's, and Atrisco not until 1880. There are several factors to be taken into account in explaining these settlement patterns and policies. In the earliest days the small population, plus the lack of knowledge on the part of the Spaniards concerning the best agricultural techniques to be used in the area, kept the settlements close to the relatively docile Pueblos. A rather symbiotic relationship seems to have developed between these two groups, and there are several instances in which the Spanish simply relocated an entire Indian group, taking over the Pueblo buildings and irrigated lands for themselves. In other cases the Spanish hired or captured and enslaved Indians to work their lands for them, and many Indians apparently defected from their Pueblos to cast their lot permanently with the Spaniards, often intermarrying with them.[2]

However, in the succeeding years, as the population was swelled through natural increase, further immigration from Mexico and Spain, and amalgamation with Pueblo and other Indians, it became both possible and necessary for the Spanish to extend their settlements to spots previously considered dangerous. According to Bancroft (1889:279), the number of Spanish more than doubled between 1770–1790.[3] Furthermore, increasing dependence upon sheepherding caused them to range farther in search of pasturage. At this point the Spaniards began to exploit the second major ecological area in New Mexico. Knowlton (1961:450) points out that by the middle of the nineteenth century Spanish-American settlements had spread deep into the plains area. Buffalo hunting on the so-called Staked Plains (*Llano Estacado*) had been engaged in seasonally by the Spanish as well as the Indians for some time before actual settlements were made, thus the area was not entirely unknown. According to E. Fergusson (1940:330):

> New Mexico sheepmen used to drive their flocks into the Llano Estacado, leaving the mountains in January, drifting down the Canadian and out onto the plains for the lambing and back again for the fall shearing.

After 1800, penetration of the grasslands occurred not only in the north, east of Las Vegas, but southward into Lincoln County as well. It appears that grazing land for their sheep was the

most important element drawing the Spanish into this area. By
the early nineteenth century, sheep were one of the chief exports
of the province (Zeleny 1944:65). But the development of trade
along the Sante Fe Trail was also a stimulant. Thus, a small
town known as La Plaza de Missouri, 17 miles west of Roswell
on the Hondo River, was founded around 1850 by Spanish-
Americans engaged in freighting goods to and from Kansas City
and St. Joseph (Shinkle 1964:277). There is also evidence that,
during the nineteenth century, Spanish settlers from the San
Luis Valley in Colorado moved southward into the plains of
what is now Union County, presumably because of population
pressure in the valley (Rendon 1953:99).

However, this Spanish foothold in the plains did not last long,
for increasing immigration of Anglos from the east—particularly
from Texas and Oklahoma—gradually pushed the Spanish back
to the Rio Grande and the northern counties from which they
had come. The newcomers were engaged primarily in dry
farming or cattle raising, or both, and the economic as well as
the ethnic conflict between the two groups was one of the factors
in the famous Lincoln County wars of 1869–1881 (Keleher 1957;
Shinkle 1964). At present, the entire eastern plains region of the
state is heavily dominated by Anglos and is often referred to as
Little Texas.

It was not until the latter part of the Mexican period, which
extended from 1821 to 1846, that the more southern areas of
New Mexico were extensively populated. Most of the Spanish-
speaking population there today are more recent immigrants
from Mexico or descendants of those who came after 1910. They
now work primarily as laborers in the large farming enterprises
of the Mesilla Valley or in mining activities around Silver City.
The discovery and refining of oil in southeastern New Mexico
have also attracted large numbers of Spanish-speaking laborers—

again primarily from Mexico rather than from the northern counties of the state.

It is somewhat ironic that the Spaniards, whose thirst for gold and other mineral riches was so great, were never to profit extensively from mining activities in what is now New Mexico. In fact, little is known about the part that mining played in Spanish colonial economy, although it has been reported that over $3 million in gold had been extracted by the Spaniards from the northern areas by the time of the U.S. conquest (Twitchell 1914, Vol. II:180). Copper mining was also carried on by the Spaniards, especially in the southwestern part of the state near Santa Rita, beginning about 1804 (Meaders 1958). But the greatest mineral wealth in New Mexico remained undiscovered or unexploited until after 1850. At the present time copper, zinc, lead, potash, uranium, molybdenum, coal, petroleum, and natural gas extraction contributes heavily to the state's gross product and total economy (LaLonde 1966). These industries are overwhelmingly Anglo enterprises, although the coal, oil, and natural gas production in the northwestern San Juan Basin has been of benefit to the Navajo Tribe, which has leased large tracts of land for mining activities (Cocklin and Geiger 1965).

The Spanish-American and Mexican population of New Mexico has traditionally been dependent upon agricultural and livestock enterprises, and this remains true for many today in spite of the fact that this population is becoming increasingly urbanized. However, it is also clear that these activities have not been sufficient to support this population for at least the past one hundred years. The story of the American conquest and occupation has often been told in terms of the rape of the land and natural resources and the consequent decline in the fortunes of the Spanish-American residents. However, it has been suggested that the northern area was already suffering from overpopulation and overuse of the available resources at the time of the American entrance during, roughly, the middle of the nineteenth century (U.S. Dept. of Agriculture 1937f:4; Holmes 1964:41; Zeleny 1944:191). Certainly, the increase in population, the land-grabs which deprived the Spanish villages of much of their grazing lands, the initiation of even more intensive livestock operations by Anglos, and the cutting of timber in the mountains on a large scale further aggravated a perhaps already serious situation.[4] On the other hand, the *gringos,* with their capital and enthusiastic plans for the development of the Southwest, opened up new areas and industries which provided wage-paying employment on a part-time basis for many Spanish-American farmers who were beginning to find that their native economy was no longer productive enough to satisfy their needs.

Railroad building in New Mexico between 1879 and 1882 not only gave employment to large numbers of Spanish but also stimulated coal mining and commerce, which in turn provided more employment for these people. In the early days the majority of such workers retained their village ties and their dependence upon the land, however unproductive. It has only been since about 1940 that a great exodus from the rural areas has been evident. But even now, many urban Spanish-Americans own a small parcel of land and a house site in some rural village; the land is often left undeveloped and is visited only occasionally, on vacations or weekends. Many retain a sentimental attachment to the land, but even this is rapidly declining as a new way of life becomes both more profitable and more enjoyable.

At the same time that the older style, small-sized, irrigated farm in the northern area has declined, other types of agricultural pursuits have developed. The eastern grasslands have been successfully dry-farmed, mostly by Anglos arriving after 1900. But cattle ranches have been of equal or greater importance in this same area. Maloney has pointed out that San Miguel and Guadalupe counties have relatively high proportions of large farms (over 1,000 acres), most of which are cattle ranches (1964:13). These large farms have developed over the past one hundred years largely through consolidation of smaller farms on the part of both Anglo and Spanish-American settlers in the area. Other areas in which agriculture is presently of importance were all relatively undeveloped at the time of the United States conquest. These include the northwestern San Juan Valley around Farmington and the southern Mesilla Valley. The first of these areas is largely owned and operated by Anglos, and the latter by both Anglos and descendants of more recent Mexican immigrants.

The Mesilla Valley was first occupied by Mexicans during the period from about 1830 to 1846, but agriculture on a really large scale was not feasible until the building of the Elephant Butte Reservoir, completed in 1915, and the Caballo Dam, which provides for the present-day irrigation of the valley. Large numbers of Mexican farm laborers came into the area between the years 1910–1930, and their descendants remain there today. By far the greatest proportion of the Spanish-speaking population of the area derives from this immigration (Johansen 1948:29).

The most recent new use of land in New Mexico has come with the development of defense projects around Alamogordo and White Sands in the south and around Albuquerque and Los Alamos in the north. The areas in the south were largely uninhabited; and although there were many small Spanish-American villages in the vicinity of Los Alamos, the population density was not great. Even Albuquerque was a relatively small city before the advent of the defense projects. These enterprises have been important in providing wage-paying jobs for Spanish-

Americans and at the same time have increased the immigration of Anglos to the state (Scotford 1953:21).[5]

Today New Mexico includes some of both the most sparsely inhabited and the most densely populated rural territory to be found in the United States. Heavy concentrations of people remain in the Rio Grande Valley and in the valleys of the other permanent streams and intermountain basins where water is available. One writer says:

> Even today, the northern Hispanic uplands are still substantially the most densely populated of any of the major divisions of New Mexico, the place-names here are three times more frequent than the State average, and the cultural imprint of this early settlement phase is unmistakable (Van Dresser 1964:55).

The *Llano Estacado* and the plains of the Pecos River are also heavily populated (Winnie 1955:11).

The northern Rio Grande Valley centers on Albuquerque, a metropolitan area of about 325,000 inhabitants. The valley, including the Espanola Valley, had an estimated total population of about 405,000 in 1965 (Gordon and McConville 1965:4). Yet the majority of its inhabitants have little direct dependence upon the land. Albuquerque is now an industrial city in its own right and is probably the largest city—at least in the United States—which lives on the atomic energy industry (Hamilton 1957–58:323). The population of the city, which has long been the largest in the state, was 10,000 in 1908 and still only 43,000 in 1938 (Linder 1939:34). Gordon and McConville (1965:4) have pointed out that, in addition to the heavy federal government involvement in defense research, Albuquerque owes its large size and sustained growth rate to a combination of factors including (1) a large supply of good ground water; (2) a favorable transcontinental transportation focus; (3) a heavy tourist trade; (4)

a number of institutions of higher learning; and (5) a climate and a natural and cultural environment aesthetically pleasing to many immigrants.

But with all these favorable characteristics, Albuquerque still owes its present large size to developments occurring during and after World War II. Rapid urbanization has taken place only in the last two decades. The small Spanish agricultural villages have lost people to the thirty or so towns in the state, and the majority of newcomers has also moved into the urban centers. "New Mexico's development," says Hamilton, "is part of a larger development and . . . the state is by no means the sole arbiter of its economic destiny" (1957:325). The 1960 economic activity in the uplands area alone was estimated at $70 or $80 million, of which $30 million was funneled from outside the state. A little less than $15 million represented government net payments, either in the form of welfare subsidies or wages for government employees (Van Dresser 1964:59). The next largest component was the livestock and farming industries, which together yielded a census record value of about $17 million; tourism brought in about $16 million; forest products about $7 million; miscellaneous manufacturing, $8 million; and mining, about $2 million (*ibid.*).

But the primary concern here is with people—and most especially with that group labeled the "forgotten people" by George Sanchez in 1940. No longer forgotten, it is time to trace the effects of conquest, domination by a foreign culture, modernization, and, finally, industrialization upon this group and its Spanish heritage. In a sense it can be said that whatever the fate of individuals, either in the past or in the future, a permanent niche has been carved into the cultural pattern of the Southwest to accommodate a tradition which will not soon be forgotten. The maintenance of this tradition, despite all, is one of the most significant differences between New Mexico and the other states in which the Spanish-speaking reside today in large numbers.

Notes

[1] See Culbert (1943) for maps showing the distribution of the Spanish population in New Mexico in 1744 and 1940. Ramsay (1951) gives this distribution for 1950, which to the author's knowledge is the latest such synthesis.

[2] Defections from the Pueblos cannot be documented statistically, but some writers have described these as case studies. *Cf.* Aitkin (1930:363) and especially Dozier (1961:122ff. and 144); and Dozier (1966:184). Dozier has also stated, "Spanish sources apparently lumped these Pueblo defectors together with the 'Genizaros,' i.e., more properly, ransomed Indians from nomadic tribes. Apparently the population of these Indian displaced persons was large up to the middle of the 19th century" (personal communication).

[3] This phenomenal increase in the Spanish population is difficult to understand unless one admits the possibility or probability that increasing numbers of Indians and mestizos were being counted as Spaniards (see note 2). Zeleny, however, assumes this increase to have been the result of immigration alone (1944:27). Probably both factors were of some importance. See also Sifuentes (1940:27).

[4] For a detailed analysis of the effects of the new Anglo settlement on the already precarious ecological balance in the state, see Harper, Cordova, and Oberg (1943).

[5] For a recent, clear account of the state's dependence upon defense-related activities, see Hawkins (1966); Walker (1966).

Chapter II

LANGUAGE, RACE, AND CULTURE

Although the main concern in this book is with the Spanish-speaking population of New Mexico, it is necessary to describe these people not only in terms of themselves but in relation to other population components. That is, in order to understand this group, the characteristics which set it off from other groups in the state and which make it culturally and socially visible must first be identified.

The people in this group are sometimes designated as Spanish-speaking, and for the sake of convenience the term has been retained in this study. But it should be noted that while this term not only covers a large variety of linguistic behavioral patterns, it also fails to characterize a large number of Spanish-Americans in New Mexico today who no longer speak Spanish with any fluency. Some of these, in addition to speaking English, have retained a kind of Spanish-English mixture which may be used only for communication with fellow New Mexicans of similar background. Others, speaking perfect English, have completely forsaken the tongue of their ancestors. A few, usually among the more educated intellectual class, have made a point of learning to speak both English and Spanish well, but they are, unfortunately, rare. In the rural villages, as well as in the lower-class areas of the larger cities, there are persons who speak a relatively pure form of Spanish (sometimes termed "archaic") and who get along with difficulty in English. This last group, once typical of most Spanish-Americans in the area, is today rapidly diminishing.[1]

It has been estimated by various persons that the majority of the members of this population still learns English as a second language (Edmonson 1957:25; Johansen 1941a:58; Manuel 1965:187; Oppenheimer 1957:61). In Albuquerque a special linguistics program was introduced in 1966 into one elementary school in a lower-income, largely Spanish-American neighborhood. This program, based on one used in Miami for Cuban refugee children, was designed not only to teach English but to help overcome pronunciation habits which produce an accent in speaking English. Many Spanish-American leaders recognize that in order for individuals to raise their socioeconomic level they must speak English well. As long ago as 1932, Senator Dennis Chavez of New Mexico said:

> English is the language the native must employ in getting a job and in keeping it. I love Spanish traditions, I love the people and the ancestors I hail from, and no one is prouder of his background, but I am prouder still of the ideals and traditions symbolized by the Stars and Stripes, so without apologizing for the past, I insist that in New Mexico the teaching of English should be stressed (quoted in Lahart 1958:71).

It has been generally agreed that the education of the Spanish-American population as a whole has been inadequate. The reasons for this are many—Samora mentions only a few when he says:

> In brief, the available literature and other sources suggest that such factors as inferior facilities and teachers, inadequate counseling,

lack of encouragement from the staff, and differing curriculums have resulted in inferior education for this population, or, in many instances, a very low educational achievement (1963:149).

Other observers have pointed to the effects of malnutrition, unequal distribution of school funds which results in poorer schools in the Spanish-American areas (Knowlton 1961:26), embarrassment because of poorer clothing (Sjoberg 1947:2), and a generally low socioeconomic status which gives few background opportunities and little motivation to the Spanish-speaking student (Barrett and Samora 1963:13; Manuel 1965:187; Samora 1963:145,149; Tireman 1930:624). Many of these factors are, of course, interrelated and have the same causes.

Lack of ability in the English language has been seen as both a cause and a reflection of this disadvantaged background, and thus, of poor performance in school (Barela 1936:17; Loar 1964:56; among others). Burma reports, "According to Albuquerque teachers, 'lack of speaking knowledge of English on entering school' and 'failure to read English with comprehension' were the two most important factors in the retardation of Spanish-American children" (1949:136). In earlier years, one way of trying to overcome the problems inherent in this situation was to teach in Spanish. In 1876 it was reported, "Education is making slow headway. Until 1871 there were no public schools in the Territory, but there are now no less than 133 with 5625 pupils. In twelve schools both English and Spanish are taught, in ten English only, and in 111 Spanish only . . ." (Rideling 1876:19). And as late as 1928 Bohannan stated, "The teachers in these public schools are Spanish-Americans and practically all of the instruction in the schools is carried on in the Spanish language" (1928:2). It is not uncommon even today to find persons in the northern villages who remember only Spanish having been used in their own primary education during the early 1930's.

The trend has been clearly in the direction of more English and less Spanish for some time. In 1915 the first jury trial without an interpreter was held at the district court in Socorro, ". . . making a historical landmark and veritable epoch in New Mexico history" (*Albuquerque Journal,* "50 Years Ago," Oct. 12, 1965). But the emphasis on learning English has had the effect of wiping out the Spanish language altogether in those families in which the young children are spoken to only in English—much to the distress of their Spanish-speaking grandparents with whom they are sometimes totally unable to communicate.[2]

Yet it remains true that the Spanish language, however poorly spoken and however divergent from other forms of modern Spanish, is still the primary symbol of the cultural dichotomy between Anglos and those of Spanish and/or Mexican heritage. It is undoubtedly important as a factor in maintaining the well-known solidarity and cohesiveness of the Spanish in-group. Many persons, perfectly able to speak English, prefer to speak Spanish when with other bilingual persons. The ups and downs of the Spanish-language press are interesting in this regard. In 1920 there were 108 newspapers and secular periodicals published in Spanish in the United States. Thirty of these were published in New York, twenty-two each in New Mexico and Texas, and less than ten in any other state (Stowell 1920:76–77). In 1931 there were nine weekly newspapers and one illustrated monthly magazine published in Spanish in New Mexico (Barker 1931:94). After this date the record becomes sketchy, but it appears that one by one these newspapers either ceased publication, started using English as a medium, or joined forces with other papers. Thus, the *Bandera Americana* expired in 1938, *El Independiente* ceased publication in Spanish in 1947, and *El Nuevo Mexicano* became consolidated with the Santa Fe newspaper, *The New Mexican,* in 1958. *The New Mexican* carried an announcement in the form of a news item on May 4, 1958, which said:

> Signalling the effective integration of New Mexico's Spanish-American and Anglo-American populations through the amalgam of the English language, EL NUEVO MEXICANO will be consolidated with THE SUNDAY NEW MEXICAN May 4, 1958. . . . Now, in 1958, with the older members of the households of "los gente" [*sic*] usually proficient both in English and Spanish, but with the younger generation able only to read English, there have been "majority movements" in most homes for the family to take an English rather than a Spanish newspaper.

Interviews during 1965 with the managers of three newsstands in Albuquerque who handled Spanish-language newspapers and magazines printed in Mexico or other parts of Latin America indicated that few of these papers and magazines are purchased by local Spanish-Americans. The managers stated that most such publications were of interest primarily to students at the University of New Mexico or to Mexican citizens visiting or newly arrived in Albuquerque.

However, in June, 1966, a weekly newspaper entitled *El Hispano* began operations in Albuquerque. This is to this writer's knowledge the first locally published Spanish-language newspaper to appear in New Mexico since 1958. *El Hispano* is printed in what its editors claim is "universal Spanish," and it includes a section designed to teach New Mexicans how to correct local usage so as to conform to the Spanish spoken elsewhere today. At its inception, there was some discussion in its pages about using "local Spanish" as the medium of expression, but this idea later disappeared in favor of the "universal Spanish." The paper covers local news of interest to Spanish-Americans, as well as digests of national and international news. The editors—a Puerto

Rican, a Cuban, and a Spaniard—regard this paper as filling a need for a medium of written communication among the local Spanish-Americans.

Many educators have pointed up the difficulties experienced by the child who enters school without sufficient knowledge of the language of instruction. This problem is not limited to New Mexico but is found in many countries about the world today where minority ethnic groups are being brought into the orbit of industrial civilization in the process of development. Many of the problems encountered are very similar. In all cases, there is a tendency for the children who lack familiarity with the formal language of instruction to do poorly in school, lose their motivation, drop out, and forfeit the opportunity to raise their standards of living by means of a superior education. It must be remembered, of course, that in all cases this is not necessarily disastrous for such children. If their own rural community is thriving, if there are few jobs available in cities, if there is no perceived advantage to be gained by becoming educated, then the problem is not so crucial and the nation can afford to put it aside temporarily for more pressing problems.

In New Mexico the Spanish-speaking—especially those in the rural villages of the north—have not always felt the need for extensive formal education. It has only been since about 1930 that the great rural-to-urban movement has become of major importance in New Mexico, and the greatest change has come since 1946. Before that time, the bulk of the rural population remained all their lives in their own villages—leaving for a part of the year to do wagework, perhaps, but even then moving almost exclusively among other Spanish-speaking persons. A minimum of English was necessary and only the basic skills in reading and writing.

Before 1930, most of the children in northern rural New Mexico were being taught in Spanish in spite of the fact that the state law required the use of English as the basis of instruction. During the 1930's, Senator Chavez and others began to raise an outcry, demanding that the Spanish-speaking be taught exclusively in English so that they might be prepared to compete with Anglos on common ground. Many contemporary young adults of Spanish ancestry grew up during this period, and many of them today feel they owe their success in the business or educational worlds to the fact that their parents forced them to learn English well. Many of these same people feel that their experience was more difficult than it need have been; consequently, they have resisted teaching their own children any Spanish at all. But for each child who succeeded in overcoming the barriers, there were unknown numbers who fell by the wayside and grew up without the necessary skills for making a living in today's world.

It is clear that the trend toward the city and away from the farm is continuing in New Mexico as elsewhere and that a good knowledge of English is necessary not only in and of itself but also as a tool for learning professional skills and securing good employment. But at the same time, many people, both Hispanos and Anglos, are disturbed by the present situation. Not only does the Spanish-American child miss a great deal of his heritage and learn more slowly when he is taught in a foreign language, but a large part of the population is forfeiting potential skills when they are denied the opportunity to become educated bilingually.

It has been shown by studies carried out among bilingual children in Wisconsin (Polish-Americans) and in Canada among French-Canadians that the performance of such children in school is often superior to that of the monolingual child. However, this bilingualism presupposes skill and fluency in two languages.

In the United States today, bilingualism can be a positive advantage in many ways. Jobs for persons fluent in two languages are open with the State Department and other government agencies, in businesses with branches in foreign countries, in teaching in foreign countries, as interpreters for the United Nations and for international meetings of professional groups, and in a variety of other areas.

In addition, the value of bilingualism is apparent to anyone who has traveled for either pleasure or business. Not only is one's physical comfort increased, but his status in the eyes of his hosts is raised when he is able to communicate with them in their own language. The days are long past when North Americans can isolate themselves, linguistically or otherwise, from the rest of the world. It has not only become politically and economically necessary to "include ourselves in" as a people, but it is also becoming fashionable to do so on an individual level. Persons who speak a foreign language gain in social prestige and may be called upon in their communities to undertake responsibilities and hold positions of honor.

The citizens of New Mexico—both those whose native tongue is Spanish and those from English-speaking homes—would do well to consider ways and means of developing their human resources to the highest extent possible; that is, by offering all of the state's young citizens the opportunity to become bilingual. This would contribute to the increased development of the state as a whole and would give those who go forth to other states and other lands a significant advantage in the world of tomorrow which, to an increasing extent, stresses internationalism.

Another way in which members of this minority group are often identified is on the basis of having a surname of Spanish derivation.[3] There are several sources of possible error in using this criterion, most of which have been noted by previous writers (Heller 1966; Winnie 1960). First of all, there are, of course, many persons with Spanish surnames who are not of Spanish-

American or even of Mexican heritage. Taking the United States as a whole, large numbers of Puerto Ricans (mainly concentrated in New York), Filipinos in the western states, American Indians in Arizona and New Mexico; some students and others from Latin America; and finally, the recent large influx of Cubans (concentrated primarily in Miami), all of whom often have Spanish surnames. It has been found, however, that in the five southwestern states (Texas, New Mexico, Colorado, Arizona, California) studied in the Mexican-American Project, and most especially in New Mexico, both the total number and the percentage of persons in most of these other categories are not of great significance.[4] The figures given in the 1960 U.S. census report refer only to the five southwestern states, of course, and thus eliminated many of the above groups.

The total number of persons with Spanish surnames can be further reduced and made more specific for our purposes by applying two other criteria used in the census—place of birth and the label "non-white." The majority of the foreign born with Spanish surnames in New Mexico are from Mexico. The United States census listed 10,613 total foreign born with Spanish surnames in the state in 1960. In October 1965 there was a total of 12,238 Mexican nationals in the state.[5] Only 994 of these were in Bernalillo County, the remainder being located primarily in the southern areas of the state. The proportion of foreign-born persons in the total population of New Mexico has never been very high, and the largest portion of this group has always been from Mexico. From 1880 to 1920 the proportion was about 7%, after which it declined rapidly until by 1940 less than 3% of the state's total population was foreign born (Greer 1942:284–286). This rose again to 4.2% in 1950 and dropped to 3.9% in 1960. For several decades now, the great majority of this group has been concentrated in the mining areas around Silver City and Gallup and in the cotton-growing areas near Carlsbad and Las Cruces (Leonard 1943:31; Walter 1947:15).

In addition to those born outside the United States, the census also enumerates those born here but of foreign or mixed parentage. In 1960 in New Mexico, there were 31,732 persons of Mexican extraction alone. This shows that many of those who immigrated in preceding years stayed on to contribute to the present-day Spanish-surname population. However, it should be pointed out that in earlier years many of the immigrants from Mexico stayed in the state only a short time, so that the 7% noted previously should be interpreted with caution. Broadbent (1941:24) notes:

> Thus in the period following the first World War, the Southwest besides being the chief area for Mexican settlement in the United States became gateway and temporary stopping place for increasing numbers of Mexicans who moved on into the northwestern United States. The migrations of Mexicans within the Southwest tended gradually to become a migration through the Southwest into the industrial East and northern great plains. As the centers of Mexican population in the Southwest had served as a recruiting point for labor in other parts of this one area, in like manner the Southwestern states became a reservoir of Mexican labor migrating to the rest of the nation.

Another problem involved in using the criterion of Spanish surnames to identify the population being studied is that it fails to include some individuals who are culturally and socially part of this group. In New Mexico there are some families who acquired a non-Spanish surname through intermarriage with Anglo males in the early days of the United States occupation. After the Civil War many young men from both the north and the south elected to remain in the territory of New Mexico where they had served and fought. Many of these also married into

Spanish families. The children of such unions were usually brought up in a purely Spanish atmosphere and, except for their surnames, adopted little from the culture of their Anglo fathers. Intermarriage has continued to occur—has even increased in recent years—and the pattern is still predominantly that of Spanish females marrying Anglo males (see Chapter VIII). In a study conducted as part of the research for this book, it was found that the percentage of mixed marriages in Bernalillo County increased from 4.6% in 1930 to 11.0% in 1964. Three-fifths of the mixed marriages involved Spanish women and Anglo men. However, it seems likely that the offspring of most of these modern marriages are brought up as Anglos rather than as members of the minority group. Many of the marriages which have occurred since World War II involve servicemen temporarily stationed in the state. After their tours of duty are terminated, most of these leave for other parts of the nation, taking their Spanish-speaking wives with them.

Heller (1966:6) mentions Anglicization of names as another process which might eliminate persons who otherwise would be included in the Spanish-speaking group. Interestingly enough, the author found little evidence of this in New Mexico, in spite of persistent questioning of informants. Only two cases came to the author's attention, and there are more instances than this on record in which non-Spanish names have been Hispanicized (Swadesh 1964a). The general feeling among informants was that if individuals or families felt strongly enough to change their names, then they probably were so completely acculturated as to be otherwise invisible among the masses of Anglos.

The matter of race identification is of some interest, for even though it is often stated in terms of color (as in the designations "nonwhite" and "white"), it is clear from various contexts that ethnicity or culture is in fact the crucial variable. Thus, in the census of 1930 enumerators were instructed to classify as Mexican all persons of Mexican origin who were not definitely white, Negro, Indian, or Japanese. This had the effect, in New Mexico especially, of eliminating from this class the bulk of the population of Spanish Colonial descent, most of whom consider themselves to be white Americans of Spanish, not Mexican, ancestry. More objectively, the Bureau of the Census also recognized in 1960 that "Ethnically, the population of Spanish-American and Mexican descent ranges from Indians to those of unmixed Spanish ancestry, with many persons being of Spanish-Indian ancestry." [6] The category of "white persons of Spanish surname" in the 1960 census, then, appears to include only those individuals who are clearly not Indian on the basis of their culture and self-identification, regardless of their physical features and color. It is well known, of course, that many Indians, especially in the Pueblos, have Spanish surnames and also speak Spanish as their second language.

The distinction between Spanish and Indian has apparently been something of a problem to census takers ever since Spanish Colonial days. Not only did many from the Pueblos defect to the Spanish way of life, but many of the Plains Indians became Christianized and settled down into village life. The towns of Abiquiu, Belen, and Tome have the reputation of having been founded by so-called *Genizaros*—i.e., Hispanicized Indians (Bancroft 1889:280; Chavez 1954:xiv). In addition to the out-and-out defections, there were many cases of intermarriage; the offspring of such unions were sometimes raised as Spaniards and sometimes as Indians. Some of these unions resulted from the capture and enslavement of women by both groups. In spite of overwhelming evidence to the contrary, there is still current among some social circles in New Mexico the myth that the Spanish-Americans of this state, as contrasted to the Mexican-Americans elsewhere, are Caucasians of relatively unmixed strain (Edmonson 1947:16; Zeleny 1944:335). Nevertheless, virtually all scholarly sources agree that the great majority are at least mestizo, while Johansen (1941b:150) goes so far as to say, "It is necessary to recognize that the Spanish-Americans of New Mexico are predominantly of Indian ancestry." Walter also labels them ". . . mostly mestizo, with Indian blood predominant" (1952:326). He further suggests that this admixture gives them a social visibility sufficient to set them apart as a distinct racial group.[7] A recently organized association which exhibits many of the characteristics of a genuine nativistic movement has proclaimed and glorified the mestization process which has produced today's "native" New Mexican. These people disclaim membership in either the Indian or the Spanish categories, pointing to the Laws of the Indies which legitimized the offspring of unions between the two races.[8] They prefer the term "Indo-Hispano," which reflects the two original cultures and symbolizes their union. Indians in New Mexico, on the other hand, generally do not associate themselves with either this group or its ideology. But it is patent that in any particular case, the distinction between Indian and Hispano may be difficult or impossible to make. Thus, individuals have been known to claim Spanish ancestry when dealing with other persons they believe to be of Spanish descent, and Indian when with members of that group.

In the final analysis, as is frequently the case in other parts of the world,[9] racial classification for social purposes is most often made on the basis of cultural characteristics. Even though the two groups borrowed freely from each other's cultural inventory in the early days of Spanish conquest and, therefore, share a number of culture traits and complexes today, the differences are considerable. Furthermore, the Indian has enjoyed (or suffered from?) the protection of the United States government in a fashion never granted to (or inflicted upon) the Spanish-speaking population since the time of their conquest. This controlled status has also served as a symbol of the opposition between the two groups. Sources differ on the amount and kind of hostility between Indian and Hispano today, but there appears to be little love lost between them.[10] Self-identification based on participation in one or the other sociocultural system is probably the best means of distinguishing individuals. Indeed, as Indians continue to become acculturated and urbanized, many of them will probably pass over into the ranks of those called Spanish-Americans in New Mexico (Walter 1947:16).

The most striking and important characteristics which separate the Indian culture from the Hispano today are those which have to do with the maintenance of an Indian dialect, certain religious beliefs and ceremonies, peculiar kinship structures, and various art forms, including both music and the plastic and graphic arts.

On the other hand, both groups share a fairly similar diet based largely upon wheat, corn, beans, chilies, and mutton; both adhere largely to the Catholic faith while at the same time engaging in religious practices not considered to be strictly orthodox by that Church; both have lived in highly nucleated, tightly organized, and isolated villages, practicing irrigation farming and some herding; and both have suffered conquest and loss of prestige as well as land at the hands of the Anglo government of the United States. Although it is clear that the Spanish-Americans are engaging in a rather massive rural-to-urban migration at the present time, Indians also are becoming more urbanized—a phenomenon even less well documented than the former (cf. Dozier 1966:183). And finally, both, in spite of inevitable gradual change, have resisted acculturation and assimilation into the larger, dominant, Anglo world within which they live as social and cultural enclaves in the Southwest. Dozier has suggested reasons for the persistence of Pueblo culture (*op. cit.*), but that is not the concern of this study.

Heller (1966:21) attributes the slow rate of assimilation of Mexican-Americans to the fact that the group has deep-lying historical roots in this country. She points out that the twentieth-century Mexican immigrants who came to the United States found here an indigenous Spanish-speaking population of long standing. "They have not founded immigrant colonies so much as they have 'moved in with their relatives'" (*ibid.*). Furthermore, the proximity to Mexico has facilitated a continual contact which has served to maintain and even strengthen the Latin culture of the Southwest. Edmonson wrote, "much of the traditional Hispano culture may be changed or even swept away within a generation but for the imponderable factor of contacts with Mexico" (1957:52).

There is ample evidence to indicate that throughout the Spanish Colonial and Mexican periods there was a great deal of intercourse with Mexico. The annual trading caravan called *la conducta,* or *el cordon,* has been described by various historians.[11] These trips brought into New Mexico items such as sugar, coffee, oranges, dried fruits, silks, linens, ladies' clothing and adornments, crockery, religious articles, and even Indian servants and Spanish or Mexican wives (as described in Jaramillo 1941). Many features of social organization, as well as other specific culture traits, were shared with Mexico. Folklore and song, baptism, wedding and funeral customs, the *compadrazgo,* the *cofradía* organization, Passion plays, secular dances, courtship customs, protection and seclusion of unmarried women, inheritance rules, beliefs concerning health and disease, witchcraft, extended families living in multi-family dwellings, male authoritarianism, and many other items were either identical or very similarly patterned in both areas. Also, as in Mexico, the people at the top of the class hierarchy were those with greater wealth in land or livestock, or both; they tended to be of purer Caucasian descent; they were somewhat better educated; and in many cases they were either of the military or descended from military leaders. The lowest class was composed of Indian slaves and servants, poor mestizos, and rural peasants, regardless of race. This traditional culture shared with Mexico will be examined further, as will some of the ways in which New Mexico has diverged from the parental patterns in recent years. At the same time this may throw light on the alleged "uniqueness" of the Spanish-American in relation to other groups of Spanish descent in the Southwest today.

Notes

[1] A cautioning note in regard to the so-called archaisms is in order. Consider the following quotation:

> A familiar notion of American folk-linguistics is that the Southern highlander speaks "pure Elizabethan English." This is manifestly untrue. They do have a number of conservative traits of language . . . but these are counterbalanced by many innovations not found outside the area, as well as by innovations that they share with other regions. "Pure Elizabethan English" became extinct with the Elizabethans, but its elements persist, mixed with various innovations in ALL English dialects (Gleason 1961:404).

The same argument holds for Spanish linguistic forms in New Mexico. Furthermore, on the alleged purity of New Mexican Spanish, Edmonson says, "Although many Hispanos tend to pride themselves on the purity of their Spanish, their dialect clearly embodies a large part of the Nahuatl vocabulary of Mexican" (1957:16).

[2] The *Albuquerque Journal*, June 22, 1966, carried a story about two elderly women who were taking English lessons so they might converse with their grandchildren and great-grandchildren. See also Marden and Meyer (1962:138) and Weaver (1965:148).

[3] This, in fact, is the way in which the Mexican-American Study Project has gone about locating the bases for its samples. (The Mexican-American Study Project, under the auspices of the Division of Research, Graduate School of

Business Administration, University of California, Los Angeles, has issued eleven Study Reports.) Most statistics in this and other studies are based upon the *U.S. Census of Population, 1960, Persons of Spanish Surname,* Final Report, PC (2)-1B.

[4] The census does distinguish white from nonwhite persons of Spanish surname. Nonwhite includes Negroes, American Indians, Japanese, Chinese, Filipinos, Koreans, Hawaiians, Asian Indians, Malayans, Eskimos, Aleuts, etc. Persons of Mexican birth or ancestry who are not definitely of Indian or other nonwhite race are classified as white. For the five southwestern states, the percentage of nonwhites in the total Spanish-surname population was only 2%. New Mexico and Arizona had somewhat higher percentages (about 4% each) because of the larger number of American Indians living in those states. See *Persons of Spanish Surname, op. cit.,* Table A-2, p. 202. There seems to be no good way of distinguishing among those within the category labeled "white," which does include some persons not of Mexican heritage. According to Joan Moore of the Mexican-American Study Project, the number of non-Mexicans turning up in the sampling procedures used for Los Angeles was very small (personal communication).

[5] This information was given the author in a letter dated October 20, 1965, from the El Paso District Office of the U.S. Dept. of Justice, Immigration and Naturalization Service.

[6] See *Persons of Spanish Surname (op. cit.,* p. viii).

[7] For scholarly opinions on this, see Anderson (1909:156); Chavez (1954); F. H. Ellis (1955:56); Francis (1956:56); Hurt (1941:48); Johansen (1941b: 150); Kluckhohn and Strodtbeck (1961:205); Leonard (1943:16); Walter (1952:326); Woodward (1935:24).

[8] This group, known as the *Alianza Federal de Mercedes,* has, as its primary and declared objective, the regaining of the landgrants originally made by the Spanish and Mexican governments.

[9] For an interesting and almost parallel situation involving Indians and Ladinos in Guatemala, see R. N. Adams (1957).

[10] Zeleny (1944:43) claimed that Pueblo Indians discriminated against Spanish-Americans by barring them from ceremonials which others were permitted to see. Many Spanish-American informants in this study freely admitted their own prejudice toward Indians. On the other hand, Anderson (1909:156) declared, "The Pueblos and Mexicans are generally on good terms with each other and, instead of decrying their aboriginal blood, Mexican families have been known to declare it openly, and produce documentary evidence of the fact, in order to enter their children in the government Indian schools where the students are instructed, boarded and lodged without a cent of expense to the parents." Also, in reference to the Navajo and Spanish-Americans, Kluck-

hohn and Leighton (1951) imply an ambiguity in the attitudes and behavior of each group toward the other. Thus, they note that Spanish-Americans will frequently assist and shelter Indians in trouble with the law, but that on the other hand, "gangs of adolescent or young adult Spanish Americans often waylay, beat up, and rob Indians (especially intoxicated ones) by night, as they would not dare to treat Anglo-Americans" (p. 78). (See also Dozier 1961.)

[11] See E. Adams (1954:92); Austin (1931:142); Bancroft (1889:278); Dickey (1949:11); Jones (1932:277–278); Lummis (1891:770); Minge (1965:107); among others.

Chapter III

EARLY SETTLEMENT AND TRADITIONAL CULTURE

The earliest European settlement of New Mexico was made by a relatively small group led into the area from Mexico by Juan de Oñate in 1598. As mentioned in the Introduction, the descendants of this group and others who had joined them at irregular intervals were completely ejected from the area in 1680 by the Pueblo Indian Revolt. Thirteen years later a successful resettlement was made under the leadership of Diego de Vargas. Both of these conquering groups were composed of a small elite of military leaders, common soldiers, a large number of Spanish-Mexican farmers, some wives, and a number of Indian retainers (Chavez 1954:xiii; Woodward 1935:28–30).

Three general types of settlement seem to have been made. One was the administrative and military center, represented by Santa Fe and Albuquerque which were established according to the gridiron plan centering on a plaza, similar to countless other such towns all over Spanish America. McWilliams (1943:137) and Loomis (1943:13) suggest that this plaza-centered town was typical of all Spanish settlements in New Mexico. Bunting, however, has said that in this area the term "plaza" or "placita" connoted the idea of a fortified place rather than a central square. By constructing contiguous houses about a central open area, windowless outside walls could serve as a defense barrier (1964:3). Weaver also describes the early settlement of Abajo (a pseudonym for the northern village which he studied) as follows:

> At first, land was abundant, grazing ranges were open, and the colonists settled in three small placitas. Each placita consisted of a series of houses built wall-to-wall encircling a small enclosure. Each resembled a small fortress, and this was probably its early function (1965:13).

Dickey (1949:41) describes the same sort of multiple dwelling unit for defense. He then goes on to point out that:

> Those communities which experienced little molestation from Apaches and Navajos, gradually gave up the fortified patio in favor of houses planned on straight lines or an L-shape. When the population of an hacienda approached the status of a village, its families separated into small-house units, each responsible for a patch of ground. Repeatedly the central government found it necessary to warn these settlements against making themselves vulnerable by scattering their houses up and down the watercourses.

The last quotation brings us to the second type of settlement pattern—the *hacienda*. Little is actually known about this particular type in New Mexico during the early days, although many writers seem to assume that it was similar to the well-known hacienda complex of Mexico. Thus, Austin says:

> There was an hacienda with its enclosed *patio* for the *patron* and contiguous to it, rooms and patios for the servants, two or three such, according to the estate, opening into the other, and finally into walled enclosures for the domestic animals and the herdsmen. Often there was a *torreon* near the entrance for outlook and defense, pierced for the *arcabuceros*. In later times, when the

raiding tribes had been subdued, about the middle of the eighteenth century, the house of the *hacendado* was two-storied, including *salas* for dancing, and extending itself by wings as the sons of the family brought their brides home. Every such estate was self contained, manufacturing its own utilities (1931:142).

Even though it is probable that some haciendas existed on which life was fairly opulent and luxurious, a cautioning note should be made, for it is clear that many of the settlements called haciendas in the literature were in fact merely extended-family multiple dwellings or small villages in which the inhabitants had built their houses contiguously around a central patio for purposes of defense, as described above. Many of these units must have been quite small, as is apparent from reading Bailey's account of a Spanish survey made in 1695 of the region near the town of Chimayo, which had been inhabited before the 1680 revolt. He describes an

hacienda that once belonged to Miguel Lujan. There the houses were still standing and in them lived the owner with his family. He cultivated and irrigated only sufficient land for one family and raised a suitable number of cattle. This hacienda bordered upon that of Marcos de Herrera, whose family claimed also another hacienda below . . . beyond that was a hacienda belonging to Juan Griego, the most desirable then viewed because of its capacity to house two families and its abundant pasturage . . . (in another) were two excellent pieces of land which were inhabited by three families . . . the hacienda of Pedro de la Cruz was visited, which boasted a one-room abode and only enough land for one colonist and his family (1940:207–208).

The account goes on in this fashion, but quite clearly the term "hacienda" here means "small farm." Most of these were probably inhabited and worked by the members of an extended family. (See also Dickey 1949:1, quoted above.)

Several scholars distinguish between the communal village and the patron-dominated village, which might very well be termed an hacienda. Knowlton (1961:451) suggests that the patron-dominated village type predominated in the south and the east, while several writers confirm the greater importance of haciendas in the so-called Rio Abajo, or the area from Bernalillo to Socorro.[1] It is also quite likely that the size and elegance of some of these farms increased during the latter part of the eighteenth century and the first part of the nineteenth, when the fear of Indian attacks had lessened. According to Murbarbarger, great haciendas were established in what is now Arizona following the discovery there of precious metals. She writes:

> The Spanish hacienda of San Bernardino, near the present Arizona-New Mexico boundary, about seventeen miles east of Douglas, is said to have embraced, at its peak, around 100,000 cattle, 10,000 horses, and 5,000 mules. Its patron *grande* lived in almost regal splendor in an elegant adobe mansion 100 feet square, surrounded by flower-filled gardens and orchards of oranges, limes, pomegranates, figs, grapes, apricots, peaches, and other fruits suited to this mild climate. Yet, by the time of the Civil War nothing was left of this elegance but ruins, the cause of its demise being laid to the revolt of the Indian slaves engaged in cultivating the attached fields of wheat, corn, beans and fruits (1964:147–148).

There are no known ruins in the Rio Grande area which even approach the opulence described above, and even though the "great houses" may have been only a few miles apart between Bernalillo and Socorro (H. Fergusson 1933:81), we have, as yet, little actual knowledge of them. In any case, it does seem clear from a variety of types of evidence, including the landgrant documents as well as other historical and archaeological sources, that the most prevalent type of settlement in this area was the small agricultural and livestock-raising village, which characteristically was founded along rivers such as the Rio Grande and its tributaries, especially in the northern part of the state. Many of these towns were founded close to an already existing pueblo, with which they entered into a symbiotic relationship. In some cases the Spanish simply removed Indians from their villages, taking over the existing houses, cleared fields, and irrigation ditches (Bailey 1940:206).

However, if there was not widespread luxury, neither was the area so desolate and poverty-stricken as has sometimes been assumed. Recent work by the historian Marc Simmons (1965) suggests that the local economy might have been fairly productive. The evidence concerning trade with the Chihuahua and Sonora districts shows that a considerable surplus was achieved, which enabled many to have a fairly decent standard of living. But it should be kept in mind that most of the settlers were peasants living in rural villages and actually working their land themselves. The Indians in the New Mexican area were neither as plentiful nor as productive as those in Mexico, and it was impossible for a Spanish elite to live solely from the surplus of the Indian farmers. Actually, the situation in New Mexico should not be compared directly with that in the Valley of Mexico at the time but with the more northern and outlying districts such as Chihuahua, Sonora, and Durango. Further research may reveal even greater social and cultural similarities between Colonial and present-day New Mexico and areas such as these.

It is not the purpose of this book to describe in detail the beliefs, customs, material culture, and social institutions which are peculiar to and characteristic of the Spanish-Americans of New Mexico. The reader is referred to the bibliography for suggested sources on various topics. Rather, an attempt will be made to describe, in sociological terms, the general parameters of the way of life of these people in the past. Knowlton has appropriately warned against the danger of generalizing about Spanish-Americans. He suggests that further "research may well uncover basic differences in the culture and social structure of the villages of the upper Rio Grande Valley and the Middle Rio Grande Valley in New Mexico, the northern mountain villages, and the plains villages" (1961:449).

One of the conclusions of the Tewa Basin Study (U.S. Dept. of Agriculture, 135c) was that there appeared to be differences in the social structure of the villages on the east and west sides of the Rio Grande (pp. vii–ix). Certainly it is evident that differences in history and ecological circumstances, plus the relative isolation of the villages, might be conducive to the development of differences among them. Yet it is also clear from a survey of the existing early accounts, and more recent anthropological and sociological studies, that certain themes, patterns, and institutions were fairly common throughout the territory or a certain portion of it. Leonard and Loomis (1941) say, in regard to San Miguel County, "The same problems and characteristics are found in all. Actually, the native villages . . . are strikingly similar" (p. 2). The purpose in delineating these major patterns in the following will be to present a background and context for a discussion of acculturation and a better understanding of the present-day situation in New Mexico.

The small northern Spanish villages were relatively isolated not only from the larger centers such as Santa Fe and Albuquerque but also from each other, and each one formed an almost self-sufficient unit, both in terms of economy and in regard to social structure. Like all peasant communities everywhere, however, they were not, in the final analysis, completely isolated, and they were partially dependent upon a "larger tradition" which gave them certain characteristics (Foster 1953b; Redfield 1953). Even though they produced most of the foodstuffs by which they themselves subsisted, built their own houses of local materials, manufactured furniture and other household items, and even many of their own clothes and ornaments, nevertheless, there were certain trade items which reached even the most remote village. Some of these were such luxuries as the silk shawls, so admired and coveted by the ladies, and the *retablos* or religious pictures portraying favorite saints. It is true that not everyone could afford such items, and local artists and craftsmen produced copies of the imported items, which in time resulted in distinct artistic traditions based upon, but distinguishable from, the European originals.[2]

There were also some items which were necessities for the kind of life led in the village, but which could not be produced locally. Prior to 1779, each incoming settler was given the basic equipment considered essential to successful farming in the region. According to Blackmar each settler was

. . . entitled to receive a house-lot, a tract of land for cultivation, another for pasture (commons) and a loan of sufficient stock and implements to make a comfortable beginning. In addition to these, he received two mares, two cows and one calf, two sheep and two goats, two horses, one cargo mule, and one yoke of oxen or steers; one plow point, one spade, one axe, one sickle, one wooden knife, one musket, and one leather shield (1891:164–165).

Although, as Leonard has noted (1943), this policy was probably seldom carried out with any degree of completeness, it remained an ideal and gives some notion of the kind of basic European technology upon which the early Spanish settlers depended.

Most of the plots held by individual farmers were small enough to be cultivated by a man and his immediate family. It appears that grown sons may have remained, together with their wives and children, until the death of the father, at which time the father's land would be divided among them.[3] In some villages daughters also might be given a portion of land as a dowry, the management of which was given to their husbands. In other villages daughters might be given livestock, furniture, and other household goods, but not land, which was reserved for male heirs only (Maes 1941:10). During the first hundred years or so, as settlements gradually increased in size and the land available in the original grant was allotted and subdivided through inheritance, small groups split off from the parent villages and founded new settlements. Frequently such a group would be small in the beginning, but they would request enough land to accommodate additional settlers up to a certain number, after which that village would be closed to newcomers.[4]

By the middle of the eighteenth century the northern limits of Spanish settlement were the village of Chama, on the river of that name, and the villages near the present boundary of Colorado, on the Rio Grande (Culbert 1943:175). But a map of the inhabited places in New Mexico in 1844 shows the Spanish-speaking population still concentrated in an area within a fifty-mile radius of the present town of Santa Fe or at the headwaters of the Rio Grande and Pecos River (Leonard 1943:31). Within this fifty-mile radius, the concentration was evidently quite great, and irrigable land in the river valleys was becoming scarce. Thus, in 1855, the largest farm managed by a single wealthy owner consisted of 1,721 acres in what is now Bernalillo County. Most plots were ten acres or smaller (Dickey 1949:8). Leonard noted that at the time of his study the landholdings of each of the sixty villages in the Upper Pecos watershed were small, ranging from one-fourth of an acre to twenty acres (1943:34).[5]

One of the specifications often made in the grants to groups of settlers was that "a person who will not reside in the town with the family belonging to him and who shall remove to another settlement shall lose all right he may have acquired to his property" (Hurt 1941:30). The right of the town officials to exact communal labor from the settlers was also sometimes specifically noted in the petitions. Communal labor and mutual aid seem to have been the primary bases upon which the social structure of these early agricultural villages was founded. Together the settlers built houses, maintained irrigation ditches, grazed their livestock, cared for their sick, buried their dead, and celebrated the holy days of the Catholic religion. Neglected by both church and state, each village developed a relatively autonomous system for maintaining law and order, socializing the children, perpetuating the faith and their culture in general.

The *cofradía* organization of the Catholic church was very early transplanted to New Mexico, as well as to other parts of the New World, and it is likely that the so-called Penitente Brotherhood, a somewhat later development, was an outgrowth of these earlier religious and beneficent societies.[6] Even without the sacraments of the church, which often had to be foregone in the absence of a priest, the rituals of life continued. In addition to the patriarchal extended family, the *compadrazgo,* or system of godparenthood, was also apparently an important institution, serving to strengthen rights and obligations among kinsmen.[7] There seems to have been some tendency toward village endogamy, and marriage between cousins was not frowned upon.

Recreation consisted largely of the celebration of the various life crises and of the holy days of the Catholic calendar, including the day of the village's patron saint. In addition to religious observances, conducted by officers of the *cofradía* or by a priest—if one was available—there was feasting and the inevitable dancing (except in the event of a funeral, which was, however, a kind of social occasion also). For the men and boys, there might be an occasional trip into the nearest larger population center, and for some, an opportunity to accompany the once-a-year *conducta,* or trading caravan, to Mexico.

The necessity to defend themselves from periodic Indian raids was also a factor in the social structure of some of the villages—especially those on the peripheries of the settled areas. The towns of Abiquiu, Belen, and Cebolleta, among others, were continually being attacked and were, in fact, purposely founded as buffer communities (E. Fergusson 1940:257; Kluckhohn and Strodtbeck 1961:180; Swadesh 1964a, 1964b).

Some villages retained the tightly nucleated settlement pattern, traces of which may sometimes still be seen today. However, in those areas where the Indian menace was not severe, and especially after 1850 in still other areas, the line settlement bordering a stream, and in later days the highway, appeared.[8] Although the flat-roofed, low, box-shaped adobe house, a composite of Spanish and Indian ideas and materials, was and still is popular in many areas, another type found in the far north and especially in the more mountainous locations was the large, wooden, often two-storied structure with gabled windows on the second floor, pitched roofs, and covered *porticos* or outside porches running the length of the building.[9]

Frequently these houses were enlarged as sons brought home wives and increased the size of the extended family. A similar type of arrangement is also observed in the simpler adobe houses, which may have as many as four or five separate doors and compartments extending in an L-shape. A more modern solution, but one which reflects basically the same type of social structure, is the house-trailer. One may find these permanently parked in the backyards of many homes in the rural villages today—one such household visited during the course of this study included three house-trailers in addition to a large two-storied house like that described above. Two married sons and one married daughter lived with their spouses in the trailers, while the elderly head of the household lived in the main structure with an unmarried daughter and three other unmarried kinsmen.

Although livestock was brought into New Mexico by the very earliest Spanish settlers, the primary emphasis in the first century or so was on farming of wheat, maize, beans, chili, and other vegetables, and fruits. Sheep were always more important than any other domesticated animals. Thus, Bancroft says:

> Of live-stock, sheep formed the chief element, these animals being raised in large numbers, both for their wool and meat though there are no reliable statistics extant. Horses and cattle were also raised, but the former were always scarce in the province on account of the numbers sold to and stolen by the wild Indians. I find no definite indications that cattle were raised to any great extent for their hides and tallow (1889:275).

It is impossible to date exactly the period when sheepherding began to outstrip farming as a way of life for the Spanish *campesino*. However, the population figures given by the official reports and reviewed by Bancroft (1889) indicate substantial increase toward the end of the eighteenth century, and this information coincides with that concerning the founding of many new settlements on the periphery of the former occupied area during this same period. Thus, the population was gradually moving out into the plains around Las Vegas (Town of Las Vegas founded 1835), east of the Sandia and Manzano ranges into the Estancia Valley (Estancia 1819, Manzano 1829), the Upper Pecos watershed (late 1700's) and westward into what is now Sandoval County (Jemez Springs 1798). Some writers have suggested that there was increased use of the available grassland during the Mexican period (1821–1846), and Zeleny (1944:65) notes that by the early part of the nineteenth century sheep and wool had become important exports of the territory. There is even some evidence that there were cases of localized overgrazing at this early date—a forerunner of the disaster which was to befall the state one hundred years later. Thus, E. Fergusson reported that:

> In 1827, the stock-raisers of Sante Fe and Albuquerque had two hundred and forty thousand head of sheep on the tax rolls—twice the number that can be supported on that range now [i.e., 1935] (1935:334).

But it was not until after the annexation by the United States government that stock raising became really big business in New Mexico. Some of the important determining factors were (1) The Indians were gradually conquered—a circumstance which not only opened up new areas for settlement but created a market for meat, since the government agreed to supply rations to many of the formerly nomadic groups. (2) The United States army itself had to be fed. (3) The eastern markets were made more accessible by building of the railroads.[10] (4) Large numbers of settlers and speculators from the east arrived and went into the stock-raising business to turn a quick profit. (5) Continued and increased population pressure sent the Spanish-American population out into the grasslands, and even many of those who remained in agricultural areas turned to herding on a larger scale. Calkins tells us that:

> The older generation of settlers in the Cuba Valley (settled between 1868–1878) were farmers, but their sons went into the stock industry. The only cash at a time when money was entering the economy for the first time was to be had in livestock (U.S. Dept. of Agriculture 1937a:14).

Two well-known social institutions, for which there is little evidence during the early colonial period, seem to have developed along with and perhaps in consequence of the rise of the livestock industry. The first of these is the *patron* system, which has been highly touted as being typical of Spanish social structure in many areas of the New World, and there are even those who feel that subservient attitudes toward and extreme dependence upon those in authority are part of the personality configuration of those of Spanish descent.[11] However, there is little to indicate that the early farming villages described were anything but egalitarian. Although a few of the landgrants were given to individuals, by far the largest number was in the names of a group of settlers (Leonard 1943). Certainly there were some differences in status, depending upon sex, age, and individual characteristics, but no *patrones* in the true sense of the word. Saunders describes it well when he says:

> Having found a way of life with survival value, the Spanish-American villages continued it generation after generation. One acquired status, prestige, and esteem by conforming to community expectations. In time, if one were of the right sex and belonged to the right family, one might attain a formal or semi-formal position of leadership. If not, it was of no great concern. The privileges were few, but so were the responsibilities. Leadership was nothing to aspire to; neither was it anything to shun (1954:50).

However, there is evidence that with the increasing dependence upon sheep and the influx of population onto the plains and other areas new social forms developed. Toward the end of the Spanish regime and during the Mexican regime many large grants of land were made to individuals for grazing purposes. During this time the power of the *ricos* increased at the expense of the lower classes. Zeleny claims that many of the grants of land to large proprietors during this time deprived the common people of much of their land (1944:82; see also Charles 1940:21). According to Fabiola Cabeza de Baca Gilbert, a native daughter, there was no set pattern for determining wealth and social position, but

> . . . on the Llano, in the days of the open range, there were men who ran thousands of head of cattle and sheep. The Baca brothers from Upper Las Vegas—Don Jose, Don Simon, Don Aniceto, and Don Pablo—jointly were running half a million head of sheep in the 1870's (1954:x).

And it is from this period that one begins to get descriptions of types of settlements which sound like the stereotyped Mexican hacienda. Thus, the same writer recalls the following from her childhood:

> Surrounded by the homes of Don Jose's sons and empleados, the Gonzales hacienda was a village in itself. Don Jose ran thousands of cattle on his domain. I remember hearing during conversations that in 1906 he had branded one thousand colts. There were many other ranchos on our way to Las Vegas, but the Gonzales hacienda stands more vividly in my memory than the others (Gilbert, *op. cit.*:135–137).

The town of El Cerrito in San Miguel County was founded in the early part of the nineteenth century. Two of the settler families owned large flocks of sheep, and most of the other families worked for them. Gradually, other families acquired herds of their own, since land was plentiful and sheep multiplied (Leonard and Loomis 1941:10).

The second institution probably deriving from the spread of livestock raising as a major economic base is the *partido* or tenant-herding system. This has been interpreted as a kind of feudal or share system, and it has undoubtedly sometimes worked as such in the case of small operators who, through convenience or necessity, turned over a portion of their herd to a friend or relative on a share basis. However, as has been pointed out by others, when used by the large owners, it was a form of financing which bore a definite relationship to other modern forms of business enterprise. According to studies in the 1930's (U.S. Dept. of Agriculture 1937b), the system operated as follows: The owner supplied a breeding herd to his tenant. The renter agreed to return twenty lambs for every hundred ewes in the herd at the end of an agreed-upon period—usually one year. The tenant further contracted to rent rams from the owner, sell his lambs and wool through the owner, and stand responsible for all operating expenses and losses. The renter was also required to return upon demand a breeding herd of the same size and age as that originally handed over to him.

In exchange, the tenant was entitled to all the wool, all the lambs in excess of the twenty-per-hundred ewes, and the right to graze his own sheep on the owner's land along with the rented sheep. However, he paid for these grazing rights at a specified rate. Clearly, the large owners could not lose!

Although this system sometimes helped a small operator or family to build up a herd,[12] it also effectively maintained a distinction between the large owners and those with small or no herds. Thus, according to a government report,

> Tenant herding, as it is now found, begins from a concentration in the ownership or control of the grazing resources which renders the development of independent livestock enterprises virtually impossible and renders the survival of small independent livestock operations difficult in the extreme (U.S. Dept. of Agriculture 1937:2).

Although there is evidence that the system was known and utilized as early as 1760, it did not become really important until much later. Charles reports, "The general impression of the older sheep men is that the partido system reached its zenith about 1905 and then started to decline" (1940:33). This would correspond with the rise and fall of the sheep industry as a whole in New Mexico. Thus, although sources differ, it appears that the number of sheep in New Mexico increased between 1800 and 1840 to an estimated million and a half, then declined to 377,000 in 1850. There was only a slight increase until the 1870's, when the real boom began. By 1880 there were almost four million sheep in the area, a figure which did not appreciably decline until after 1910.[13]

There can be little doubt that the *partido* system was closely related to the *patron* system. Charles says:

> The patron looked out for the well-being of the partidario and his family. He encouraged frugality and good management, made advances for subsistence if necessary, attended at weddings and christenings, secured medical attention when needed and always had their interest and comfort at heart (1940:55).[14]

Several sources indicate that *patronship* was a late development in New Mexico in general. Leonard (1943:118 *passim*) has an especially interesting and illuminating discussion of this. He points out that class distinctions in the early days were based primarily upon family and blood lines and favor with the Spanish crown.

> Later, with the rise of the *patron* class among the Spanish-Americans, however, the channels of circulation between the layers of the social pyramid became more open and the caste element became of less importance. A man with some ingenuity and business acumen might rise within a few years from the laboring class to the exalted status of a *patron*. Economic position came to be a dominant factor in social status (*op. cit.*).

More recent studies seem to confirm this and emphasize the importance of livestock in determining wealth and status.[15]

Indeed, even now sheepherding remains an ideal way of life for the Hispano—although it is no longer a particularly lucrative pursuit. Virtually all contemporary accounts by social scientists comment upon the people's stated preference for this occupation, and Hollywood a few years ago presented a charming, but romanticized, version of such a life which bears little resemblance to the actual circumstances of most Spanish-Americans today.[16]

However, various factors combined to help destroy the basis for the sheepherding industry among Spanish-Americans. There is good evidence that between 1870 and 1900 many Anglos moved into the rich eastern plains area and through force and chicanery deprived the Spanish-Americans of much of their grazing lands. The best-known instances of this maneuvering are described in relation to the so-called Lincoln County wars (1869–1881). Although this wild-west fracas is today best known because of the participation of the famous or infamous Billy the Kid, the real issues seem to have been competition between sheepmen (primarily Spanish) and cattlemen (predominantly Anglo). But even after 1881, when some semblance of law and order was established, the Spanish continued to suffer. One authority described the situation in 1885 as follows:

> . . . for several years past, but few Mexicans have been allowed to live within these limits peaceably and without any molestation, for any considerable length of time; that many Mexicans have been killed out-right, without provocation, several have been wounded, and many more driven away from their homes by intimidation and threats of shooting, assassination, and mob violence . . . (quoted in W. A. Keleher 1945:90).[17]

Today this area, along with nearly the whole eastern plains area of the state, is heavily dominated by Anglos, and the term Little Texas is applied to it in recognition of the origin of the

majority of the settlers and of their cultural patterns. Dry
farming and cattle ranching are today the primary economic
pursuits in this area. Although Anglos predominate in the
extreme east, it should be pointed out that in the area around
Las Vegas, where the plains begin, there are many Spanish-
American cattle ranchers as well. It appears that the early conflict
was not based entirely upon ethnic differences and that some
Hispanos managed to come out quite well. (See pp. 45–46 for
descriptions of Gilbert.)

In addition to the loss of land through trickery and deceit,
some holdings melted away because the Spanish-speaking population was ignorant of the United States government requirements
in regard to registration of land claims and was unable to pay
taxes. Much has been written concerning the era of New
Mexican history following the U.S. conquest in 1846 and the
subsequent difficulties in establishing rightful ownership of lands
granted by the Spanish and Mexican governments. In few cases
were actual boundaries known with any certainty, and in some
instances the same area had been granted to more than one
applicant.[18] Furthermore, many of the original titles had been
lost or destroyed through the years, and confirming information
from the archives of the viceregal and Mexican governments
was frequently missing, inadequate, or ambiguous.

In short, the problem of how to secure justice for the previous
inhabitants and at the same time open up previously unused or
inefficiently used lands to Anglo settlement was enormous. There
seems to be little doubt that in spite of good and honorable
intentions on the part of most of those who set the policies and
made the judgments, there were in fact many individuals who
suffered deprivation of lands. Most of the "deals" made were
within the letter of the law—but it was a United States law,
little understood by most of the people involved. Many, needing

cash desperately, sold portions of their land at fantastically low prices within short periods after receiving confirmation of ownership. Others, choosing to live in old Mexico, willingly abandoned or sold cheaply their shares *in absentia*. Most of the buyers were Anglos, but some were also Hispanos who took advantage of their poorer, lower-class countrymen.[19]

The final blows to the economy based upon livestock had their origin in a slow, but inevitable man-made shift in the ecological balance of the area. The tremendous buildup in the number of animals led to serious overgrazing, which effectively destroyed the natural grass and shrub cycle and led to widespread erosion of the topsoils. In addition, the large-scale cutting of timber in the forest areas led to a more rapid runoff and consequent floods, which contributed further to the destruction of the grass cover, made farming more difficult, and destroyed much property. In one case an entire village was permanently destroyed.[20] According to most authorities, the effects of overgrazing occurred prior to 1910 and were recognized by the national government during the first decade of the century, if not before. Johansen (1941b) reported that the Mesilla Valley benefited from a reclamation project which was carried out between 1910 and 1920 and which included the construction of Elephant Butte Dam. Although the area as a whole has developed remarkably since that time, depending largely upon large-scale cultivation of cotton, it is important to note here the effects upon the Spanish population of the area. The overall trend has been in the direction of a more highly commercialized type of farming—larger holdings cultivated with modern machinery and techniques. Johansen says:

> While specific quantitative data are not available, there exists evidence that many of the original Spanish-American farmers (most of whom had settled in the area during the Mexican period),

in the process of commercialization were removed from their land
through foreclosure . . . (1941b:44).

Most of these dispossessed persons became part of the farm
laborer population, whose ranks were swelled considerably by
immigration from Mexico.

Reclamation in the Albuquerque area also led to widespread
loss of land by small owners, the majority of whom were Spanish.
In 1937, 8,000 people lost their land titles because they were
unable to pay taxes and assessments on the Middle Rio Grande
Conservancy District Project—a much needed program, true, but
one which these people had no part in voting on and no way of
paying for. The federal government did try to remedy the
situation somewhat by buying some of this land from the state
and offering it to those rural communities most in need of
assistance.[21]

Another action—designed to aid in reversing the destructive
forces then in operation but which has been much resented by
the Spanish-American stockmen, among others—has been the
creation of national forests from the public lands and the
restriction of grazing thereon. As early as 1892 Congress established the Pecos River Forest, now part of the Santa Fe National
Forest. Further large amounts of land were set aside during the
next sixteen years. In 1906, what is now called the Carson
National Forest was formed from all or parts of the Las Trampas,
Santa Barbara, Mora, and F. M. Vigil grants.[22] Today roughly
10 million acres, or about one-eighth of the total land area in
New Mexico, is within the boundaries of the national forests.[23]
Further grants of public lands were made to railroad companies,
and some were transferred to the state in aid of public education.
Burma (1954:16) and Knowlton (1964a:209) say that since 1854
Spanish-Americans have lost 2,000,000 acres of private land and

1,700,000 acres of communal land. Wolff (1950), in describing cultural change in a northern village says, "The most far-reaching event was the establishment of the National Forest early in this century. It eliminated sheep and goats by pre-empting grazing lands and pasture; thus indirectly eliminating spinning, weaving and related skills" (p. 53).

In 1934 the Taylor Grazing Act was passed which set up mechanisms intended to protect the rights of small operators. Permits (termed "preferences" by informants) were issued to the stockmen, the number based on a percentage of the animals already owned. These preferences may not be sold—although they may be "given away" when one sells an animal. A few stockmen have been able to build up their holdings by buying animals—and thus, preferences—from their poorer neighbors who found that the risks involved in owning a very small number of animals simply made their endeavors not worthwhile. Nevertheless, even today the average small livestock owner tends to be suspicious and resentful of the government and its representatives in any matter regarding his animals.

During the summer of 1965 one informant stated that in his opinion the government was trying to drive everyone out of the stock business. In support of his belief he described a number of what he termed "tricks," especially designed to discourage the smaller operators. Among these were the raising of fees, adding of new fees (for such items as fences, e.g.), the reducing of the number of animals each owner was permitted to graze, and the shortening of the grazing season. Other informants expressed distrust of the forest ranger, feeling that his primary function was to spy for the government. The local Stock Association, the organization through which many details are handled, was thought by several informants to be dominated by the local forest ranger without whom they are not supposed to meet. However, other informants pointed out that the local townsmen often meet in secret without the ranger in order to hash things out.

It is clear that stock raising, upon which so many have come to depend not only financially but also for status in the eyes of their fellows, has gradually become an illusory and impractical means of achieving either wealth or social position. Still, many cling to a pitiful one or two animals more as a symbol than anything else. Edmonson (1957:47) says:

> New Mexican Hispano culture is firmly based on sheep and cattle ranching and the necessity of change in this fundamental economic pursuit has been a powerful factor in social change generally. The rancheros who are left are scarcely able to support themselves from their small holdings; most of them augment their income by occasional labor for other ranchers, farmers, companies or the government.

Wage labor came to be (1) the means by which the Spanish-American was able to survive while maintaining his unproductive and inadequate fields and herds, and (2) a further agent in the destruction of this way of life. As early as 1909 one astute observer commented upon the effects of wage labor and prosperity:

> With the coming of great American manufacturing concerns, the younger element of the natives is drifting into mechanical employments, yet sheep, goat and cattle raising are still the chief means of livelihood to the many. Since the great advance in the price of sheep and wool a few years ago, the rural New Mexican has grown prosperous beyond all expectation and with this new condition, a change is rapidly coming over him. He is acquiring a fancy for the piano, the phonograph, the Easter bonnet, tinned goods, embalmed hams, steel ranges, modern furniture, granite-ware cooking utensils, and a thousand other things he formerly never dreamed of as being necessary to his happiness (Anderson 1909: 158).

It has taken a long time for wage labor to replace sheep-herding; and, indeed, it has not yet completely done so. Yet the story of the gradual decline in this industry is also the story of the change in many other aspects of the sociocultural system of which it was an important integral part, if not its basis. In succeeding chapters some of the specific ways in which this traditional culture has changed during the past five or six decades will be considered. At the same time that the processes of cultural breakdown or disorganization have been going on, there have been trends leading to a new synthesis, a modern reorganization retaining and combining some of the old traits with the new.

Notes

[1] See Adams and Chavez (1956); H. Fergusson (1933:81); Zeleny (1944:66).

[2] Although there are many books and articles dealing with the arts and crafts of New Mexico, the best comprehensive volume on the subject is by R. F. Dickey 1949, *New Mexico Village Arts.*

[3] Although sources differ, this practice may have been of relatively recent origin. Thus, Perrigo says, "Beginning in the Mexican period, when primogeniture had been abolished, the practice of dividing the arable fields among heirs was initiated. A land grant which once sufficed for a family presently was cut up into strips of only a few acres each for the families of sons and grandsons" (1960:370). The practice of leaving all lands to the eldest son would have forced younger sons out of the village, and as long as there was vacant land upon which to settle and form new villages, this would have been an efficient and functional practice. The time of the change in the law suggested here is significant in that it also coincides with the period during which population pressure was becoming a problem. This would have had the effect of increasing the number of persons and families living in any given village, while decreasing the standards of living for all—a situation which did, in fact, develop. E. Fergusson (1940:259) assumes equal inheritance to have been dictated by Spanish law. Atencio (1964:46) says all children always inherited equally in spite of Spanish law favoring primogeniture.

[4] Callon (1962:7) writes, in regard to the town of Las Vegas, "As per the stipulation of the grant they selected a townsite, two community gardens, an

easement to a convenient watering place and distributed land to each petitioner. No one was given more land than he could till and keep in good condition. The remainder of the land was for common pasture or to be granted to new settlers who could prove their need of land for the sustenance of their families."

5 See also Bohannan (1928:4); Burma (1954:14); Rusinow (1938:95); New Mexico Rural Council Study (n.d.:2).

6 Much of the literature concerning the Penitente Brotherhood is sensational and inaccurate. Myra Ellen Jenkins will soon publish a book based upon the 1935 doctoral dissertation by Dorothy Woodward. In the meantime, this dissertation and a shorter article by Fray Angelico Chavez (1954) are the best scholarly sources.

7 Only a few of the contemporary sociological and anthropological accounts include much material on the *compadrazgo*. Weaver (1965) is both the most recent and the most inclusive. See also Edmonson (1957) and Kluckhohn and Strodtbeck (1961). A recent Master's thesis (Vincent 1966) at the University of New Mexico outlines and summarizes the existing sources and gives new data on *compadrazgo* in the modern urban environment of Albuquerque.

8 See, for example, *A Pilot Planning Project for the Embudo Watershed of New Mexico* (1961:46–47,56), hereafter referred to as Embudo Report; Weaver (1965:13,135).

9 This style of housing is certainly not the earliest. Thus, the Embudo Report (see note 8) describes Rio Lucio—"Rio Lucio's houses are a good example of the post-colonial changes in local housing construction. Yankee-introduced steel tools were used to shape and ornament the boards which new Yankee-built sawmills began to turn out inexpensively. Adobes began to acquire gabled roofs of wood, wooden floors, front porches, and relatively elaborate wooden trim. Particularly noticeable were paneled doors, louvred or paneled window shutters, and door casings decorated with elaborate moundings. Pitched roofs replaced the old flat dirt roofs" (*op. cit.,* p. 51).

10 The railroad-building era in New Mexico began about 1875. The Atchison, Topeka and Santa Fe reached Albuquerque April 22, 1880. Not only did the lines of the Southern Pacific establish a junction at Deming, New Mexico, March 10, 1881, but the Santa Fe joined these lines, forming the first all-rail route across New Mexico. For further details, see Arsdale (1932). He says: "Railroad building in New Mexico from 1878 to 1911 brought a fourfold increase in population and a development of resources" (p. 6).

11 Examples of this type of interpretation are found in Hawley and Senter (1946:137); Russell (1938:36–38).

12 This interpretation, as might be expected, is more commonly found among the members of the upper classes involved. See, e.g., Gilbert (1954:57).

13 Figures on the number of sheep in New Mexico at various dates up to 1940

may be found in Charles (1940); Donnelly (1940); and, more recently, Irion (1959).

[14] See also U.S. Dept. of Agriculture (1935b:6); Kluckhohn and Strodtbeck (1961:204).

[15] See especially Edmonson (1957:54); Kluckhohn and Strodtbeck (1961:205); Burma (1954:12).

[16] *And Now Miguel,* Universal Film Exchange, World Premiere, June 1, 1966, Albuquerque, New Mexico.

[17] See also Keleher (1957); Shinkle (1964:36).

[18] This occurred, for example, in the well-known case of the Las Vegas Town Grant and in the Estancia Valley at Manzano. In each case a group of settlers was given a grant of land located in the middle of a previous grant to an individual. See Callon (1962:11–16); Bergere (n.d.).

[19] The following sources include valuable information and interpretations of various aspects of the land claims problem in New Mexico: Bancroft (1889, Vol. 17); Bloom (1903); Burma (1954); Fierman (1964); Holmes (1964); Horn (1963); Keleher (1929 and 1945); Knowlton (1964); Leonard (1943); Perrigo (1960); U.S. Dept. of Agriculture (1937g); Welch (1950); Westphall (1947). See also a recent account by Rubel (1966) which describes a similar situation in the lower Rio Grande Valley in Texas.

[20] See Harper, Cordova, and Oberg (1943). San Marcial was the village; for details, see Calkins (1937a).

[21] Laughlin (1940:280 *passim*). See also U.S. Dept. of Agriculture (1937d, 1937g).

[22] Embudo Report (n.d.:23).

[23] Data from National Forest Areas, U.S. Dept. of Agriculture, Forest Service, June 30, 1964.

Chapter IV

SOCIAL SYSTEM

In this chapter the characteristics of the interpersonal relationships which bind Hispanos one to another in various kinds of social structures will be considered, as well as those which articulate Hispanos, both as individuals and in groups, with the broader society in New Mexico and elsewhere in the United States. The Spanish-speaking population of this state may in no way be considered a homogeneous unit, as was suggested in the preceding chapter. There are several important divisions which reflect different vested interests but which nevertheless cross-cut this population in different directions or dimensions, thus preventing it from being hopelessly split into schisms. Kroeber long ago noted a similar structural situation among the Zuni. He commented in 1917 (p. 183) as follows:

> Four or five different planes of systematization cross-cut each other and thus preserve for the whole society an integrity that would speedily be lost if the planes merged and thereby inclined to encourage segregation and fission. The clans . . . , the fraternities, the priesthoods, the kivas, in a measure the gaming parties, are all dividing agencies. If they coincided, the rifts in the social structure would be deep; by countering each other they cause segmentations

which produce an almost marvelous complexity, but can never break the national entity apart.

The principle remains generally the same among the Spanish-Americans of New Mexico today, although the types of groupings are different. Thus, among this population we must recognize the distinctions between rich and poor, between rural and urban dwellers, between Catholic and Protestant, and between Democrat and Republican, among others. These cross-cuttings are also important in that they form links between Spanish-Americans and Anglos and because they underlie social class distinctions. While each of these will be discussed in turn, it is first necessary to examine those units which seem to demand primary loyalties and which serve to increase the solidarity of the Hispano group.

Kinship

All sources agree on the importance and solidarity of the family group among Spanish-Americans. Although the nuclear family may be considered the basic kinship unit, most Hispanos would include other relatives besides parents and siblings as members of their *familia*. Grandparents, parents' siblings and the latters' children, termed *primos hermanos,* are all considered "close" relatives; and indeed, there seems to be a great deal of social interaction with such persons throughout life. Rubel's recent work on Mexican-Americans of South Texas (1966) gives a picture which is essentially the same as that encountered in New Mexico. Within the family different statuses are assigned on the basis of sex, age, generation, type of kinship bond, and to a certain extent individual behavior. Thus, although an eldest brother would ordinarily be held in the greatest amount of respect by a sibling group, he could lose this position by behaving in a fashion deemed immoral, through laziness, or through failure to fulfill his kinship obligations. However, he would continue to be considered a kinsman regardless of his behavior.[1]

Studies in both rural and urban areas of New Mexico indicate that most social intercourse occurs among relatives. Loomis, in 1940, described the informal groupings in a rural village: The extended family proved to be the most important unit in such areas as economic cooperation and recreation. It has repeatedly been mentioned as a primary agent of socialization and social control. In spite of the fact that in the twenty-six years since Loomis' study many changes have occurred, recent studies by Weaver (1965) and Vincent (1966) indicate that the extended family has by no means become a thing of the past. That it is still highly viable and functional in many aspects of life does not, of course, mean that it is still the same sort of unit it once was.

Loomis himself, in a 1958 restudy of the same village, pointed out that the status roles of parents and children were changing and that the younger generation exercised more independence in choosing marital partners, residential patterns, occupations, etc. The process of disorganization (or reorganization) of the Spanish-American family system has apparently been in operation for some time, however. In 1946 Moore (1947) found that divorce, desertion, and broken families had been increasing steadily among Spanish-Americans in a suburban Albuquerque neighborhood over a ten-year period. He also noted that ". . . a number of children are leaving their families and are moving elsewhere, thus destroying the old family solidarity which had existed for years" (p. 53). These general patterns were further confirmed in another study, in 1956, by Cassel.[2] One would expect such changes to occur earlier in the urban zones, yet Johansen noted a similar process in the villages and hamlets of Dona Ana County as long ago as 1942. At the same time he stated that the family was still the most important single factor in the social organization of these population centers.[3] Hurt, on the other hand, in reporting on a northern village during the same time period, said:

> The household and family institutions show the least amount of disintegration of various aspects of this culture. Orphans, unmarried children, and older people without income are taken care of by attachment to functioning households (1941:125).

Kluckhohn, in describing a rural northwestern village in 1936, emphasized that all emigrating family members are kept track of forever (1961:192). Edmonson also noted the fact that family solidarity continues even though some members spend "all or part of their time in other, larger towns, such as Albuquerque or Phoenix" (1957:46). In reference to two closely intermarried upper-class families, he says, "They do take care of a large circle of 'poor relatives' . . . ," which suggests that kinship relations may still take precedence over property relations.

Atencio has recently denoted the disorganization and dispersal of the extended family as a major problem in connection with the efficient economic use of much of the land in the northern part of the state. Many individuals have retained title to small portions of family land, which they apparently cling to primarily for sentimental reasons. He claims that:

> When the members of a disorganized extended family are geographically separate yet all have claims on the various plots of land, it is difficult to turn that land into productive use. Since yield is insufficient for an adequate livelihood, the owners do not want to farm it, yet no one else can have legal access to it by lease or sale as the titles are vague and claims to it are numerous. One member is responsible for the water rights and taxes, and he will inevitably fail on one or the other with the result that the land falls to the State or an alert land speculator (1964:48).

Sjoberg in 1947 said that "the extended family no longer is the basic unit of economic protection [in San Jose, a section of Albuquerque]," yet he also pointed out that the idea of reciprocity among family members still persisted. He noted that those on relief were frequently aided by children and other relatives—especially in the matter of housing. Sons typically provided quarters apart from their own home in contrast to daughters who tended to bring their parents into their own homes (Sjoberg 1947:36–37). Kluckhohn suggested that urban adjustment by Spanish-Americans was at least partially facilitated by the continued cooperation among members of collateral kinship groupings in the cities (1961:227).

It seems safe to say that, although certain aspects of the former strongly knit family organization of the Hispano way of life have changed, the extended family unit remains important in ways unparalleled in the Anglo world. Indeed, several investigators have suggested that persons who cannot be fitted into some kinship category may be treated with suspicion, withdrawal, and perhaps even shown overt hostility.[4] As Weaver has said recently, "Spanish-American society is kin-based society and the most lasting, deepest ties are those between kin-related members" (Weaver 1965:76). Kinfolk continue to call upon each other for economic assistance when necessary, for advice, moral support, and simple companionship. The functions of socialization and social control have to an increasing extent been taken over by other agencies, but even in these areas the role of the family has not been superseded completely. It is only when the extended family is considered as a corporate property-holding group that one may speak of its nearly total disorganization. In part, this is related to the tendency toward greater dispersal of the family members, and this in turn has to do with the decreasing dependency upon the traditional agrarian economy. As was clear in Atencio's comments quoted previously, there exists a conflict today between the emotional identification with the land and the larger family group and the impossibility of a dispersed group acting as a unit in the economic utilization of the land.

Even the *compadrazgo,* commonly used in Latin-American countries to extend in a ritual manner the network of kinship relations, has here the effect of reinforcing or intensifying family relations. Both Weaver (1965) and Vincent (1966) have shown that most of the sponsors for baptism are chosen from within the family circle itself. Furthermore, this appears to be as true of the urban as of the rural zones today. Visiting and mutual-aid patterns show the highest amount of interaction among those persons related through *both* a biological and a ritual kinship tie.

Community

The second primary social unit to which Hispanos become attached is the community. This has in the past usually been the village, but today, as urbanization proceeds rapidly, the city neighborhood in many ways replaces the village as the most important territorial identification. It is true that the rural community might also be considered a kinship unit, since its members were frequently interrelated by complex ties of consanguinity and affinity. Thus, according to Leonard and Loomis, "Few families in El Cerrito cannot claim at least a third cousin relationship to every other family" (1941:8). A preference for village endogamy has tended to perpetuate this situation. In former days it was not at all unusual for cousins—even first cousins—to marry. It is important to note that, given equal inheritance by all the children, such marriages could be used to consolidate family lands which might otherwise be fragmented and lost.

However, not all Hispano villages followed this pattern, and the whole subject of the interrelationships in the forms of property, inheritance, marriage, and kinship systems among the New Mexican Spanish peasantry would make a fascinating study.[5] In the case of at least one village, it has been recorded that only males inherited land and that marriages were with non-village women who went to live in their husbands' village (Maes 1941:9–10). This had the effect of creating a localized land-holding patrilineal descent group. The existence of numerous New Mexico place names derived from particular patronymics suggests that this structural type may have once been more frequent than at present.[6]

Another alternative, still ascertainable through present-day genealogies, was the system involving what anthropologists would term an exchange of wives through a broader region including several nearby villages. Leonard (1943:113) says, ". . . there developed in time, all over the Spanish-American area, a pattern of highly integrated, extended or consanguine family groups. These larger kinship groups almost deserve to be called clans."

Weaver (1965:40) reports a similar concept he calls *La Sangrelidad* from the northern rural village where he recently worked. This term, which might be translated "the blood relatives," refers to persons who belong to the same bilateral kin group as opposed to those of other similar groups. Since bilateral kin groups are ego-oriented with overlapping member-ships, and clans are usually defined as unilineal exogamous discrete units, the former is probably a better term to describe the actual patterning of relationships among these Spanish-Americans. Weaver also notes that the emphasis is on patrilateral kin, and this characteristic might at first glance give the impression that one is dealing with clans. A closer examination of the data clearly indicates, however, that this is not now and never has been the case in New Mexico. Most anthropologists would probably prefer to classify the system as one having bilateral kindreds with a patrilateral skew.

Regardless of the type and degree of interrelatedness along kinship lines, all observers agree that the individual identifies strongly with his natal village and retains a sense of loyalty to it throughout life, even though he may reside elsewhere temporarily or permanently. One way in which this strong community solidarity is expressed and reinforced is through inter-village rivalry, which often breaks out into open physical violence. Most informants remember many instances during their youth when fights occurred between groups of young men from neighboring towns. Weaver mentions such conflict in some detail (1965:151–152). He also notes that this intercommunity strife is generally limited to teenagers and school-age children. Other informants have noted that these fights very frequently arise in connection with sexual competition. Thus, young men may visit a neighboring village with the idea of looking over the girls or crashing a dance party, only to meet opposition from the local swains— either because they wish to protect their sisters' and female cousins' honor or to defend their own interests. As such, this pattern may be considered as part of the system of courtship and marriage.

In the urban situation, two different patterns of regional identification may be observed. As Loomis has noted, "Most large cities in the Southwest are interlaced with cliques of Spanish-speaking people who once lived in villages" (1958:58). These rural-to-urban migrants not only tend to seek others from their own region within the city, but they seem to retain ties with the villages themselves. However, such linkages are perhaps better understood if considered as kinship, rather than territorial ties. As has been shown, it is sometimes difficult to separate these dimensions. The relationships are important not only in terms of the adjustment of the migrant, and their effect on the social structure of the city, but also in relation to the village and its place within the broader social system. Information, as well as goods from the outside world, filters into the rural areas through these linkages. Loomis has pointed out that such contacts were important to the rural dwellers in obtaining relief and making use of other governmental facilities during the Depression (1958:62). Individuals seeking office in either state or national elections also find these ties of kinship and community invaluable.

There is some evidence to suggest that in former years the linkage between the village and the outside world was largely through a leadership figure known as the patron. Frequently there were one or two families in each village who held this position by virtue of the fact that they had greater wealth in livestock or land or both. The patron also frequently owned the only store in the village, selling goods on credit to the villagers who may also have been his employees. Clearly, this gave him some power over them. In addition, since the patron was also probably better educated and better acquainted with the outside world and governmental personnel and regulations, he was generally in a position to advise and even to command the people under his influence. He was not necessarily a tyrant, however (Charles 1940:55).

In return, such leaders could expect loyalty, hard work, and support for their political candidates from the villagers. Even though the classical patron complex as described above has now all but disappeared from the New Mexican scene, largely due to changes in the economic base which supported it (see Chapter III), there are still some aspects of patronship apparent in the ideological system. Thus, both the poor rural Hispano and his equally poor city counterpart may turn for leadership to individuals whom they perceive to have more wealth, power, knowledge, and prestige than others. Such individuals may be Hispanos or Anglos, they may be employers or professionals such as lawyers or medical doctors, or perhaps simply wealthier, more prestigious neighbors. Frequently nothing but frustration results from the situation in which only one member of a two-way relationship perceives it in terms of a patterned set of reciprocal obligations. Inevitably the person whose life is not oriented toward nor dependent upon these dyadic contracts will not behave in an appropriate manner. This, in turn, will cause misunderstanding, hurt feelings, and inconvenience to the one whose expectations have been built upon the ideal operation of a system which is not general throughout the area or throughout the total culture. The non-Hispano, when faced with patron-expectations on the part of the Hispano or even when he is a mere outside observer of such a relationship between two Hispanos, is likely to react with disgust and disdain.

However, certain aspects of patronship survive in the political system. Leonard and Loomis suggested that since it is the county politicians who are thought to control effectively the sources of public relief and employment, in some measure these men have come to take the place of the patron under the old system.[7] Astute candidates recognize this pattern and make use of it during campaigns. Indeed, state as well as municipal and county campaigns are largely concerned with the candidates as *personalities* and emphasize the extent to which they will take care of their constituents. The heavy dependence of the New Mexican economy on government spending and employment is also an important factor in that it increases the effect of the spoils system in determining local political behavior. The matters of how the candidates intend to govern, the basic issues for which they stand, or even their technical competency to fulfill certain positions are of far less importance to many voters than other personal characteristics (see Judah 1961). An individual votes for the man who will "take care of him and his" through *personal* rather than formal institutional means. Some politicians who have done this have been attacked on charges of nepotism and worse.[8] Others, who have tended to relate to their constituents more through impersonal means, have been accused of "selling out" their people.

Although often considered to be typical of Latin Americans in general, this situation is probably more understandable in terms of the structure of the society involved, rather than as a product of a particular culture, or even less as a reflection of a personality type. Certainly the political history of many non-Latin areas in the United States shows similar processes to have been at work elsewhere. As Holmes has put it, ". . . if the ethnic flavor differs somewhat from that in most states, it is mainly in the spicing, much as chili differs from clam chowder" (1964:73, 74). New Mexico has no monopoly on political corruption, which can indeed only be called corruption when viewed in a particular social context. In fact, the personal element in politics, which is frequently dubbed "bossism," can be viewed as an institution in and of itself, which functions to protect a group that for one reason or another is set apart from the dominant majority. Edmonson has suggested that for the Hispano villages, this system ". . . tends to cushion cultural differences and to slow the process of cultural change" (1957:52).

This is not to suggest that the Hispano villagers are now or ever have been naive when it comes to politics. Holmes has criticized anthropologists and other social scientists for not recognizing the political nature of many social institutions that existed before U.S. conquest. Thus, he says:

> The assignment of herd or guard duty, determination of the type and priority of repairs to an irrigation system, the assignment of

water rights, and the organization of a joint venture of several families or villages are all of an order of activity likely to result in specific institutional arrangements. Merely to list such activities is to make obvious their political nature. Several formal organizations of a broad membership arose in many areas to perform the needed or desired activities. These organizations also provided a training of considerable utility for those who grappled with the problems and requirements of the new polity (1964:37–38).

Holmes also demonstrates that the voting records of the past fifty years indicate a lack of uniformity and an absence of monopoly in political power which he takes as evidence of the lack of bossism. He suggests that "there must often have been alternative sets of leadership in active competition" (1964:31).

Actually, most anthropologists and sociologists would probably accept this point of view, with some modifications. Many observers have described factionalism on the village level and related it to political activity. Wolff (1950) has specifically denied that bossism played a role in the village in which he worked. Ramsay found little evidence of authoritarianism in politics in the counties possessing a high percentage of Spanish-speaking citizens (1951:50). Edmonson states that the system of factions is likely to remain a feature of the Hispano political system in New Mexico for some time to come (1957:52), and Weaver makes much the same point (1965:205). This tendency toward factionalism has frequently been considered a hindrance to effective cooperation rather than a mechanism serving to check and balance political power and thus provide better government. However, this is not necessarily inconsistent with the views expressed above in relation to personalism in politics. Rather, it is precisely in his role as a mediator between the villagers and the impersonality of the outside social structure that the local politician succeeds or fails in the eyes of his constituents.

The rights and obligations involved in kinship and patronship
will probably continue to be important in determining political
behavior at least for a time, for these have proven to be time-
honored means of assuring loyalties in both directions. The point
that needs more emphasis is that although this system may not
always assure the best possible government for *all* persons involved, it is not necessarily either corrupt or naive, and it has
served as one means of integrating the Hispano villages and
their inhabitants with the impersonal, foreign, and dominant U.S.
sociocultural system. Without some such mechanism these villages
would likely have been even more "forgotten" by the larger
society than they have been. As long as any remnant of the old
village system remains, the author would predict that patronship
will survive there. It may also survive, but with a shakier base,
in the city *barrios*. As will be shown in Chapter VIII, however,
new forms of organization are developing in the latter, and these
may prove more viable.

La Raza

The third dimension of social solidarity is that commonly known
throughout the Southwest as *la raza*. Although the literal translation of this would be "the race," this fails to communicate its
actual meaning for those who use the term. The concept appears
to have little or nothing to do with heritable physical characteristics so often associated with race by lay persons, and which
indeed are used as the bases of biological classifications of race.
Thus, it is difficult or impossible for most informants to describe
the physical characteristics of *la raza*. The majority would probably find it amusing to be asked to do so, although some of the
newer activist groups place high value on what they term
"brown" skin color and other physical characteristics of the
mestizo. Nevertheless, it seems difficult for most Hispanos to

verbalize their attitudes, and investigation turns up many seeming inconsistencies. Thus, one informant stated emphatically that the term does *not* cover persons from Mexico. She thought it *might* include Spaniards from Spain, but she was somewhat unsure of this since she and her family mostly use the term in reference to very close relatives and friends—their "own small circle." Later in the interview, however, she extended this primary group to include her whole village and wound up by describing a young immigrant male from Mexico who had come to her community about twelve years ago to work as a sheepherder for a local family. He is now considered to be a permanent member of the community—everyone likes him, though he is still unmarried, speaks no English, and is definitely one of the less privileged in the village. He, in my informant's opinion, is unequivocally a member of *la raza.*

When one tries to pinpoint the concrete elements by which an individual may be identified as a member of *la raza,* or by which to define the group as a whole, many problems arise. A speaking knowledge of Spanish is frequently taken as being symbolic of group status.[9] Yet there are today an increasing number of Hispanos who speak Spanish very poorly or not at all, and, of course, there are some non-Hispanos who speak Spanish. The same sorts of problems arise in relation to Spanish surnames. Informants seem to agree that some degree of Spanish ancestry is a *sine qua non,* and in the last analysis this does seem to delimit best the criteria actually used by the people in identifying one of "their own." Thus, even in regard to those persons who for one reason or another prefer to deny their Spanish background, one informant said, "They're members of *la raza* anyway, like it or not!" And on the other hand, some individuals with no known Spanish ancestry but who speak Spanish fluently and interact frequently with Hispanos might be considered as part of *la raza.* In the majority of cases, however, the members of *la raza* are known by their Spanish surnames, their Spanish language, their Spanish-derived culture, and their association with other persons of like characteristics. These elements give them a kind of mystical common bond, the importance of which cannot be overemphasized. It is, in the long run, beyond the kinship and community ties, the major unit with which the individual identifies regardless of differences in socioeconomic status, residence patterns, religion, color, etc. The translation "the people," meaning "my people," seems appropriate. Marden and Meyer (1962:140) have noted that there is much similarity and much cohesiveness to this group, no matter where they are:

> Thus, in California, the two most popular leaders are a New Mexican and a Coloradan; in New Mexico, a Texas-Mexican has done wonders in rallying the Hispanos for much-needed reforms in government. In Texas, a New Mexican has been in the middle of the state Latin-American leadership.

It is certain that appeals to the mystical cohesiveness of *la raza* are consciously made by politicians and others in vying for the support of the Spanish-speaking group. An organization, formed in Denver in the fall of 1965 for the purpose of alleviating some of the worst problems due to poverty and cultural deprivation among the Spanish-speaking there, purposely contrived a name whose initials would spell "LA RASA" (Latin American Research and Service Association). The Ford Foundation is currently sponsoring what is known as the Southwest Council of La Raza, with headquarters in Tucson, Arizona (see Chapter VIII).

Even though *la raza* as an organizing principle incorporates and supersedes the dimensions of kinship and community discussed in the foregoing, it is necessary to stress that this concept becomes important only vis-à-vis the Anglo world. In other words, unlike the kinship group and the community, *la raza* is in no way a structured corporate unit, nor for the most part is it so considered by the Spanish-speaking. It is true that politicians and others with an occasional axe to grind may make emotional appeals to the "members" of *la raza* to stick together, to cast their votes along ethnic lines, etc., but in fact they seem never to have done so. This becomes particularly clear in an examination of voting behavior through the entire course of statehood and even before.[10] But in other areas as well, there is evidence of much disagreement and internal division within *la raza*.

Rubel has discussed anxiety and disaffection as being characteristic of social relations among Americans of Mexican descent in a south Texas city (1966). He links these traits with a type of social system called the "atomistic society," which is defined as one in which there is a lack of cooperation between nuclear families.[11] It is somewhat difficult to compare the situation in New Mexico with that in Texas, since there are no comparable studies of Spanish-speaking enclaves in cities dominated by Anglos in New Mexico. However, it seems to the author that the apparent divisions within the Spanish-American group in New Mexico may be better explained in quite different terms. First of all, no evidence is seen, from the literature nor from the author's own research in New Mexico, of the hostility, lack of trust, and general disaffection among unrelated persons such as that described by Rubel. Certainly, sharp verbal attacks may be made upon individuals with whom one has a quarrel, and there may be feuds between two factions of a village or between villages, as mentioned before, but hostility or belligerence has not seemed to be a general theme of the society. More recently, hostility has been apparent among the militant youth toward the "establishment Hispano," but this seems a new development, and one which reflects poverty and generation differences.

In order better to understand the way in which the concept of *la raza* operates, some of the structural mechanisms must be discussed which tend not only to unify this group and prevent it from losing its identity altogether, but which at the same time make it difficult for it to act as a corporate unit.

There are, as mentioned above, several principles of division which *cross-cut* the Hispano group as a whole. The most important ones include rural versus urban, rich versus poor, Catholic versus Protestant, Democrat versus Republican, educated versus uneducated, Spanish versus Mexican, acculturation versus tradition. Of course, some of these may not be independent variables; and though some produce two mutually exclusive categories, most of them, as analytic tools, merely allow placement of persons along a continuum upon which arbitrary dividing points may be delineated. The major point to be emphasized is that most of these do vary independently; and, with the exception of the last two items enumerated, they also vary within the Anglo population.

Thus, Spanish-Americans continually find themselves aligned with some Anglos against some Hispanos because of certain variations in interest. At no point are discrete units produced which always coincide with each other in opposition to all others. Even the family may find itself divided along such issues as urbanization, education, and acculturation. Similarly, villages may be cross-cut by religious and political differences. Thus, in religious matters, a Protestant Hispano may identify with a Protestant Anglo as opposed to a Catholic Hispano. This can be interpreted as an integrative mechanism, and it is suggested that it is precisely through such means that the Hispanos of New Mexico are in fact thoroughly enmeshed today in the broader society. It is true that from the point of view of the state or area as a whole, ethnicity may also be seen as a classifying principle. But today it is merely one of many cross-cutting divisions. Therefore, for some purposes, *la raza* may be a unifying concept or principle, but like Catholicism or poverty, it is not sufficiently strong to override the commitments and interests represented by the other divisions mentioned.

Social Class and the Legend of Cultural Differences

Ranked or stratified social classes have apparently been a part of the total social structure in New Mexico since the very beginning of the Spanish-Colonial period, and ethnic differences seem to have been important among the criteria used for assigning class membership then as now. In the early days the conquered Indian slave or servant was at the bottom of the social scale, along with those mestizos brought from Mexico or born in the new colony. The *Genizaros,* Christianized and partially Hispanicized converts from the nomadic groups, also swelled the lower-class ranks, but the "wild" roving brothers of these people will not be considered since they remained outside the effective boundaries of the Spanish-Colonial society. It might also be said that the Pueblos, even though converted to the Catholic religion and subject to the laws of the Spaniards, remained effectively outside the social system of their conquerors. The two societies were linked at various points but not really united or integrated into one system (Spicer 1954). Nevertheless, there seems to have been a constant flow of defectors from the Pueblos who did become assimilated into the Spanish population at the lower end of the social scale.

The upper class was small and of relatively pure European or Caucasian stock, since the men of this group could afford to bring Spanish women from Spain or Mexico as their wives. They were the noblemen and officials appointed by the crown and later by Mexico to conquer and hold the land, search for wealth, and maintain order among the citizens. Some of them were granted large tracts of land which they pledged to settle. There was also a group of small farmers, of both Spanish and Spanish-Indian descent, some of whom settled on the large landgrants of the upper class, and some of whom were granted lands upon which they formed villages. Some writers have referred to these farmers, along with the common soldiers, as a middle class (Leonard 1943:110; Senter 1945:35), reserving lower-class status for the Indians and mestizos—particularly those who were the servants or slaves of the upper classes. This model may well reflect the earliest situation, but time seems to have achieved a cultural, social, and racial blending of the original lower-class groups, and by the time of the conquest by the United States, a two-class system appears to have been in effect (Zeleny 1944:321). The lower class was distinguished by the darker complexion of most of its members, by a lack of formal education, by a low income and poor standard of living, and by a low degree of participation in the power structure of the colony. It is significant that these are still the characteristics of the lower class today.

The development of a true middle class began only after annexation when new patterns of land exploitation, opportunities for wage labor, and finally, after about 1871,[12] public educational facilities opened the way to economic advancement and upward social mobility. The middle class has continued to grow, largely being recruited from the rural areas of the northern part of the state and, more recently, from the urban lower class. The processes of modernization and urbanization and their effects upon acculturation and assimilation will be discussed in further detail in Chapter VI.

At this point the author's primary concern is with the structure of stratification itself, including the relationships among the

classes. This new middle class is distinguishable from both the
lower and upper classes on the basis of certain patterns of behavior, and particularly in terms of world view. Although
acculturation to Anglo culture patterns may be said to cross-cut
the social classes, particularly in the urban areas, in many respects it could be said that the middle class tends to be the most
"Anglicized" today. Members of this group speak only English
in their homes; place a positive value upon higher, especially
technical, education; frequently reside in middle-class Anglo
neighborhoods; send their children to dancing school and to
summer camp; sometimes become Protestant; usually change
their dietary patterns; and increase their participation in Anglo
voluntary associations. They are often described by other Hispanos as *agringado* or *inglesado* (Madsen 1961), or *americanizado.*[13]

Since most of the members of the middle class have risen from
the lower class, many of them still have contact with members
of the latter—particularly with relatives "left behind." Moreover,
psychological stress often develops through a confusion of roles
and identities. Some of the values of their former way of life
remain with them, yet they find them incompatible with their
new goals. Even though many of these people would like to live
in large, modern, and more comfortable houses, for example, they
do not wish to leave their old neighborhoods. Yet since the latter
are frequently run-down, are assigned low property values, and
may even be zoned as commercial sections, they are not willing
to build or improve upon already existing houses in these areas.
In the long run, many do leave for Anglo neighborhoods, but
they return on Sundays to the old neighborhoods to worship in
a Spanish-language church, have dinner with their parents and
grandparents, etc. Little by little they become immersed in the

affairs of their new neighborhoods, however, and return less often than before.

Since the members of this class are still not secure, either financially or socially, they are frequently highly critical of other persons of Spanish surname whose behavior does not conform to either the old Hispano or the new Anglo middle-class patterns they are trying to emulate. This group frowns upon dirtiness, ignorance, laziness, sexual laxity, civil disobedience, crime, and violence. They recognize that both Anglos and Hispanos are frequently guilty of any or all of these, but they also are patently aware that Anglos are likely to pounce upon Hispano failures and generalize them to include the entire ethnic group. In their efforts to protect themselves from such stereotyping, they are quick to attack other Hispanos, frequently in the name of Hispano dignity. When possible, they will dissociate themselves, not only as individuals but as a group, from the lower classes, claiming that the latter are not in fact Hispanos at all, but "Mexicans."

Thus a new dimension has been added to the conception of social class in the Southwest in this century. The old stigma of Indian ancestry has been replaced by a condescension toward those presumed to be of Mexican, as opposed to New Mexican, descent. This reflects what might also be called a statewide pre-occupation with the supposed cultural uniqueness of New Mexico and what has been referred to as the New Mexico legend. This legend, accepted by most New Mexicans today on faith, as it were, has become part of the New Mexican cultural pattern. As is usual with legends, this one serves a number of functions within the culture, the most important of which is to define social position and to avert discrimination, real or imagined.

In New Mexico from earliest times there were some cultural distinctions among the different social classes, but they were not too unlike those found elsewhere. The lower classes apparently borrowed more items directly from the agricultural Indians who lived under circumstances similar to theirs. However, it is clear that Mexico was considered by all as the cultural center and homeland. Her ways and fashions were copied as well as possible by the upper-class settlers—especially those in the larger towns— and many of these fashions eventually filtered down to the more rural and lower-class countryside. (See Chapter II, pp. 28–30.)

This pattern was reinforced during the Mexican national period from 1821–1846, when numerous new settlers moved into New Mexico, many settling in the more southern reaches of the state from Socorro southward, especially in the Mesilla Valley. That there was some emigration to Mexico as well is not generally recognized. In 1874 when an eastern cattleman desired to buy a portion of the Baca Grant in the Estancia Valley, most of the heirs were living in Mexico City (Bergere n.d.). At the time of the U.S. conquest, numerous villages along the lower Rio Grande were relocated in order to preserve the Mexican citizenship of the villagers. It has often been suggested that the majority of the Spanish in New Mexico at the time of the U.S. conquest was pleased with the change in government. In spite of the fact that the occupation in 1846 was a bloodless event, only a few months later a number of Mexicans in league with groups of Pueblo Indians staged an attempted revolt against the new Anglo leaders.

Zeleny has pointed out that the distinctions between the rich and the poor were further increased during the Mexican regime, and she suggests that this insurrection may have been a symptom of the rising social consciousness of the Indians and the lower class against the *ricos* (1944:82–84). Perhaps it was primarily the upper-class long-time residents who were happy about the new government. It is certain that many of the upper class survived the conquest extremely well, cooperating with the Anglos and furthering their own interests at the expense of the poorer classes. Clearly, this would have been objectionable to the latter, and some sort of protest might have been expected. In the long run, however, most of the Hispanos probably accepted the situation because it was clearly inevitable, and there was no place else to go.

During the early decades after the conquest there is little evidence that the Mexican population was looked down upon or discriminated against on the basis of their ethnic differences per se. Intermarriage between Anglo men and Mexican women was apparently quite common and not restricted to any particular social class. Business and commercial mergers between Anglos and Mexicans occurred frequently; and in politics, combinations of Anglos and Mexicans worked together in each of the major parties. The original constitution of the state explicitly provided for the protection of the rights of the Spanish-speaking population.

However, there is also evidence that this acceptance or tolerance of the so-called natives began to change about the turn of the century. Larrazolo, a naturalized New Mexican, born in Mexico, believed that he was defeated in his race for Congress in 1906 because he was a native (Cordova and Judah 1952:4). However, in 1919 this same man was elected governor. It has been shown that following World War I the Spanish-Americans grew in political strength as a result of their being organized in the American Legion (Armstrong 1959:33–34). It was also in the years immediately following World War I that the term "Spanish-Colonial" first came into general usage in the Southwest to refer to the early pioneers and their culture (Austin 1931). Before that, the term "Mexican" had been used for all Spanish-speaking persons. The author believes the substitution of the term "Spanish-

Country church at Peña Blanca.

(Opposite page)
(*Above*) The two-family adobe house in a rural setting is similar to those found in many Indian pueblos today.
(*Below*) Church and graveyard at Truchas, New Mexico.

Some Spanish-Americans find security and contentment in their bicultural patterns for living.

A Penitente *morada*.

One of the many northern Spanish-American villages nestles against its hills.

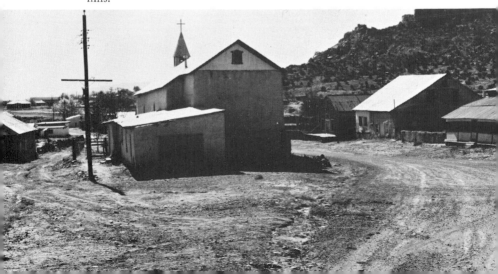

The teenager—a product of two worlds—sometimes member of neither.

Children like this silently plead for understanding and help in keeping up with their English-speaking peers in an Anglo world.

A rural general store is also home for these girls.

The urbane sophisticated Hispano retains his Catholic faith.

An urban family, happy and united in spite of obvious poverty, relaxes with friends.

This adobe house hides a yard full of potentially useful items, including a trailer for visiting kinsmen or a married child.

(*Left*) Members of the Alianza preparing for the march on Santa Fe, July 4, 1966. Their headquarters building appears in the background.
(*Right*) Alianza members display a sign recounting one of their grievances in regard to nineteenth-century land losses.

American" is directly related to an increase in prejudice and discrimination discernible during the 1920's and 1930's.

In New Mexico, among those of Spanish heritage, three general patterns or techniques exist for countering felt discrimination. The first is to dissociate oneself completely from Mexicans, denying any historical relationship or similarity between their culture and that found in New Mexico. This reaction is usually identified with the upper classes—especially the urbanites—but it is also found to some extent in the country. It emphasizes the grandeur and glory of the way of life of the Spanish *conquistadores,* from whom most such persons claim to be descended in virtually an unbroken line. Many of these people are quite successful by Anglo worldly standards and may achieve considerable prestige within their communities, although they will probably not move in Anglo social circles. In the past many of them have been made to feel the pain of discrimination, and their defense has been to gild and glorify the past which is now lost to them forever. Many of the symbols to which they cling perhaps never existed in colonial New Mexico, but the belief in the past does serve the purpose of alleviating feelings of inferiority and furthering social and ethnic solidarity.

A second pattern to counteract felt discrimination is to take on as fully as possible the Anglo way of life and cultural paraphernalia. This appears to be most typical of, though not confined to, the middle classes, most of whom have risen from the lower. Although this group is not, for the most part, concerned with the glories of the past, they too will reject lower-class Hispanos as Mexicans, particularly if their moral code seems different. One informant in this group stated that the Spanish-speaking on welfare were all Mexicans, as contrasted with the Spanish, whose characters were superior.

Finally, the third general pattern in dealing with discrimination is typical of primarily the lower class and is based upon the principle of an eye for an eye. It tends to group together all Spanish and Mexicans and is frequently openly antagonistic to Anglos as a class, as well as to the *agringado* group. There is a recent movement entitled the *Alianza Federal de Mercedes,* which promises to sue the state of New Mexico or the federal government, or both, to secure justice for the heirs of the original land grantees who were frequently swindled of their land.[14] This movement may be interpreted as an attempt to organize and improve the status of the lower-class *Mexicano* group. Edmonson (1957) points out that:

> . . . much of the traditional Hispano culture may be changed or even swept away within a generation but for the imponderable factor of contacts with Mexico. Hispano New Mexico has been thoroughly willing to borrow heavily from Mexican culture in even the recent past. The continued existence of Mexicano ethnic identity in New Mexico may well hinge on this (p. 57).

Not only are persons in this class more tolerant of recent immigrants from Mexico, but they object less to the term "Mexican-American" when applied to themselves. They recognize the obvious cultural similarities between themselves and those south of the border, and they respect the modern Mexican nation. They are also becoming aware of the fact that they share a minority-group status with Mexican-American populations elsewhere—particularly in California and Texas.

For the social scientist concerned with analyzing the socio-economic and cultural characteristics of the Spanish-speaking population of the United States, it is important to understand the bases underlying the class structure among Hispanos in New Mexico and the differences between this population and that found in other states. But as Marden and Meyer (1962:140) have said, quoting George Sanchez,

> In the last analysis these are all Spanish-Mexican peoples, with all that that implies. These people, in New Spain and then in Mexico and in the U.S., have been consistently disadvantaged peoples, much in the same boat as to socioeconomic circumstances. These common antecedents have given a fundamental sameness to their culture, and as a consequence to their behavior. Therefore, they are all mexicanos, they all belong to "la raza."

It should be emphasized that the present status of the middle- and upper-class Spanish-speaking groups in New Mexico appears to be considerably higher than in other U.S. areas such as California and Texas.[15] It has not always been so (Zeleny 1944). It also appears that as the Spanish-speaking people rise in the socioeconomic hierarchy their political power declines. This may be related to the process of acculturation which leads more individuals to align themselves according to interests other than the preservation of the ethnic group, as well as to the fact that their numerical majority has steadily declined in recent years. It may fairly be said that in this sense the New Mexican situation is different from that in other areas. But the primary differences seem to be in the social behavior relating the classes to each other and to the larger Anglo social structures of which they form a part.

Notes

1 For descriptions of family organization, see especially Burma (1954); Hurt (1941); Johansen (1942, 1943); Kluckhohn and Strodtbeck (1961); Walter (1938).

2 There is a series of interesting small studies of the Albuquerque area. See, in

addition to Moore, Cassel (1956); Johnson (1948); Sjoberg (1947); Waggoner (1941).

3 Johansen (1942:154).

4 Edmonson (1957:56); Kluckhohn and Strodtbeck (1961:192); Weaver (1965).

5 Colorado State College, under the direction of Paul Kutsche, started a long-range study program along these lines in 1966, working in an isolated northern mountain village.

6 Such names as "Los Lunas," "Los Griegos," "Los Cisneros," "Los Padillas," "Los Vigiles," "Los Trujillos," etc. See Pearce (1965:92–93).

7 Leonard and Loomis (1941:59). The subject of patronship has been a popular one among observers of New Mexican society. On the role of the personal patron in the political sphere, see especially Barker (1931:88); H. Fergusson (1925:112); Edmonson (1957:63); Leonard (1943:68); Russell (1938:36); Sjoberg (1947:-49); Zeleny (1944:213). Since the 1930's and the New Deal, there has been a tendency among many of the Hispanos to look upon the government itself as well as its representatives as a more impersonal type of patron. On this concept, see Donnelly (1940:244); Judah (1961:1–3); Johansen (1941b:165); Loomis and Grisham (1943:34); Perrigo (1960:370); Weaver (1965:159).

8 Lahart (1958:100) quotes a newspaper account in which Dennis Chavez, former U.S. Senator, was accused of nepotism. Also see Rubel (1966) for comparable material from a Texas city.

9 The *Albuquerque Journal* (October 27, 1966) reported on a confrontation between a Spanish-American government official and a group of Spanish-Americans accused of breaking the law. "Zamora testified the mob failed to grab him at first but 'then two ladies saw me,' and cried in Spanish, 'There's another one.' I told them in Spanish 'Get your hands off me' . . . when they heard I could speak Spanish they said, 'Here's one of ours, don't hurt him,' Zamora testified."

10 See, e.g., Judah (1961:5–6); Edmonson (1957:50); Holmes (1964:325); among others.

11 Rubel (1966:207).

12 Compulsory school attendance was enacted as early as 1860 (Horn 1963:84), but Rideling tells us that until 1871 there were no public schools in the territory of New Mexico. By 1876 there were 133, with 5,625 pupils (Rideling 1876:19). Previous to this a number of private schools and some so-called public schools had been established, but these were attended primarily by children of the upper classes. See Mayfield (1938).

13 See Dickerson (1919) for an interesting contemporary point of view on this, and Grebler (1966) for an up-to-date synthesis.

14 See chapters V and VIII for a full description of this organization.

[15] Broom and Shevky (1952:154) report that formerly in California those individuals who had advanced substantially, either economically or in educational status, frequently used terms such as "Spanish," "Colonial," or "Californian" instead of "Mexican" in reference to their ancestry. This situation has changed in that state, and there are some indications that certain elements in New Mexico are changing in this same direction. See chapters V, VI, and VIII.

Chapter V

VOLUNTARY ASSOCIATIONS

With the growth and dispersal of the Spanish-speaking population within the United States and with their increasing participation in the industrial-based society of this country, they are apparently turning more and more to the large, non-kinship kinds of institutions for mutual aid and community action, which may be grouped under the term "voluntary associations." Clubs and organizations of various sorts provide a means by which individuals may achieve the sense of belonging to an in-group in an otherwise cold and impersonal world. From a functional point of view, organizations may also operate as pressure or action groups within a national or local community to bring about culture change through legislation or other socially approved means. By definition, voluntary associations are joined because one has a personal interest in the activities, aims, goals, or symbols of the club. Also, some such clubs limit their membership to those acceptable to the group as a whole—again common background and interest dictate the rules of recruitment.

Many students of Hispanic-derived culture patterns in the United States have commented that voluntary associations are few and that the Spanish-speaking as a group are not characteristically joiners.[1] It is true that not many Spanish names appear on the rolls of the more usual types of Anglo clubs such as the nationally known men's service clubs, college fraternities, women's clubs, country clubs, etc. However, a careful perusal of the literature, plus the field notes from current research, indicates a wide variety of clubs and associations in the southwestern area in which Hispanos do in fact participate. Indeed, there is plenty of evidence to indicate that in New Mexico the Spanish Colonials had pretty much the same "joining" habits as did their contemporaries in Mexico and in Europe. The earliest associations, apparently founded almost immediately after colonization, were the *cofradías* or *confraternidades* (lay brotherhoods) sponsored by the Catholic church. The most complete accounting of these comes from the visitation of Dominguez in 1776. He lists the confraternities of Our Lady of Light, the Poor Souls, the Blessed Sacrament, the Rosary, and the Third Order of Saint Francis, the last not properly a confraternity at all but operated in a similar fashion. Dominguez notes that the Confraternity of the Poor Souls had been founded as early as 1718 in Albuquerque (Adams and Chavez 1956). It is perhaps significant that the religious societies noted by the visiting priest were limited to the three Spanish parishes of Santa Fe, Santa Cruz de la Canada, and Albuquerque. There was none in the Pueblo Indian Missions, as has been noted by Fray Angelico Chavez (1954:109).

The primary purposes of these organizations were to maintain the church and the statues of saints, to conduct religious activities in the absence of priests, and to provide mutual aid during times of crisis for the members. The famous *Penitentes* probably derived from this type of organization, as is indicated in part by the full and proper name, *La Confraternidad de Nuestro Padre Jesus Nazareno,* by which the members themselves refer to their society. This society apparently developed in New Mexico much later than those mentioned earlier and combined the features of the already existing confraternity organization with scourging and bloodletting taken from the Spanish penitential tradition. Madame Calderon de la Barca describes such a rite in Mexico City in the 1830's. Chavez further suggests, ". . . it is significant that certain villages in which the Penitente movement was strongest were also greatly populated by *Genizaros* [Spanish and non-Pueblo Indian mixtures]" (*op. cit.,* 116). However, the total geographical area finally covered by this society extended from southern Colorado to the Pinos Altos Mountains in the south (Woodward 1935:ii). *Penitente* chapters were found in most, if not all, of the northern Spanish settlements during the last half of the nineteenth century and the first part of the twentieth. Although many chapters have long since ceased to exist, there are still many small towns where the groups are very much alive and functioning as in the past. In addition, there are many other church-associated societies which operate today as before to maintain the Catholic religion and to provide assistance to the members upon death of a relative, illness, etc. Such groups in Albuquerque and other cities may also function as social clubs—giving parties, raising funds, and even participating in community action programs.

There are also now, and have been in the past, many other organizations which function in a similar fashion but which are not connected with religion. Some of these have developed into supra-local institutions, covering the entire Southwest. One of the earliest of these was the *Alianza Hispano-Americana,* founded at least as long ago as 1894 (Officer 1964:53). This society, like so many other similar ones, collects dues from its members, from which payments are made to stated beneficiaries upon the death of a member. In addition, the organization publishes a magazine entitled *Alianza,* which reports the affairs of the association and news of interest to *la raza*. The *Alianza Hispano-Americana* states that it is "dedicated to the social, economic, and fraternal progress of the inhabitants of the southwest" (*Alianza*, December 1942).

Of a similar nature were the *Sociedad Cervantes* and the *Sociedad Española de Beneficiencia Mutua* mentioned by Brown (1945:274) and the *Fraternal Aid Union* which was in existence as early as 1915 and probably earlier (Cochrane 1915:37).

The idea of cooperating in groups for specific purposes for the mutual benefit of members is not at all new to the Spanish-Americans of New Mexico. In addition to the church-oriented groups mentioned, the villagers have long known various kinds of community organization, including the Ditch Association for purposes of building, maintaining, and regulating the flow of water in irrigation ditches. This has been mentioned by many writers, but Dickey (1949:7) has a particularly good discussion of the structure of these groups and mentions the fact that there had been a precedent for this type of organization in Spain. Weaver (1965:48) describes a present-day Water Supply Association in the community he studied, which clearly is historically linked with the ditch association practice. Hurt also mentions a Water Commission in the town of Manzano, which again reflects the continuing extreme importance of this valuable resource to the economy of the rural Spanish-American in the state (1941:137-138). Of a similar nature are the livestock associations, found in many northern villages, which function to further the interests of those engaged in this type of activity to the mutual benefit of the members. These may have developed after the formation of the national forests and the consequent regulation of grazing and herd sizes by the federal government.

Hurt (1941:171) mentions a men's society in one small town which was only "indirectly connected with the church, having its own officers and managing its own finances." This organization was responsible for the construction of a large community building in which plays and dances were held. Saunders and Samora (1955) mention that there were health cooperatives in New Mexico sponsored by the Farm Security Administration, which paid the medical bills of members.

There is also mention in the literature of vigilante organizations operating especially in the northern counties at various times in the past, although no systematic historical account of these groups exists to this writer's knowledge. Among these were societies organized to protect the citizens of various villages from bandit gangs, or *gavillas,* which brought terror to parts of Taos, San Miguel, Mora, and Colfax counties during the 1890's (Jaramillo 1941:21–23). *Las Gorras Blancas* (The White Caps) was another organization operating in San Miguel County especially, which seems to have been aimed at sabotaging the efforts of Anglo homesteaders to carve up the wide expanses of former grazing lands in the area (Jaramillo 1941:23; A. J. Martinez n.d.). Weaver (1965:172) mentions a similar organization, known as *La Mano Negra* (The Black Hand), functioning in the northwestern part of the state as late as the 1920's. These groups were probably involved in more formalized politics as well, although this seems not to have been their primary purpose.

Loomis and Grisham (1943:26) describe a more generalized Community Council, which handled a variety of matters of concern to the entire village. Today's counterpart to this structure is the community action group, of which there are several functioning in Albuquerque, Santa Fe, Las Vegas, Taos, and perhaps elsewhere. These are frequently given impetus and assistance by personnel of the local Office of Economic Opportunity, and in some areas by persons who were associated with the Peace Corps and Vista which operated training programs at the University of New Mexico from 1964–1967 and 1966–1969, respectively.

Another very interesting rather recent development is the club known as Life With Pride, an organization of women receiving Aid to Dependent Children. This organization was begun by a local welfare worker in 1964 to encourage these women to help each other by sharing their problems and in taking advantage of existing opportunities to educate themselves so that they might eventually become financially independent. The idea spread rapidly in Albuquerque and soon there were several chapters with from 20 to 40 members each. Meetings are held regularly at which guest speakers discuss topics ranging from birth control to household management and better personal-grooming techniques. The club also strongly encourages its members to attend classes at the local vocational institutes. Although these groups are not restricted to Spanish-American women, most of the members are of this heritage.

The concept of mutual aid runs throughout these examples and can be seen as the basic principle underlying such well-known organizations as the League of United Latin American Citizens (LULAC), the G. I. Forum, the Good Americans Association founded in 1958 in Denver, and many others. LULAC, for example, arose from a previously existing association called *Orden Hijos de America* (Sons of America), which

. . . was founded in San Antonio in 1921, and seems to have been the brain-child of two or three Mexican-Americans of influence in the Mexican quarter of that city. The constitution of this organization restricts its membership exclusively to citizens of the United States of Mexican or Spanish extraction, either native or naturalized, and its central purpose is stated to be that the members use their influence in all fields of social, economic and political action in order to realize the greatest enjoyment possible of all the rights and privileges and prerogatives extended by the American Constitution (Weeks 1929:260).

Similarly, the G. I. Forum was founded in Texas in 1948 to combat discriminatory practices against the returning Mexican-American World War II veteran. However, the association's aims and objectives are headed by the desire to "develop leadership by creating interest in the Spanish-speaking population to participate intelligently and wholeheartedly in community, civic and political affairs." [2] Chapters now exist in all the southwestern states, as well as in many others. These groups operate as social and civic improvement organizations, but they concentrate upon the problems of the Spanish-speaking and, as such, are ethnic mutual-aid societies.

There are other groups being organized throughout the Southwest today. Many of these are directed toward one or two specific issues, such as the improvement of education, or community organization. Thus, there are LA RASA (Latin American Research and Service Association), founded in Denver in October, 1965; the Latin American Educational Foundation, the Association of Mexican-American Educators, the Mexican-American Political Association, and others (see Chapter VIII).

Organized labor has never been a strong force in this not highly industrialized state, but Spanish-Americans have probably been as active as others in this area. As early as 1890 there was a society known as *Los Caballeros de Labor,* composed almost entirely of Hispanos. Not much is known of the activities of this group, but it has been suggested that it was primarily concerned with political matters (A. J. Martinez n.d.). Most of the labor union activity has been centered in the mining areas in Colfax, Eddy, McKinley, and Grant counties and in the city of Albuquerque (Holmes 1964:13). According to Maes (1935:139), unionism was stronger in 1912 than in the 1930's when he was writing, and he attributed this weakness in part to the conflict between Spanish and Anglo interests at the time.

In 1934 the *Liga Obrera de Habla Español* (League of Spanish-Speaking Workers) was organized in New Mexico. Its primary concern was with the problems of the Spanish-speaking worker in the mining industry and in farm labor, but accusations of communism were made against the group while still in its infancy, and it seems not to have lasted long (Maes 1935:139; Stevenson 1936:68; Swayne 1936:32). This special organization of Spanish-American laborers is probably best viewed as an outgrowth of the social situation which obtained in New Mexico during the 1930's, when discrimination was fairly overt and feelings often ran high on both sides. World War II and its consequences changed this situation considerably, as will be described in greater detail in the next chapter. Suffice it to say that during the 1940's many New Mexicans left the state to work in defense industries elsewhere, and many others learned industrial and craft skills either directly or indirectly through service in the armed forces. This further enhanced their sophistication and interest in the world at large (Samora 1963:24; Watson and Samora 1954:415). Since the late 1940's the Spanish-Americans have been well represented in the existing labor organizations in New Mexico, and in 1965 there was a number of labor leaders with Spanish surnames, including the state executive secretary of the AFL-CIO.

During the past few years an organization known as the *Alianza Federal de Mercedes* (Federal Alliance of Land Grants) has been gaining members and, recently, much publicity. Although not generally so recognized by the public, this organization and its activities exhibit many of the characteristics of a revitalization or nativistic cult movement. Wallace (1956:265) defined revitalization movements as ". . . deliberate, organized, conscious efforts by members of a society to construct a more satisfying culture." Nativistic movements are, to Wallace, ". . . revitalization movements characterized by strong emphasis on the elimination of alien persons, customs, values, and/or material . . ." (*ibid*:267). It is generally accepted that such movements must be analyzed in relation to culture change, but Smith (1959:11) has said, ". . . cult movements should be distinguished from other phenomena of culture change because they are *deliberate, conscious* and *organized* and are responses to social and economic dissatisfaction" (emphasis supplied). This characterization purposely says nothing about the contextual features of the movement, which may include messianic, millennial, revivalistic, militant, or reformative features, or various combinations of these.

The *Alianza Federal de Mercedes,* later renamed the *Alianza de los Pueblos Libres* (Alliance of Free City-States) and hereafter referred to as the Alianza, may be seen to include all these features. In spite of the fact that the Spanish-Americans have undergone extreme social and economic deprivation during the past century, there appear to have arisen no true nativistic cult movements among them until now.[8] It seems worthwhile to describe and analyze the social and cultural aspects of this organization as part of the total New Mexican pattern on the one hand and as an example of a nativistic cult on the other.

The Alianza was founded and is led by Reies Tijerina, a dynamic young Spanish-speaking man in his forties. Born in Texas, and one of eight children, he claims to have New Mexican ancestors, and a few years ago married a young Spanish-American woman from New Mexico. Throughout his childhood he lived in poverty, moving with his family as a migrant laborer from the cotton plantations of Texas to the beet fields of Colorado. He had little formal schooling, especially after his mother died when he was still a young boy. He recalls intermittent periods, however, when he was able to go to school, and tells of going through garbage cans in order to find something to take with him for lunch. In public he often insists that he had no formal education at all. This image better fits his role in the movement and should be understood as such. It makes him more acceptable to his followers, most of whom have little education themselves.

At some point Tijerina joined a Protestant fundamentalist religious sect and, after a period of training in a Bible school in Texas, went to California where he engaged in preaching. He dates the beginnings of his present activities to a dream he had while working in California. This dream not only gave him directions as to the course he must pursue in organizing his people, but also prophesied his success. Today he de-emphasizes his Protestant faith and background out of deference to the majority of his followers who are Catholic, but he frequently quotes the Bible and makes references to Jesus Christ and his followers.

After several years of preparation, which included a period of study in Mexico of the historical events pertinent to the Hispanos in this area of the world, and after engaging in at least one unsuccessful attempt to organize a group of poverty-stricken rural Spanish-Americans in Arizona, Tijerina came to New Mexico where he began to preach a doctrine welcome to the ears of the long-suffering conquered people.

The elements of this doctrine, which constitute the goals of the Alianza, have been summarized by the author from interviews with Tijerina, perusal of the constitution of the organization, and from observation of the actions of members.

1. The Laws of the Indies provided that the landgrants made in the territory of New Spain should never be sold but should be passed on to the descendants of the original settlers.
2. The Laws of the Indies explicitly recognized the legitimacy of those persons born in the Americas, whether of Spanish or of

mixed Spanish-Indian descent. The Alianza today claims that its members are neither "pure-blood" Spaniards nor "pure-blood" Indians, but a mestizo race. Therefore, they cannot be held responsible for the wrongdoings of either original group. They also claim a status more honorable than that of many other "races," in that their "birth certificate" was given them by Philip II, King of Spain, in 1573. They prefer the term "Indo-Hispano" in reference to themselves.

3. The Treaty of Guadalupe Hidalgo between Mexico and the United States provided for the inhabitants of the territory annexed in 1848, giving them the rights and privileges of U.S. citizens. The Constitution of the United States guarantees the property rights of its citizens.

4. According to the constitution of the state of New Mexico (1911), "All the rights, privileges and immunities, civil, political, and religious, guaranteed to the people of New Mexico by the Treaty of Guadalupe Hidalgo will be preserved inviolable."

5. Those Spanish-Americans who sold their land, and especially those who allied themselves with Anglo interests to purchase lands from their more unfortunate brethren, acted illegally and immorally.

6. The problems and ills of the Spanish-speaking population of the Southwest today all stem from the loss of the bulk of the original Spanish landgrants, amounting to some 4 million acres in all (Burma 1954:16).

7. The Anglo-dominated federal and state governments have also been remiss in failing to protect the Spanish-speaking citizens of New Mexico from discrimination in the schools and in employment opportunities.

8. The Spanish-Americans should band together, as have other minority groups (Indians and Negroes) in the United States in recent years to seek redress for their wrongs in the courts of the United States and to secure equal rights under the laws of this country.

The Alianza has taken various steps toward achieving its goals. First of all, largely through the personal charisma and dynamic speaking ability of Tijerina, it has secured dues-paying members whose contributions support the organization and, to an unknown extent, its leader and his helpers. It is impossible to say how many members there may be at the present time, but the organization claimed 20,000 as of July 1966. By June 1967, the number was estimated by the press as 3,000. Each of these figures represents an extreme; the true membership may be near 10,000. The members are drawn primarily from New Mexico, but they represent several other states as well. At first the members paid $1 per family per month, plus a $10 initiation fee, which was a later innovation, not having been collected until the early part of 1966. Each family was also assessed a lump sum of $100, which could be paid in monthly installments, to help defray court expenses. Since October of 1968, however, after much adverse publicity, accusing the leader of "milking" his poor followers, these assessments and dues were abolished.

The organization maintains an office and meeting hall, in which building the leader and some of his family also live. The Alianza has sponsored and paid for advertisements on the local Spanish-language radio and TV stations and has also printed large numbers of posters, handbills, and other propaganda materials which are distributed throughout New Mexico and other states without charge. At the present time the Alianza is supported by donations from individuals and some organizations, plus honorariums to Tijerina for speaking engagements. In addition to the personal efforts of the leader of the organization, there are a number of other persons who operate in the outlying rural districts to secure more members by publicizing the Alianza's message. These persons apparently work without charge and have private means of support.

Although the Alianza has as its ultimate goal the securing of all the landgrants lost through the years by various means, at first it restricted its positive action to presenting petitions to the governor of New Mexico and to the President of the United States via New Mexico's Spanish-American senator. But then a "march" was made on the weekend of July 4, 1966 from Albuquerque to Santa Fe to dramatize the Alianza's mission and to present a petition to the governor of the state. Later, during the autumn of the same year, a small band attempted to take over a portion of the national forest lands in the north which they claimed was really theirs anyway. The group was quickly routed by authorities, and state and federal charges were brought against the Alianza leaders on several counts, ranging from the illegal killing of a deer to assaulting two U.S. Forest Service rangers. Five members were convicted on these charges, and an appeal to the Circuit Court was unsuccessful. It is likely that this will be carried eventually to the U.S. Supreme Court.

All these early efforts were largely ignored, "deferred for future reference," or simply put down as the work of hoodlums or madmen. But in June 1967, the Alianza burst into the national spotlight in the so-called insurrection at Tierra Amarilla, a small county seat in northern New Mexico. Again, as in the previous year, the Alianza had threatened to close off a portion of the federal lands, set up an independent "republic," and issue visas to "foreigners" who might wish to enter. The state district attorney, in order to prevent such an occurrence, forbade the holding of a proposed mass meeting and proceeded to arrest several persons allegedly on their way to take part in it. Two days later members of the Alianza staged a raid on the county courthouse where their friends were being held, and in their efforts to set them free, two lawmen were wounded.

The result of all this was to land Tijerina and several of his followers, including members of his own family, in jail, facing charges as serious as kidnapping and assault with intent to commit murder. At the same time, the incident generated a tremendous amount of controversy among New Mexicans and others as to the causes of the raid, the character and purpose of the Alianza, and the plight of the lower-class rural Hispano. In the fall of 1968 in a dramatic trial during which Tijerina served as his own defense attorney, a jury found him innocent of these charges.

The overt aspects of the movement, most of which are already of public record, parallel in many respects similar civil rights movements among both Negro and Mexican-American minorities elsewhere in the United States. However, there are some other, less well-known facts which place it fully within the category of those described elsewhere as nativistic cult movements.

There are, for instance, several supernatural elements in the movement. In addition to the dream-revelation which provides support and sanction for the leader's actions, some of his followers contribute to the classic prophet motif by telling a legend which they claim has been current among the Spanish-speaking in the state for generations. According to this, their ancestors foretold a time when large numbers of persons would come "laughing" from the east and take their land by force, thus destroying the happy life of the Hispanos. They would suffer for many years, but they were urged to maintain courage and to watch for a leader who would also come out of the east to lead them against the enemy who would be forced to return "crying" to their original homes. Incidents have been told of old men who, after hearing Tijerina speak at public gatherings, have gone to him on their knees to kiss his feet, proclaiming him the messiah of the legend. Research by this writer did uncover one reference to such a legend in the literature of the past century, but it was probably also handed down by word of mouth.[4] In any case, it is not important whether the story has had continuous currency or has only recently begun to circulate. Each one who hears it feels certain he must have heard it before, and he dutifully passes it on. It is also perhaps significant to note that prophecies of a messiah who will lead his people out of adversity back to a former and better way of life have long been recorded among American Indian groups (Fletcher 1891:58).

The actual militant character of the more esoteric doctrine has also not generally been recognized by the public and is usually played down by Tijerina when talking with the press. He has been quoted as threatening violence toward Anglos if his demands are not met, but he has consistently retracted or denied such statements in public. Privately, however, and to his followers, he definitely preaches the coming of the millennium as a violent occurrence. He tells his people that they must be prepared to sacrifice and that it may take a long time, but that in the end the Anglos will be frightened and will move out of the area willingly. In the press, he is usually quoted as saying that the Anglos won't have to move out but that they will have to pay rent for lands illegally held or purchase them at their current valuation. The constitution of the Alianza clearly states that the group expects compensation not only for the lands but for the profits earned by the "foreign violators" through the years. These profits and benefits include the fruits of agriculture, of livestock herding, of water, mineral, and timber exploitation, and gains realized through the construction of highways, railroads, cities, factories, etc. (*Constitución Nacional de la Alianza Federal de Mercedes,* Capítulo VI, Art. VI, página 9).

Tijerina is also explicit (in private only) about how the details of the apportionment will be handled when the millennium comes. He states that no lands will be owned individually, as this would be in opposition to the original Spanish directives.

Rather, the Alianza will hold all lands in trust for the people and will hold tribunals to determine who should be allotted the use of a plot of land for life. In this he clearly provides a way of distinguishing among: (a) members of the Alianza, who will be given first preference and who will share equally; (b) those of Spanish descent who, even though not members of the Alianza, have not opposed its operation nor have denied their Spanish heritage; and (c) those "black sheep" who have worked against the best interests of their own people or who have tried to pretend that they are Anglos rather than Hispanos. Those in the second category may be forgiven if and when they see the light and join the movement, but the last group may expect some harsh but unspecified treatment. Any funds deriving from successful negotiations with the government will be divided among the organization's estimated 5 million potential landgrant heirs—provided they are not classified as "traitors" to the cause.

In addition to securing redress in the matter of the landgrants, the organization also stresses certain other aspects of the pre-conquest past. Thus, another matter upon which they are presently agitating concerns the use of Spanish as a language of instruction in the grade schools. For many years this has been a difficult problem for local educators. It is well recognized that in the past instruction in many schools of the outlying areas was conducted almost wholly in Spanish by teachers of Spanish ancestry, while in other cases English was stressed to the point that the incoming children, not familiar with the language, soon fell far behind their Anglo peers. Clearly, in any "either/or" situation the Spanish child is bound to lose out, for he must be able to use English fluently in order to compete as an adult for jobs in a life-pattern which is increasingly dependent upon wage labor or employment of some sort.

Although the Alianza is correct in pointing out that there are still many children who lose valuable time and enthusiasm for school in the early years because of the fact that they have not learned English at home, it is probably unrealistic to insist, as the organization has, that *all* elementary school teachers in New Mexico be fluent in Spanish as well as English. This is clearly more in line with the general nativistic viewpoint of the organization and is not merely a matter of civil rights. In addition to the Spanish language, the group holds up as symbols of its solidarity those foods such as the wheat tortilla, green chili, pinto beans, and tamales, claiming that they represent the mixture of the Indian and the Spanish in New Mexico, being wholly native to neither cultural tradition. It has also been pointed out to the author that the New Mexican Spanish language itself is unique.

As might be expected, there has been considerable opposition from various quarters to the organization and to the prophet himself. Some of this has come from the better-educated and more affluent Spanish-Americans who are embarrassed by the more extreme aims of the group and who feel that total acculturation is the best road to assimilation. Many of those who would not go so far as to advocate complete acculturation are nevertheless disinclined to associate with the Alianza because of their extreme views on mestization, their unrealistic demands, and their general lower-class background and orientation. These are the Spanish-Americans who consider themselves to be descendants of the upper-class colonials and who most vehemently disclaim any Mexican influence on their racial and cultural heritage.

Typical of the reaction of such groups opposing the Alianza is the message on a poster found tacked to a tree on the campus of the University of New Mexico in May 1966. It read as follows:

We true Spanish are white, and we are Catholics. We fight communists. We don't care for foreigners, Negro or White, to come and lie about our race. The only race problem is the one brought in by dirty communists who try to pass as Spanish to get our landgrants.

The prophet himself is frequently attacked, either by name or by implication, as in the above statement. To the charges of being a communist and/or a wetback (illegal entrant from Mexico) or foreigner is frequently added that of operating a confidence racket for personal gain. None of these charges has been substantiated by any concrete evidence, even though Tijerina's background has been thoroughly investigated by state governmental authorities with the assistance of the Mexican government and the FBI. Most reactions such as these are irrational and are based upon purely emotional responses to the organization's efforts to change the *status quo*.

However, there is another type of opposition, just as interesting to the social scientist, which comes from the highly educated intellectual liberal individuals and groups. Individuals of this type usually become frustrated in their attempts to understand and/or assist the organization's cause because of its seeming irrationality, illogic, and lack of clear "democratic" structural principles. Thus, a prominent local historian, a champion of the Hispano population, has attacked the group because there seems to be little historical validity to many of their claims. She points out that many members of the Alianza are not descendants of any Spanish or Mexican land grantees. Many fear that there are "outside influences" which are reopening this old landgrant issue for pecuniary gain and/or political motives.

Some members of the local board of the Commission on Civil Rights, always eager to help any disadvantaged person or group obtain a fair hearing and due process of law, became alienated after a personal appearance before them of the prophet himself. This group apparently expected a formalized civil-rights-type protest movement, which, although stemming from similar causes in the overall social milieu, does not necessarily, or even usually in the United States, have the same characteristics as the militant nativistic revivalistic movement being described. Not being familiar with the latter, most of the board members found themselves in little sympathy with this prophet and his organization. They were prepared to listen to him and his spokesmen as representatives of a minority group fighting discrimination using by now well-known protest techniques, most of which are actually founded on logical principles of action leading to realizable ends. But a total lack of communication developed between the two groups, and the encounter ended with the prophet walking out of the meeting and refusing assistance of any sort. The members of the board, equally disenchanted, were relieved to see him go.

The sociological and anthropological analysis of the movement described is of considerable theoretical interest, since true nativistic cult movements are most often reported from non-Western, fairly primitive groups. In this case, furthermore, there have been over 100 years of contact with concomitant domination of the Spanish-speaking group by a foreign power. With the possible exception of the Penitente groups, which might well be viewed as having nativistic overtones but which were neither messianic nor millennial, there have been, to our knowledge, no movements comparable to the Alianza in the entire history of contact with the United States.

The "relative deprivation" theory should have led us to expect such a movement during the 1930's, when the socioeconomic status of Spanish-Americans in New Mexico appears to have hit an all-time low. Yet, none appeared. However, there are some other elements that are probably of importance in attempting to explain why such a movement has developed at this particular time and place—in New Mexico of the 1960's. First of all, even though the Spanish-Americans of the state as a whole are probably better off than ever before, both economically and in terms of their relations with Anglos this does not hold for all persons who may be so designated. Indeed, many of the more successful and most comfortable Hispanos are those who have in large part abandoned much of their ancestral culture, including the Spanish language. Yet, the bulk of the poverty-stricken lower class in New Mexico is today, as it has been since 1846, made up of Spanish-speaking persons. There is indeed prejudice and discrimination evident against this group. Although it can very well be argued that the disapprobation is oriented along class rather than ethnic lines, it seems to those affected that they suffer because of their Spanish or Mexican heritage. This segment of Hispanos is perhaps even more deprived today in relation to the Hispanos who are better off. Furthermore, some feel that for the first time many elements of Spanish-American culture are in danger of disappearing—the anxiety over this eventuality among many Spanish-Americans of all classes is reflected weekly in the pages of *El Hispano,* one local Spanish-language newspaper. (The Spanish language itself is the *symbol* of the entire culture.)

At the same time, the rise of civil rights movements has undoubtedly influenced the organizational structure of the Alianza and may also have been important in its origin. The use of techniques such as the protest march, the sit-in, the seeking of publicity, the holding of annual conventions, and so forth, seem to derive from the broader immediate surroundings in the United States as a whole. Mexican-American groups in Texas and in California also have organized in recent years along the lines of

civil rights movements, and their modicum of success in manipu-
lating the environment has been an incentive to the Alianza.
Recently, Swadesh (1968) has analyzed the Alianza in relation
to its civil rights aspect.

It is difficult to predict the future of the Alianza, for, though
young, it now seems to be in serious trouble. It appears clear
that to the extent that it continues its more excessive demands
for the return of the landgrants and the expulsion of Anglos, it
will continue to be opposed by the established power groups—
both Anglo and Hispano. But if it takes a more moderate course
and at the same time aligns itself with movements now developing in Texas and California designed to better the conditions of
Mexican-Americans, and most especially those in the lower-class
brackets, it may have some success. It has already been successful
in attracting the attention of the state and federal governments
to the plight of the poor rural Hispano. As Wallace has observed:

> In most instances the original doctrine is continuously modified
> by the prophet, who responds to various criticisms and affirmations
> by adding to, emphasizing, playing down, or eliminating selected
> elements of the original visions. This reworking makes the new
> doctrine more acceptable to special interest groups, may give it a
> better "fit" to the population's cultural and personality patterns,
> and may take account of the changes occurring in the general
> milieu (1956:275).

Although at the present time the leader of the Alianza does
not seem ready to modify his basic doctrine, he may well do
so in the near future if he is to save the movement. There have
been many criticisms in recent months—some stemming from
fairly powerful interests—and these may force his hand. However,
regardless of what the outcome may be, the movement's history
may prove to be enlightening as further data on nativistic cults

in general. It may also be that the public and its governmental representatives may be more understanding of the movement if they recognize that it is not an isolated phenomenon, but one which has occurred scores of times in history under similar circumstances of deprivation. And finally, whether the movement lives or dies, it is important to this particular discussion because it represents a new type of organization, underlaid by a different set of principles than we have seen before among the Spanish-Americans of New Mexico. It is significant that although the concept of mutual aid among members of *la raza* is an important rallying point and underlying philosophy of the Alianza, it does not function as the older type of society, providing benefits to individual members who undergo hardships.

There are a number of veterans' associations which have a high degree of Hispano participation in the Southwest. These include the Veterans of Foreign Wars, the Disabled Veterans, and especially the American Legion. Just after World War I the American Legion was organized in New Mexico by the late Senator Bronson Cutting, who used it as a political tool to further his own career, as well as the interests of the Spanish-speaking in the state (Armstrong 1959:34–35). Actually, this period, just following World War I, might be seen as the beginning of Hispano participation on a large scale in Anglo-oriented voluntary associations. This would coincide with a general acculturative process which was commented upon by Gamio in 1930 (p. 211) as follows:

> There is a universal agreement that the younger Spanish-American people are much more intelligently sympathetic with the American ideals as a result of education in the mission schools and the public schools, and by new business and social contacts with the Anglo-Americans and to a very considerable extent by the experiences of the World War.

Zeleny, who did a sociological study of Albuquerque in the early 1940's, noted that Spanish-Americans were almost totally excluded from fraternal orders such as the Elks, Greek letter societies on the University of New Mexico campus, the Rotary Club, and the Junior Service League. Some societies maintained separate chapters which segregated Anglos from Hispanos. This was true for one social organization on the University of New Mexico campus—Phrateres—and was also generally the custom in the veterans' organizations as well as in the churches (Zeleny 1944:328–329).

There is no doubt but that prejudice against persons of Spanish or Mexican ancestry was particularly rife during the 1930's and early 1940's and that discriminatory practices affected Hispanos at every level of the social scale. Most informants can cite cases of individuals who sought membership in such groups but were blackballed—presumably because of their ethnic background. However, it should also be noted that the majority of Hispanos probably were not interested in belonging to such clubs, which served somewhat different functions than the Spanish-American dominated groups mentioned above. Certainly the Anglo fraternal orders may also be interpreted as mutual-aid societies, but the aid proffered to individual members is most frequently of a non-material nature. Membership in these groups is most often used as a means of establishing or reaffirming one's social position in the middle- and upper-middle-class business and professional world dominated by Anglos. As such, most Hispanos in the state during the 30's and 40's would have been excluded on other than ethnic grounds. It should be remembered that lower-class Anglos are also rigidly excluded.

However, the total situation has changed in Albuquerque in the past twenty years. Today, almost every voluntary association one cares to mention has at least one person of Spanish descent on its roll, and some have a great many. This includes such prestigious organizations as the country clubs, the Junior League, the Petroleum Club, the Albuquerque Symphony Women's Association, the Rotary, Kiwanis and other service clubs, and sororities and fraternities on the University of New Mexico campus. It is true that participation in these groups by Hispanos is very low, but this would seem to reflect economic status as much or more than ethnic position. The formal and informal financial obligations imposed upon members by these groups would exclude a great many persons. It is likely that there may be persons of Spanish origin who can well afford to belong, and who might very well be acceptable to the other members, but who do not seek membership simply because their world view does not emphasize this type of social participation as a value—in other words, they are not acculturated to Anglo middle-class standards. Officer has dealt with this point at length in a work which refers to the Spanish-speaking in Arizona (1964:379, 394). See also Samora (1953) for a discussion concerning the joining habits of Spanish-Americans in a small southern Colorado town.

This attitude of not seeking membership seems particularly relevant in the case of the men's service clubs, which, like the Chamber of Commerce, are made up primarily of business and professional persons. Throughout the state of New Mexico, while research for this book was being done, it was noted that Spanish-American businessmen in general eschew membership in the Chamber of Commerce, which is open to everyone who cares to join and can pay the fees. The reason for this seems to be that the typical small Hispano businessman continues to conduct business along more personal lines—his clientele comes from among his friends, relatives, *compadres,* neighbors, etc. The advantages of belonging to a group which proposes to increase business in the community at large through quite impersonal means are not readily apparent. At the same time the personal association with other members of the group is similarly only of value to the highly acculturated individual.

There are other areas in which upper-class Hispanos do not highly participate, but this nonparticipation cannot be explained on the basis of prejudice and discrimination. For example, in the 1965 Santa Fe Opera season, out of 554 contributors to the opera, only eight had Spanish surnames—and this in an area of many wealthy and upper-class Hispanos. Similarly, in Albuquerque during the same year, out of 380 listed as "Dons," "Associates," and "Friends" of the Albuquerque Civic Symphony, only eight had Spanish surnames. Two Spanish surnames were found out of forty-one on the Board of Directors, however.

Another intellectually oriented association, the Pan American Round Table, has a high proportion of Spanish-Americans. Thus, in 1965 fourteen of the thirty-seven members were in this category. This women's club, part of a national organization, emphasizes good relations with our Spanish-speaking neighbors south of the border and also stresses the value of Latin-American cultural patterns. Membership is by invitation only, and it is clear from an analysis of the roster that the group constitutes something of an intellectual elite. Local honorary members have included the wife of the president of the University of New Mexico and wives of Latin-American scholars on the faculty. In the Sante Fe chapter the proportion of Spanish surnames is also quite high, but it is interesting to note that in that city many of the members have Spanish surnames through marriage only.

At a somewhat lower level of prestige, there are other clubs with a high proportion of Hispano participants. A key informant estimated that about one-third of the members of the local Elks Club were of Spanish origin. This same informant, himself a recently initiated member, stated that this was a recognized means of gaining prestige among Hispanos striving to achieve middle-class status. Since here again entrance is contingent upon a favorable vote of the membership, the applicant, regardless of ethnic background, will most probably have a world view, way of life, income, education, and ambition similar to that of most of the other members—in other words, his interests and social position will be generally comparable. It is also significant to note that the informant specifically mentioned the fact that the Elks admit only Caucasians and that this provision appeals to those Spanish-Americans who fear being classified with Indians, mestizos, or Negroes.

One of the most striking modern developments is the participation of Spanish-surname college students in fraternities and sororities at the University of New Mexico. The following table shows their year-by-year increase in membership. It should, in fairness, be pointed out that not all the Greek letter societies are equally hospitable to new members of Hispano background. Informants among the student body during this study stated that there was always greater discussion when a Spanish name came up for consideration, and that such individuals were admitted only if they were particularly outstanding in the characteristics valued by the organizations; these include wealth, physical attractiveness, scholarship, and "family background." It was also stated that if there was any suspicion of Negro admixture the individual would not be considered. It is interesting to note that all the five Anglo informants from different Greek letter societies interviewed for this study felt it very likely that local Spanish-Americans as a class could have Negro ancestors. Since New Mexico has now, and always has had, a very small Negro population, this possibility seems remote.[5] The darker skin color

Table 1

*MEMBERSHIP IN UNIVERSITY OF NEW MEXICO GREEK
SOCIAL CLUBS AT FIVE-YEAR INTERVALS, 1925–1965, BY
ETHNIC ORIGIN AS INDICATED BY SURNAME*

	1925	1930	1935	1940	1945	1950	1955	1960	1965
Fraternities:									
Anglo members	113	175	207	265	215	326	367	417	425
Spanish-American members	3	3	1	2	1	7	20	26	23
Sororities:									
Anglo members	82	144	156	169	231	199	304	352	476
Spanish-American members	1	0	3	4	1	0	1	4	8
Total:									
Anglos	195	319	363	434	446	525	671	769	901
Spanish-Americans	4	3	4	6	2	7	21	30	31
Percentage of Spanish-Americans	2.5	0.94	1.1	1.4	0.44	1.3	3.1	3.9	3.4

sometimes observed among Hispanos most often derives from
Indian ancestry, but this fact is apparently not well recognized,
or, if recognized, not admitted.

It was also noted that individual fraternity and sorority
members from outside New Mexico tended to be more tolerant
of people with Spanish surnames per se and that active members
frequently accepted such an individual when the alumnae would
not. One fraternity which pledged a large number of Spanish-
American boys during the 1950's came to feel that their prestige
had declined as a result. It was said that some Anglo boys had
turned down invitations to join this group because of the high
percentage of Hispano members.

On the other hand, it is clear that acculturated Hispanos are very much accepted today. One girl related the fact that she had made a bet with her father that she could secure a bid to a sorority, and did so, despite her parents' insistence that it was not possible. Her father had attended the University of New Mexico and had been unsuccessful in achieving membership in a Greek society during the 1940's. In the early 1960's an Hispano was president of the student body at the University of New Mexico and also president of his fraternity—one of the most prestigious both locally and nationally. This man, like many others of his generation, has become thoroughly acculturated to and assimilated into the general Anglo-dominated culture, yet he has not found it necessary to deny or resent his Spanish-American heritage.

It seems clear that New Mexican Hispanos today, as formerly, do join voluntary associations of various kinds. Yet, different patterns of affiliation can be detected among them, depending upon social class, place of residence, and degree of acculturation. Rural Hispanos in the northern part of the state restrict their club activities to religious and community organizations, which seem to serve their individual needs for mutual aid, recreation, and psychological security. From the point of view of the village social organization, these structures help to maintain social control and serve the economic and political necessities of the society, as well as to maintain community solidarity.

In the southern counties, where the major population component is from Mexico, these types of organizations seem less important, but the secular supra-community mutual-aid societies there have had a long history (Cochrane 1915). In the cities, it is true that until recently participation has resembled Rahm's description of Mexican-Americans in El Paso, Texas. He says, "Concerted action on a neighborhood basis is unheard of. People don't participate in community affairs or community organizations. Very few parents show up at PTA meetings, Scout pack meetings, or at church, social, or action groups" (Rahm 1958:11). Today, with increasing economic resources and acculturation, even this picture is changing, at least in Albuquerque.

However, it must be remembered that Spanish-Americans, like anyone else, join those organizations which benefit them. Most Anglo organizations have not served the needs of Hispanos who have different life styles and goals. But as these change, so do both the joining habits of the Hispanos themselves and their acceptability as a class to the Anglo-dominated organizations. And finally, in addition to joining more and more of the existing Anglo groups, there is evidence that the pattern of organized activity for generalized as well as for *specific* goals seems to be increasing in importance among Hispanos. Thus, groups like the Alianza, although superficially organized for the specific purpose of regaining lost lands, have a broader purpose in fighting discrimination and dissatisfaction among lower-income, less-privileged sectors. This new concept of organization seems related to the general trend toward modernization which has been gaining impetus over the past twenty years, or since World War II, and which will be discussed in detail in the final chapters.

Notes

[1] This characteristic has been discussed or mentioned by many, including the following: Cochrane (1915:38); Edmonson (1957:63); Holmes (1964:136); Johansen (1941b:157); Judah (1961:10); Loomis and Leonard (1938:7); Madsen (1961:19); Rubel (1966); Saunders and Samora (1955:394). Madsen and Rubel refer primarily to Mexican-Americans of South Texas, while Cochrane and Johansen are concerned with southern New Mexico, the population of which seems generally more like that of the Texas Mexican-Americans. The last

source refers to a small town in southern Colorado. See also Officer (1964) on Arizona.

2 Pamphlet entitled "What You Should Know About the American G. I. Forum," issued by American G. I. Forum of the United States.

3 The *Penitentes* organization can be interpreted as having some nativistic elements in its composition, but it cannot truly be called a nativistic cult in that there was no overall organization, no messianic leader, no doctrine of returning to the past or of eliminating an oppressor. Although it did serve to reinforce the solidarity of Hispanos in the face of increasing Anglo domination, this seems a concomitant feature of its mutual-aid functions, which seem to have been primary in most instances. For further information on this, see Woodward (1935).

4 Bancroft (1962:317, N11). "Gregg tells us . . . 'it was prophesied among them [the Pueblo Indians] that a new race was about to appear from the east to redeem them from the Spanish yoke.' " This comment was made in reference to the revolt of 1837–1838, which might also be interpreted as a nativistic movement but about which we have too little information to use for comparative purposes.

5 There are reports that Negro cavalry troops were stationed near Taos in the northern part of the state during the 1870's to fight Indians. There also were a few Negroes stationed at Fort Union. Although some of them might have married Spanish-American girls, it does not seem likely that any large-scale miscegenation took place, given the small number of Negro men and the tightness of the existing Hispano community structure at that time. Zeleny comments upon this and implies that the physical characteristics of some villagers were changed as a result of this group's having been there (1944:333).

Chapter VI

THE WAGES OF CHANGE

It is difficult to pinpoint any particular year in history as the beginning of the modern era in New Mexico. Indeed, relative to many other states, New Mexico is still not considered to be highly developed or industrialized. However, in an attempt to set forth the major events associated with the change from a primarily peasant, agrarian, relatively isolated society to the present, the year 1821 seems a likely year with which to start. In that year Mexico won her independence from Spain, and New Mexico became her northernmost territory. The Spanish governors were replaced by Mexicans, new policies of government were introduced, and the population grew by leaps and bounds as new lands were opened to settlement, trade routes were developed, and local production was encouraged and expanded. Although there is some evidence that New Mexico may never have been as poor a colony as is usually suggested, certainly it prospered as never before during the twenty-five years of Mexican rule.[1]

One of the most important events of the new regime was the opening of the Sante Fe Trail in 1822. The resulting trade between the United States and New Mexico brought cheaper and better manufactured goods to the citizens of New Mexico, as well as added income for its government from the customs duties imposed (Zeleny 1944:91). At the same time, a market was created for local produce and crafts, thus stimulating the sheep industry and handiwork such as carving, weaving, sewing, and knitting (Callon 1962:8; Dickey 1949). Trade with other parts of Mexico continued to flourish during this period, and the existing cultural similarities increased as the northern areas became less isolated and more prosperous.[2]

However, Mexican rule was short lived, and further changes were in store for the citizens of New Mexico when General Kearny and his forces arrived and took over the area in the name of the United States of America. This occurred in 1846, and apart from a small revolt in early 1847, it was a bloodless conquest.

It has often been suggested that the majority of the Mexicans in New Mexico at the time of the United States conquest were pleased with the change in government, yet the revolt, plus some other evidence, indicates that this is not entirely true. Numerous villages along the Rio Grande in the southern part of the state were relocated to the other side of the river in order to preserve the Mexican citizenship of their inhabitants. With the Gadsden Purchase in 1856, this area also became United States territory, so these efforts were in vain. In 1874 when an eastern cattleman desired to buy a portion of the Baca Grant in the Estancia Valley, most of the heirs were living in Mexico City (Bergere n.d.). It is likely that the opposition to the United States was largely concentrated in the upper classes, and even here there seem to have been factions. Those most recently arrived from Mexico— and this included most of the settlers in the southern villages mentioned—as well as numerous government personnel and other new land grantees with large holdings were generally opposed to the new regime. There does seem to be a discernible patterning when one examines the roster of names of persons who participated on each side in the 1847 revolt.[3] Even the old-time settlers from the pre-Mexican period seem to have been split, as were local representatives of the Catholic church. One priest, the famous and influential Father Martinez, took an active part in organizing the revolt, and was later excommunicated by Bishop Lamy for this and other unorthodox beliefs and practices.[4] In the long run, however, most of the residents in the territory—peasants, *ricos,* and clergy—accepted the situation because it seemed inevitable, and there was no place else for most to go.

Under this new government massive changes were to occur, but they came about slowly at first. Anglo settlers began to filter into the territory immediately, but it was not until 1900 that the trickle became a wave, resulting in an Anglo majority sometime after 1920.[5] Bishop Lamy, the French priest-missionary, arrived in 1850 and attempted to institute reforms in the local Catholic folk religion. However, the Penitente organization, which had helped keep the folk traditions alive during the so-called secular period, that is, after 1800 when the Franciscans began to dwindle in numbers, remained viable and only slightly altered by the new circumstances. During the Civil War minor skirmishes took place in New Mexico, which remained loyal to the Union (Chavez 1954). Many of the soldiers who fought in the west stayed on, married daughters of Hispanos, and founded many of today's prominent families of Anglo surname but Spanish heritage (Westphall 1947:21).

During the 1870's and 1880's there was a great expansion of the livestock industry in New Mexico, as well as in other western states. Cattle and sheep were both important, but tended to have mutually exclusive distribution. The differing natures and requirements of the two types of animals led to different kinds of range management techniques, different patterns of land exploitation, and, eventually, to separate subcultures, each showing some hostility toward the other and extreme loyalty to its own. This conflict has sometimes been portrayed as one based upon differences in ethnicity, yet it should be emphasized that both Anglos and Spanish were involved on both sides.

Although sheep were important earlier than cattle in New Mexico, it has been claimed that by 1870 most of the cowboys in the cattle industry of the United States as a whole were "Mexicans" (Bernstein 1938:46). They were the roving, migratory hands, who roamed as far north as Montana, west to California, and east to Texas and Oklahoma searching for jobs on both cattle and sheep ranches. This type of employment has been an important source of income for Spanish-Americans, and as late as 1937 it was estimated that 2,400 men from New Mexico alone were engaged in such activity (U.S. Dept. of Agriculture 1937:22; see also Harper, Cordova, and Oberg 1943:30). The *partidario* system, described on pages 46–48, was the most popular in the sheep business, while wages for work performed or for specified time periods was the custom for cowhands.

The railroad-building era in New Mexico covered the years between 1878 and 1911 and coincided with the final subjugation of the nomadic Indians. The Atchison, Topeka and Santa Fe met the Southern Pacific line at Deming in 1881, thus joining New Mexico to the outside world in four directions (Arsdale 1937:6–7; Horn 1963:217). The Navajos returned from the Long Walk to Fort Sumner to take up residence on their reservation lands in 1868, and the Apaches were finally pacified in 1886, thereby opening the way to settlement of large areas previously avoided or sparsely inhabited for fear of Indian raids.

The effects of the railroad were many and extremely important. New towns were created and old ones stimulated by the maintenance of the railroad itself, as well as the needs of its personnel.

Furthermore, the locomotives required coal, and the mines at places such as Dawson and Madrid became important local sources of this fuel and employers of men. With the new means of transportation to eastern markets, mining of other minerals and lumbering were further stimulated, as was the livestock industry. As Arsdale has said, "Railroad building . . . brought a fourfold increase in population and a development of resources. When the railroads came to New Mexico it meant more for the permanent prosperity and rapid development of the Territory than any other event of the century" (1937:6,11).

Jobs were available for all who cared to labor—part-time or full-time. Many Hispanos used this means of supplementing their small income from farming, thus making it possible to continue life in the rural villages in spite of decreasing productivity there. In time wage labor became the mainstay, supplemented by homegrown produce.

In Colorado and California, now accessible by rail, the sugarbeet industry was developing at about this same time. The first successful sugarbeet factory was opened in California in 1870. In later years, and down to the present day, many Spanish-Americans from New Mexico, as well as *braceros* and other immigrants from Mexico, have found jobs in the sugarbeet fields and factories (U.S. Dept. of Agriculture 1937:11–21).

In New Mexico itself, the modern means of transportation brought new goods, new settlers, and new markets for New Mexican produce—chiefly wool, meat, and hides. Many individuals and families, both Anglo and Hispano, became wealthy through the exploitation of the cheap land and cheap labor available in the territory. The land flourished, and the portents of future disaster were not readily apparent or well understood.

The rich grew richer, but the poor grew poorer without realizing that this was, in fact, the case. As has been noted previously, there is evidence that overpopulation and resultant land pressure were already a problem when the United States took over in 1846. That agriculture had started to decline earlier seems likely from the remarks of Bareiro in 1832 who said that agriculture was being almost entirely neglected at that time (quoted in Loyola 1939:41). Although probably somewhat of an exaggeration, as suspected by Loyola, Bareiro's comments may well have reflected an actual diminution.

In addition to the well-known effects of overgrazing, over-cutting of timber in the mountains, and overdivision of lots among increasingly numerous heirs, there were some other factors responsible for the loss of productivity and consequent extreme poverty in the Spanish-American villages. Between 1850 and 1880 the greater use of the waters of the Rio Grande by irrigation farmers in Colorado resulted in a lowering of the water supply in New Mexico. This affected primarily the small farmers in the northern part of the territory. The southern reaches, potentially fertile, had always been dry, and the federal government moved to correct this problem first. Between 1910 and 1920, reclamation projects were carried out in the Mesilla Valley. The completion of Elephant Butte Dam in 1919 made possible a tremendous agricultural development in the area, and very soon cotton and other cash crops became important there (Foscue 1931:13). After 1910, Mexicans fleeing the effects of the revolution in their own country came in droves to work as laborers on the large farms in the valley. Many Spanish-Americans, most of whom had settled in the valley during the Mexican period, lost their small farms because they were unable to compete with the larger, mechanized agricultural production made possible by the new irrigation system (Johansen 1941b:40). Even where the farmers were not pushed out completely, the increase in mechanized farming in the rest of the country made that in New

Mexico—particularly in the northern villages—less productive and less profitable by comparison (Stevens 1964:42).

The construction of Elephant Butte Dam also had the effect of raising the water level of the Rio Grande in the Middle Valley, with sometimes disastrous results. One whole village, San Marcial, was totally destroyed by floods between 1929 and 1937 (Laughlin 1940:280; U.S. Dept. of Agriculture 1937c). In other cases valuable land bordering the river was lost or made unproductive by increasing marshiness. The average Spanish-American was prevented from mechanizing his own farm by lack of capital, lack of knowledge, poor transportation facilities, lack of a market, and by the fact that time and labor-saving devices are of minor importance when manpower is already in excess of the work to be done (Burma 1954:16; Cottrell 1955:148). Weaver has pointed out that mechanization has also affected sheepherding. The modern use of the pickup truck reduces the number of shepherds needed, but this, of course, has been a more recent development (Weaver 1965:138).

The creation of national forests, starting in 1900, had a tremendous effect upon the villages, some of which found themselves eventually completely surrounded by federalized lands. Wolff, in listing the agents of change most important in the village he studied, places the establishment of a nearby national forest first (1950:212). Regardless of the conservationists' arguments in favor of cutting herd sizes and the regulation of grazing, such measures forced large numbers of Hispanos to reorganize many aspects of their former economy and the way of life dependent upon that economy. The recent "protest uprising" among villagers in Tierra Amarilla reflects the fact that many people were unable to adjust and are still suffering from the deprivations of being forced to cut their herd sizes. Knowlton

(1967) has very recently reviewed the conflicting concepts of ownership and usage of lands held by Anglos and Hispanos today. At point after point it is clear that many of those Hispanos remaining in the rural areas maintain an ideology different from that of those making the laws and not in accordance with scientific principles of herd and farm management. As a result, the people long ago became dependent upon some outside source of cash in order to survive on their small holdings.

The opportunities for wage labor outside the home village and the income derived from it succeeded in covering up the real situation until the early 1930's, when the widespread depression decreased and almost cut off completely the available jobs. Virtually all studies referring to Spanish-Americans during the 1930's and the early 1940's testify to the importance of wagework to these people.[6] The Tewa Basin Study by the U.S. Department of Agriculture showed that in eleven Spanish-American villages containing 1,202 families, an average of 1,110 men went out of the villages to work for some part of each year prior to 1930. In 1934, only 157 men out of 1,202 families had found outside work (U.S. Dept. of Agriculture 1937f:5). When this situation occurred, the men tried to fall back upon the more traditional sources of income—farming and sheepherding—and then discovered that changes in the ecological balance, new laws, and competition with modern techniques made it impossible for farming and sheepherding to support the existing population.

Many of the Hispanos found work with the Work Projects Administration (WPA), the National Youth Administration (NYA), and the Civilian Conservation Corps (CCC) (Loomis 1942:33). Large numbers also went on relief. In one way or another, the majority of Spanish-Americans in New Mexico became directly dependent upon the federal government during this period, a fact which was, and still is, to a certain extent, apparent in their voting behavior (Holmes 1964:31; Judah 1949). As Burma has said, "It is impossible to overemphasize the value of government relief programs to the Hispano villagers. Without such programs their traditional way of life would have disappeared and they along with it" (1954:18).

But even with government help there was much change in the way of life, at least for some people. In 1939 Walter pointed out that, "During the past ten years the Spanish-speaking have lost land at an alarming rate through foreclosures and tax sales" (1939:154). And Oberg found in a 1940 study of the Cuba Valley that 32% of the 514 Spanish-American consumption units in his sample owned no land whatever, forming a landless, largely migratory, class of laborers (1940:440). There are still some Spanish-Americans from New Mexico who join every year with Mexican-Americans from Texas, California, and Mexico in the migratory farm labor force. Knowlton (1961:20) states that in 1961 around 1,000 migrant workers and families left San Miguel County alone for seasonal harvesting and other agricultural work in Colorado, Wyoming, and other western states. Of these, 95% returned. The 1960 census showed that a larger proportion of the Spanish-American labor force is in farm wagework than is true for the general population (U.S. Dept. of Agriculture 1963:19). The migratory life, in which whole families travel from place to place following the seasonal cycle, or even that which takes families from home each year to one particular type of seasonal work, has not been well studied by anthropologists, but it clearly would have some effects upon the maintenance of a traditional culture pattern.[7]

The second response to the situation, a pattern which began to appear during the Depression, was the influx of Hispanos into cities. Walter commented on this as early as 1939:

The combination of threats to the old village life has brought thousands of refugees to the suburban villages surrounding the growing urban centers of the state, especially Albuquerque, Santa Fe, and Las Vegas. Here they attempt to readjust by entering the prevailing American wage economy, but so far the effort has met with a discouraging incidence of failure (1939:156).

At that time the masses of Spanish-Americans were not well educated in a formal sense, and by-and-large they were not prepared to seek white-collar or even skilled-labor positions in cities, even when such were available. New Mexico was not an industrialized state, but in spite of the Depression, in 1936 and 1937 Albuquerque showed gains in public and business building, residence building, employment, bank clearings, school enrollments, and utilities. New industry was being developed, several chain stores had been established, and the Municipal Airport and State Fair Grounds were under construction. Certainly, there were many Spanish-Americans who profited from all this activity, but the primary beneficiaries seem to have been Anglos. (See Maxwell 1938:47.)

The year 1941 and the entrance of the United States into World War II further stimulated the movement away from the farms by providing employment elsewhere and, as such, marks another turning point in the social history of the Spanish-speaking population of the Southwest. As had occurred in World War I, thousands of Hispanos joined the fighting forces of their country, and thousands more went to work in defense plants in California (Loomis 1943). Many of those who left the state elected to stay in some other place—they found California particularly attractive. Although no figures are available, the number of New Mexican Hispanos who have relatives in California is estimated to be quite high. Over the past twenty-five years many have gone to join relatives as well, so there has been a constant outward stream of undetermined magnitude.[8] Winnie estimated that the net postwar migration of Hispanos from rural New Mexico to other states may have amounted to nearly one-fifth of the 1940 rural Hispanic population (1955:97).

By 1950, 41% of the Spanish-American population of New Mexico lived in urban areas. This trend continued and even increased in magnitude during the 1950's, so that by 1960, 61% of the Hispanos had been urbanized (Barrett and Samora 1963:4). Another way of indicating the sheer magnitude of the movement is to note that between 1950 and 1960 24% of the rural dwellers left their homes for other locations (Knowlton 1961:28). Some of the effects of this depopulation are apparent even from superficial observation of many villages today. Weaver noted that there were twenty or more abandoned houses in the village he studied (1965:44). A field survey for purposes of this study revealed that a similar picture exists in most of the smaller villages.

The Embudo Report states, "Out-migration of the [Embudo] watershed is much in evidence in Las Trampas where there are many vacant or abandoned houses. If it were not for welfare payments and a tradition of close ties to the land, villages like Las Trampas would probably be almost completely depopulated" (1961:77). San Geronimo, fifteen miles southwest of Las Vegas, was reported as having more than one-third of its 58 houses deserted as early as the 1930's (New Mexico Rural Council Study, San Geronimo, n.d.:1) and the same, or similar, comments dot the literature. Loomis gives a dramatic account of the depopulation of the village of El Cerrito, originally studied by him and Leonard in 1939 and revisited in the summer of 1956. Out of the twenty-six family units present in 1939, only four remained in 1956. In addition, there were four elderly couples whose children had all migrated. Almost without exception the migrants had gone to live permanently in Colorado, especially in the city of Pueblo (Loomis 1958:53–55).

Although the results were not quite so devastating, Weaver was informed by older residents of the village which he studied that during the 1930's when the large livestock holders were forced to reduce their herds and flocks, the young men who were dependent upon them for employment left the community—many of them for Colorado and Utah. In the case of one family, Weaver says, "Brother followed brother until only one was left of the once numerous Garza family" (1965:129,131).

At the same time that this outward migration of Hispanos was occurring, the state began to experience another massive wave of Anglo immigration, many of whom came in connection with the development of defense activities during the war. Winnie estimates that between 1940 and 1950, the population was increased by 50,780 Anglos and decreased by 31,680 Hispanos—27,960 of native New Mexican parentage, 3,720 of foreign—presumably Mexican—ancestry—(1955:145). Most of these Anglos went to the cities.

This trend continued during the 1950–1960 decade. Maloney has pointed out that during that period all but one of seven northern counties, traditionally dominated by Hispanos, decreased their percentage of Spanish-speaking persons. The one exception was Santa Fe, which, significantly, contains the urban area of the state capital and which gained both Hispano and Anglo citizens. Maloney estimates that more than 14,000 Hispanos left the six northern counties during the last decade, but that the loss was balanced by a nearly equal influx of Anglos. In the case of San Miguel County, there has been a tremendous exodus of Hispanos from the small villages, but the combined city and town of Las Vegas has remained virtually stable in size, largely through the immigration of Anglos who have replaced Spanish-

Americans leaving the county entirely (Maloney 1964:4,7). Thus, that county has become both more urbanized and more heavily dominated by Anglos, a situation which more or less parallels that of Albuquerque and Bernalillo County.

There seems to be some disagreement as to the effects of urbanization upon the Hispano migrants, mostly due to an inadequate amount of data available on the subject. In 1950 Saunders pointed out that no one had as yet studied the effects of urbanization on the Spanish-speaking population in the Southwest (1950:152). Although this statement may still be made today, there are many studies which have touched upon one or another aspect of urbanization. Walter (1939:156) mentioned that in the urban and suburban situations many of the patterns of communal mutual aid disappear. Kluckhohn says much the same thing when she comments that urban migrants become ". . . an ethnic minority (largely segregated in particular areas) which has had little of the internal cohesiveness so characteristic of the villages . . ." (Kluckhohn and Strodtbeck 1961:245). Sjoberg noted in a study of Albuquerque Spanish-Americans that, of 81 records reviewed, aid by fellow-members of the community other than relatives was listed only twice (1947:49). Kluckhohn also goes on to note that those Hispanos living in cities become secularized to an extent not seen in the villages. She points out that the recreational activities, formerly connected with the family, the community, and the church, now emphasize commercialism— "movies, dancing, drinking in taverns, and riding about in cars" (Kluckhohn and Strodtbeck 1961:243). Also, urbanites place "greater reliance upon medical treatment, the use of clinics, and other developments having to do with physical welfare" (*ibid.*).

Several studies indicate some breakdown in both the extended and the nuclear family as a result of urbanization. Many writers point out that it is the younger people who move to the city, thus changing the traditional authority structure relating parents and grown children. One aspect of this has been well described by Weaver in a general discussion concerning conflict between generations. He says:

> One might also mention the conflict which derives from the problem presented by grandchildren who have moved to the city and are no longer able to communicate with their grandparents in Spanish. Many a weekend visitor returns to his home in Santa Fe or Albuquerque remembering the tongue lashing administered by his parents because he has failed to teach his own children *la propia lengua* (the proper language) (1965:148).

Even the second-generation city dwellers continue this pattern of breaking away from the parental generation. F. Moore (1947:53) found that in San Jose, a lower-class, largely Hispano section of Albuquerque, "A number of children are leaving their families and are moving elsewhere thus destroying the old family solidarity." He found that both males and females were leaving home in search of work, but that the latter predominated. Sjoberg confirmed both of these points in a study of the same area a year later (1947:57). Barrett and Samora (1963:15) also point out that many Spanish-American females today are working, who in the rural areas would have remained at home. This increasing participation of females in the labor force is, as they suggest, indicative of change and probably also reflects higher rates of divorce and broken homes (*ibid.,* p. 18). A series of studies over a ten-year period showed that divorce among Spanish-Americans in the same section of Albuquerque increased from 3.1% of all families studied in 1936 to 5.7% in 1946.[9] In 1956 Cassel, studying attitudes toward divorce among Hispanos on Aid to Dependent Children (ADC) in Bernalillo County found that many women thought it was "the only thing to do" in many cases—clearly a modification in the traditional way of thinking on this subject (1956:150).

Besides divorce, there also seems to be an increase in the number of illegitimate births and subsequent desertion of the woman by the father of her children. This was a situation which was said literally never to occur in the traditional villages, and which certainly was extremely rare. Loomis commented on the change in this in his restudy of El Cerrito (1958:57). Cassel found that 834 out of 981 women in Bernalillo County receiving ADC were of Spanish surname. Reasons for the dependence included divorce, desertion, death, incapacitation of the father, and illegitimacy (Cassel 1956:3). Another study of ADC recipients done by Neal in San Miguel and Mora counties, which have a high percentage of Spanish-Americans, showed several interesting facts which relate to this point. She found that in about 35% of the cases the fathers had never married the mothers of their children. She also found no significant difference between the rural and urban zones of these two counties in terms of the amount of dependence upon ADC. However, it is not possible to determine from her data whether there was a greater amount of divorce, desertion, and illegitimacy in the urban zones (1951:9,12,26).

Whatever the cause, the high rates of dependence upon ADC and other types of public assistance, which continue even today, are evidence of social disorganization.[10] It is also fairly clear that as the rural villages become increasingly depopulated in the migration to the cities, some of the types of social problems prevalent in urban society also appear in the country, although probably to a lesser extent.

The nature of the sociological concomitants of urbanization among Spanish-Americans is not, however, entirely understood nor agreed upon by all observers. Burma said in 1949, "With this minority, rural-urban differences are far greater than is normal in the United States" (p. 134). Yet others have suggested that the patterns of life for the urban Hispano are not in fact so very different from those in the villages. Winnie (1955:117) pointed out that there was a very small difference between the fertility ratios of rural and urban Hispanos and urged a study designed to bring more information to bear on explaining this demographic fact in relation to culture change. Aside from Winnie, most of the others who claim that the transition to urban life is not a drastic one for most Hispanos base their opinions on largely impressionistic, qualitative observations, which are, nevertheless, of some importance in understanding the phenomena associated with urbanization. Kluckhohn reported that in the city many of the families from the village she studied live in the same neighborhood (Kluckhohn and Strodtbeck 1961:225). They rely upon each other, borrow equipment, share their food, etc. In fact, she states, "Patterns of day-to-day life are not markedly different from those observed in Atrisco two decades ago."

In contrast to his 1949 statement quoted above, Burma in 1954 said, "The rural-urban change is not an extreme one. Housing, household conveniences, and general culture are not very different in the section of the city into which the Hispano typically moves" (1954:29). Barrett and Samora (1963:4) emphasize the fact that, ". . . most of these newly urban residents are still carrying a rural, folk culture with them, creating important problems of adjustment in their new environment." A study done in Martineztown, a Spanish-American section of Albuquerque, found that as of 1966 the institution of *compadrazgo* was still highly viable and important in the structuring of interpersonal relations among city Hispanos (Vincent 1966).

How can we reconcile such apparently conflicting statements concerning the sociological effects of urbanization? On the one hand, it must be remembered that New Mexico's largest city,

Albuquerque, is under 350,000 in population.[11] Furthermore, it is a comparatively young metropolis, not highly industrialized, and has a sprawling, not very densely occupied, settlement pattern. Its lower socioeconomic sections resemble poor rural villages more than they do urban slums. A product of the automobile age, Albuquerque is bifurcated by freeways in two directions; and though distances are great, it is possible to travel from one end of the metropolitan area to another in well under an hour. Furthermore, roads in all but the most remote mountain areas of the state are generally good, and most villages are readily accessible by car on weekends. In 1941 Leonard and Loomis reported that the rural residents of El Cerrito visited relatives in the city of Las Vegas, but that these visits were seldom repaid (1941:44). This pattern seems now to have become more reciprocal—the urban residents returning to the villages for rest, recreation, and to assist elderly relatives in the maintenance of property there. Not only are the cities of New Mexico themselves less urban than most, but the migrant frequently maintains contact with his country relatives, a fact which might well be conducive to the maintenance of some aspects of the former way of life.

Another factor of importance to some segments of the Hispano population has been the frequent opportunity to become gradually immersed in the industrial world through employment, without actually having to move one's residence. The creation of Los Alamos, the Atomic Energy City, has, in the words of one writer, ". . . profoundly affected the countryside for a hundred miles around" (Scotford 1953:21). Since housing was scarce in the city, many of the Spanish-Americans recruited as workers continued to live at home and simply commuted to work daily. In addition to employment opportunities in Los Alamos itself, others were available in the several nearby towns that experienced a considerable boom as a result of their proximity to the research site. The effects of this were to urbanize the countryside, as it were— a process probably less traumatic for the individuals involved than direct and immediate transfer to an already existing city. A similar situation obtains in the southern part of the state where workers from small towns are transported by bus to Alamogordo each day.

Finally, it should be remembered that within the Hispano population several different patterns of adaptation exist. There are many for whom urbanization has meant greater poverty, social disorganization, and a loss of the moral standards highly valued in the rural environment. On the other hand, there are some who have considerably improved their situations through the acquisition of skills, higher education, well-paying jobs, and a retention of a home and family life similar to the traditional type known from the literature. It could be said of this group that, instead of changing from one mode of life to another, it has both retained the old and added the new. The process of urbanization itself, then, is not necessarily synonymous with acculturation to Anglo culture, although there are some signs that this may be the long-range trend. Indeed, as will be shown, urbanization does seem to correlate with a higher degree of intermarriage with Anglos, greater participation in Anglo social structures, and entrance into a way of life not distinguishable from that of the average middle-class New Mexican of non-Hispanic origin. True acculturation undoubtedly involves basic changes in the value system of the individuals or groups undergoing the process, and these are usually well reflected in the life styles or general culture patterns. However, many traits may be adopted and incorporated into a previously existing culture without necessarily changing the basic value system, thus giving the outward appearance of change, which may in fact be only superficial.

The following chapter will discuss in greater detail some of the characteristics of the modern urbanized Hispano population in New Mexico, stressing the major city of Albuquerque but also using materials from other cities where available.

Notes

[1] The historian Marc Simmons (1965) has recently made this point and has suggested that further research may show New Mexico to have been better off economically than is usually thought. Jones (1932:277–278) also argued this position.

[2] See especially Minge (1965), Simmons (1965), and Zeleny (1944) for further information on the cultural aspects of the Mexican period.

[3] Dr. Myra Ellen Jenkins, the State Archivist of New Mexico, has suggested this point (personal communication).

[4] For further accounts of Father Martinez and his fascinating career, see Francis (1956b); H. Fergusson (1933:122).

[5] Anglos did not settle in large numbers in all parts of the state. According to Holmes (1964:11–12):

In 1900 the 195,000 residents of the Territory were still concentrated in the traditional area of settlement along the Rio Grande. In the nine Hispanic counties of Bernalillo, Dona Ana, Mora, Rio Arriba, San Miguel, Santa Fe, Socorro, Taos, and Valencia, reside 132,000 persons—67 percent of the population of the Territory. This population and that of most of the adjacent areas was largely of native-born citizens of Hispanic surname. As late as 1915 Spanish-Americans numbered 57 percent of the state's total population and constituted 75 percent or more of the population of eleven counties; between 50 and 75 percent in three; and from 25 to 50 percent in four others of the state's twenty-six counties. By 1950 the proportion of residents of Hispanic surname had dropped to 37 percent in the state, and only ten of the thirty-two counties mustered an Hispanic population of 50 percent or more.

[6] See Burma (1954:18); Edmonson (1957); Embudo Report (1961:33,39,79); Knowlton (1961:20); Leonard (1943:34); Maes (1941:11); Weaver (1965:16); Wolff (1950:53); U.S. Dept. of Agriculture (1937f); among others.

[7] There are many studies of migratory wage laborers, though few that attempt to analyze their way of life as a distinct subculture or their social structure from a systematic point of view. See, however, Goldschmidt (1947); and

González (1961) for anthropological viewpoints. See also Larson (1937); Potts (1959); and the U.S. Dept. of Agriculture (1963) for materials on Spanish-speaking migrant laborers.

8 Several writers mention this New Mexico-to-California migration pattern, and the present research uncovered innumerable cases all over the state. See Burma and Williams (1962:48); Johansen (1941a:132); F. Moore (1947:92,94); Sjoberg (1947:47); Winnie (1955:1,103,115).

9 See Waggoner (1941:46) who includes data from 1936, as well as 1941; Moore (1946:91); Sjoberg (1947:57).

10 For the latest figures on the extent of welfare in New Mexico, see Annual Report of the Department of Public Welfare, Santa Fe, December 20, 1965. A new report, covering the year 1966 should soon be available but has not been seen by this author.

11 The population of the city was estimated at 237,283 in 1964. Bernalillo County was designated the Albuquerque Standard Metropolitan Area in 1957. The population estimate for this larger entity was only 309,536 in 1964 (Albuquerque—Population Characteristics, Report No. 3, Albuquerque Industrial Development Service, Inc., July 1964). However, estimates for the 1970 SMSA population are between 336,400 and 600,000, depending upon bases used for calculations (Community Survey 1965:17).

Chapter VII

EFFECTS OF URBANIZATION

Materials upon which this study is based were drawn, wherever possible, from the existing literature. A vast number of reports and analyses was available covering the early periods and the rural Spanish-American culture. However, as the research went forward, it became increasingly clear that many of the most important features of the current socioeconomic and cultural situation of the New Mexican Hispano had seldom, if ever, been documented. Furthermore, the events and processes described in the last chapter have led to the development of certain completely new types of behavior and social structures, most of which seem to be associated with urban, as opposed to rural, life. This chapter will present materials compiled by the author specifically to suggest and partially to fill the gaps in our knowledge concerning the present-day Hispano, the majority of whom lives in cities (Barrett and Samora 1963:4). Although the stress will be upon the process of urbanization, it will also be apparent that acculturation and assimilation are concomitant products of the modern age.

It should be made clear at the outset that this writer has no desire to become engaged in any polemic regarding the relative value of urban versus rural life. It has been shown in numerous

136

studies that many of the primary ties often thought to decline or disappear in the city in fact remain strong and viable (Gans 1959; Young and Willmott 1957; Smith, et al., 1954; Sharp and Axelrod 1956). As the writer has already indicated, the Hispanos of Albuquerque do retain many features of their strong family organization, including the *compadrazgo,* which seems to reinforce the former. Mutual-aid societies of one sort or another flourish, and neighborhood personal ties are important structural features. It is clear that *anomie* and social disorganization are not the inevitable results of urbanization. On the other hand, there is some evidence that certain social forms and types of social disorganization occur more frequently in cities.

In the following pages discussion will be limited to such topics as juvenile delinquency, participation in credit unions, increasing higher education and involvement in professional and managerial activities, ethnic exogamy, and changing religious behavior. All of these are suggested to be closely associated with urbanism, at least in New Mexico; and although most of the data come from the major city of Albuquerque, some attempt has also been made to show regional variations within the state. In most cases, any conclusions are only tentative, and the major purpose of presenting these data is to show what seem to be some major trends and to suggest areas for further research.

Juvenile Delinquency

It is interesting to note that in a study of juvenile delinquency in Bernalillo County in 1936, out of the 350 complaints referred to the probation officer, the ethnic breakdown was as follows:

Ethnic Status	Number	Percent
Spanish-American	210	60
Anglo	125	36
Indian	11	3
Negro	4	1

(Carter 1936:63). This corresponds quite well to the proportion each group contributed to the total population at that time, and suggests that juvenile delinquency was no more prevalent among Hispanos than among any other ethnic division. In 1941, Whiteman (p. 19) found that 68.4% of the delinquent girls in the State Welfare Home (now called the Girls Welfare Home) were Spanish-American. This percentage remains high today. The figures [1] for new commitments in recent years are:

1963	*1964*	*1965*	*1966*	*1967*
46	42	47	52	56

There is also a high percentage of boys of Spanish surname in the State Training School at Springer and at the detention home in Santa Fe. However, this does not necessarily mean that Spanish-American youths are any more prone to delinquency than Anglos, for as has been pointed out by local officials, more of the Hispanos are likely to be sent to these instituitons after being involved in mischief. This stems from the fact that most of these Hispano youngsters come from poverty-stricken and/or broken homes, from which it is often felt they should be removed for their own good. Youngsters from middle- and upper-class homes where both parents are present are likely to be released to the parents' custody. This coincides with the generally accepted principle that factors other than poverty are involved in juvenile delinquency among American youth. In fact, it would be interesting to compare the rate of delinquency among middle- and upper-class Hispanos with that among a comparable sample of Anglo youths. It may be that poverty per se is of more relative importance in explaining delinquent behavior among Spanish-Americans. Conversely, the type of family organization and the nature of interpersonal relations among family members in middle- and upper-class Hispano homes may be quite different from those in Anglo homes of similar economic status.

Albuquerque, like most other urban areas, has its share of territorially organized gangs to which belong not only Spanish-American but black and Anglo youths as well. Although the majority of these are boys' gangs, there are also a few made up of girls. The latter seem to be structured similarly to those of their male counterparts, and the behavior involved is virtually the same, so the following description will, in general, cover both. The primary activities of these groups in Albuquerque are fighting other gangs, drinking, indulging in sexual activities, dancing, and occasionally using narcotics.

Fighting often takes the form of arranged "rumbles" or "blows" between two rival groups, but also may result through chance encounters between individual members—especially when a group feels its home territory is being "invaded" by those who do not rightfully belong there. Occasionally too, members of one gang intentionally enter another territory, prowling about looking for trouble until they find it. The fights themselves seldom last long, but in the words of one informant, "While they last, they are real good." Many sporting events between high schools end with fights between gangs associated with each school. Weapons include knives, razors, occasionally guns, and various other types of cutting or hitting instruments. One informant described a homemade mace constructed of a croquet ball on a rope into which had been pounded nails, later sharpened to a point on the protruding end. Girls frequently carry razor blades in their bouffant hairdos. Gang attacks may be made upon individuals for purposes of revenging real or presumed insults or injuries to any member of the gang.

Research among juveniles, many of them members of gangs, as well as among law enforcement officers concerned with juvenile activity, revealed the presence of nineteen organized gangs in Albuquerque in 1965, and there are very likely more now. Each of the eight senior high schools had at least one gang, and usually more, associated with it. These gangs have names, recognized leaders, symbols by which the members are made highly visible and recognizable, and a generally agreed-upon territory which they control. Initiation usually involves performances of endurance and daring, during which the initiates prove their willingness and ability to interact with the gang by drinking large quantities of alcohol; submitting to paddlings, tatooing, and other painful rites; carrying out humiliating assignments, such as presenting themselves naked at someone's door and asking for clothes; and occasionally indulging in sexual relations in the presence of the gang members. Not all gangs include all of these activities as part of their initiation ritual, however.

The use of narcotics—especially marijuana—is also associated with gang activity in Albuquerque. Although its use is not entirely restricted to the Spanish-American ethnic group, it seems quite clear that it is largely concentrated there. Marijuana use seems to be an ingrained part of the culture of the lower-class Hispano, and many nondelinquent individuals regularly use it. Informants state that many persons grow a small patch of it, not for sale but strictly for "home use." Others, of course, engage in buying and selling, utilizing both local and out-of-state sources, including Mexico. Although the local "retail" price has remained relatively constant for years—fifty cents per cigarette or "stick" and $15 per *lata* (Prince Albert tobacco can)—it is still possible to turn a good profit by participating in this traffic.

There is a fairly complex network of interpersonal relationships by means of which distribution is accomplished. Marijuana and other drugs are not typically "pushed" on the streets and in other public places in Albuquerque. Indeed, occasional reports that this has occurred are scoffed at as "propaganda" by local informants who claim that narcotics are readily available only to those who know the ropes and who have personal contacts with individuals within the system. The use of marijuana is generally accepted as a form of vice which is not harmful to the user and no more immoral than many other items—such as alcohol, for example. The fact that its possession is illegal has only pushed the whole network underground and possibly made its use more attractive to some who enjoy the idea of engaging in the forbidden.

Heroin and other "hard stuff" is also obtainable but is not nearly so widely used as marijuana. Informants recognized the dangers of becoming "hooked," and stated that this was considered in a completely different category from marijuana. Glue and paint sniffing may begin earlier than other habits and are frequently introduced through gang activity. Informants tended to view this as "kid stuff," although they noted that it sometimes becomes hard to shake the habit in adulthood. It was generally considered that this, too, could be physiologically harmful if indulged in to excess.

Consistent with Heller's description of Mexican-American gangs in other areas, the Albuquerque Hispanos interviewed listed a large number of special slang words and phrases—most based upon Spanish—which are in current use among gang members. The Spanish gang members are referred to as *Chicanos* or *pechucos,* and Anglos as *gavaches.* Knowledge and use of this slang are important parts of acceptance by the gang, and might also be viewed as a mechanism for furthering the social solidarity of the in-group. It is interesting to note that many of the words refer to narcotics—particularly marijuana and heroin—and many others are double entendres with sexual connotations. No attempt was made to study this jargon systematically, and it is not known whether the same words and phrases would be understood by Spanish-speaking youths in other areas.[2]

All informants agreed that gangs do not jointly engage in burglary or vandalism, although individual members may frequently engage in such activity and the gang does not pass judgment on it. It was also emphasized that the object of fighting is to cause pain and possible mutilation of opponents, but not to kill, although killings do occur and may be becoming more frequent. Members of Spanish-American gangs interviewed commented that Anglo or *gavache* gangs were more likely to kill than were their own, a belief which is reciprocated by Anglos in regard to Hispanos.

It would appear that the whole matter of gang activity is complicated, for although one official interviewed said that he thought there was a correlation between dropping out of school and joining gangs, this seems to be true only in the case of some gangs. Furthermore, gang activity is not restricted to the minority groups (Spanish-American and Negro), nor to the most poverty-stricken areas of Albuquerque. The fact that most individual gangs are made up primarily of either Anglo or Hispano or black members seems possibly more related to the territorial nature of the groupings than to discrimination between ethnic groups. This, of course, reflects the residential patterns in Albuquerque. Some predominantly Spanish-American gangs have a few Anglo members, and the opposite is also true.

Until quite recently Albuquerque had a very small percentage of Blacks. As a group, they were looked down upon and discriminated against by Hispanos, and Blacks reciprocated this behavior. Yet individuals were frequently accepted across the racial boundary, and informants state that gangs often had one or two members of the other group. Rarely were these gangs composed of an equal number of Negroes and Hispanos; however, one ethnic group or race always dominated. Now there is evidence that hostility between these groups is increasing— possibly in part related to the existence of an increasingly large black population.

Rumbles and rivalries seem to reflect antagonism between ethnic groups, and certainly some of this is present. One Spanish-American informant pointed out that after a big blow with an Anglo gang, some youths might tend to take out their anger against Anglo members of their own group, but that in the abstract prejudice against Anglos was not strong. This situation, reported by Hispano youths in 1965, is clearly changing rapidly at the present time. Increasing hostility has been registered in many ways and in general might be interpreted as a reflection of greater tensions in the adult world. Superficially, this behavior appears to resemble an earlier pattern of conflict along ethnic lines.

In the 1940's and early 1950's there were just two rival gangs in Albuquerque which clearly reflected the hostility between Anglos and those of Spanish or Mexican origin. This situation is said currently to exist in Las Vegas, New Mexico—a much smaller city and one in which ethnic feelings and prejudices are still quite strong. Zeleny said that Anglo boys in Albuquerque in the early 1940's would hesitate to enter a "Mexican district" at night because of beatings which had sometimes occurred under such circumstances (1944:319).

However, in Albuquerque today, violence also occurs between two gangs of the same ethnic composition. Whatever the situation a generation ago, it would seem that factors other than ethnic conflict are now also important in explaining the presence and activity of youth gangs. One informant, an official of the police department, thought that economic deprivation and broken homes were of greatest importance in the poorer, largely Hispano, sections of the city. He noted that seven out of fourteen members of one gang listed with the police department were from broken homes or living away from home for one reason or another. He also said that among these groups, stealing, when it occurred, was often motivated by hunger.

On the other hand, this same official claimed that there was a larger number of gangs operating in the fairly affluent Heights section of Albuquerque, which is heavily dominated by Anglos and a relatively new part of town, having been built up over the past 25 years. In this area, few, if any, juveniles are starving, and most of those who get into trouble are pure "hell-raisers." Membership in gangs here, as in the older Valley section of town, is probably stimulated by a desire to seek prestige, security, and recreation. It is important to note that in all areas, only a small minority of the youth joins such gangs. It seems likely that the type of individual who needs this kind of association is a product of certain of the social changes which accompany industrialization and urbanization.

The type of gang activity described above very greatly resembles, even in some of its details, that described by Rahm (1958) for El Paso, Texas. El Paso has been actively working to eliminate gangs because they are considered to contribute to delinquency and have led to increased violence and killing over the past twenty years. In addition to the Catholic Center in which Father Rahm worked in El Paso, much effort has been channeled through the organization of the Boys' Club of America and lately through a project funded by the Office of Economic Opportunity.

In Albuquerque there are several organizations dedicated to the elimination of gangs. Here too, the Boys' Club attempts to provide other interests and channels for the boys to develop skills and win prestige among their peers. There are two branches of the club in the city—one in the Heights, serving primarily Anglos, and the other in the Valley, in a predominantly Hispano neighborhood. The clubs stress pool, basketball, ping-pong, and other athletic activities, which have led other agencies in the city to criticize their efforts since they appeal only or primarily to the boy interested in sports. The staff of the Valley branch of the Boys' Club, mostly Spanish-Americans themselves, also enforce rigidly the conduct of those attendant at the clubhouse and forbid, under threat of expulsion, any kind of roughness, swearing, or destruction of equipment. An attempt also is made to acculturate the Spanish-American boys by forbidding them to speak Spanish while on the premises, teaching them better grooming techniques, and encouraging them to compete with Anglos on their own ground.

In 1965 an organization known as SCORE (Street Corner Offense Reduction Experiment) sent representatives to Albuquerque to organize its youth in an attempt to alleviate juvenile delinquency. Claiming that the Boys' Club had made little progress, SCORE set out to infiltrate the gangs themselves. Led by a young man of Puerto Rican descent from New York, himself a "reformed" gang member, SCORE rented an apartment to which the youngsters were encouraged to come and try out more socially acceptable pursuits—especially those designed to earn a living. Unfortunately, soon after the group began to work in Albuquerque, several juveniles who had become associated with SCORE were convicted of assault and battery and sentenced to terms in the Juvenile Detention Home. This tended to lower public opinion of the group; and when it was discovered that the organization was unknown to the police department of New York, where it had presumably been founded and had great success, many others were disenchanted. From all current informants' reports, SCORE is not now operating in Albuquerque.

Another institution attempting to combat juvenile delinquency is *Esperanza,* an experimental school primarily attended by members of the Bernalillo County Juvenile Detention Home. The students themselves are given great freedom in planning the curriculum and in running the school. It is hoped to stimulate those youngsters who for one reason or another find regular schools unsatisfactory for their needs.

Of course, there are innumerable other organizations which also offer activities to teenagers in the hope of keeping them from boredom, gangs, and perhaps serious trouble. There is no evidence to indicate that Hispano youths participate with any less vigor than Anglos in many of these, including the Boy and Girl Scouts, the YMCA and YWCA, and the many voluntary associations officially sponsored by Albuquerque schools and churches. Although there tends to be some apparent segregation within these groups—largely because most of them are organized along neighborhood or residential lines—here again, some Hispanos will be found in the Heights groups and some Anglos in the Valley.

Finally, a word should be said concerning the small, informal, neighborhood youth gang which seems to be a feature of growing up in the United States in general. Rubel (1965 and 1966) has described the Mexican-American *palomilla* (literally, covey of doves) as it existed in the south Texas city he studied. Heller asserts that the nondelinquent, neighborhood gang is actually quite similar to the delinquent gang (1966:57–58), but this does not accord with the information gathered in this brief survey in Albuquerque, nor with Rubel's materials on *palomillas* in Texas.

The neighborhood gang is not only nondelinquent, but neither is its structure formal. Thus, there are no formal initiations, no formal leadership roles, no typical patterns of dress or other outward symbols of group membership such as tatooing, no gang name, and no concept of a particular territory which must be defended. (Heller does exclude the last point in discussing non-delinquent gangs.) Furthermore, as Rubel has shown, the non-delinquent gang tends to be smaller and is usually egocentric and noncorporate (Rubel 1965:92–93). That is, any given individual may have a slightly different set of friends with whom he customarily associates than does any one of these friends himself. In Albuquerque, as in Texas, it is in such groups that, ". . . a boy becomes a man and learns to express himself as such" (*ibid.*, p. 93). Typical activities of such groups include standing around on street corners watching the girls and telling stories, riding around in cars and sitting in drive-in snack bars, drinking, attending movies, games and parties together, etc. Local slang sometimes includes all of these activities under the term "messing around."

One point which should be emphasized is that in Albuquerque, at least, this behavior does not seem markedly different from that observed among Anglo youths and is probably not unique to the Spanish-American subculture. The functions of such associations would seem to be the same, regardless of ethnic origin. Neither does it seem likely that the form has been borrowed by one culture from another, but that it is an outgrowth of the peculiarities of urban living per se.

Credit Unions

Membership in the nonprofit credit union as a means of providing savings or securing loans or both to cover emergency needs is becoming of increasing importance to Hispanos in New Mexico—especially to the middle-class salaried urban worker. In many ways this type of organization seems to form a bridge between the personal, face-to-face mutual-aid societies like those discussed in Chapter V and the completely impersonal bank or savings and loan association. Many credit unions are organized about a nucleus of persons bound together by common interests of other sorts. Thus, some are made up of employees of a particular firm or factory, community residents, or church members.

The first credit union in the United States was organized in a Catholic parish in New Hampshire in 1909. A spokesman of the Catholic church has said, "It was only natural that the greatest growth of credit unions since that time paralleled the industrial expansion of America." [3]

The first credit union in New Mexico was organized in 1945 by a Catholic priest in a section of Albuquerque known as Barelas, largely populated by Spanish-Americans. Although this particular group is no longer extant, three other parishes with large numbers of Spanish-American members have active unions at the present time. In 1965 there were 118 credit unions in New Mexico, 33 of which were located in Albuquerque. Of these, six were listed by an official of the New Mexico Credit Union League as being made up largely or predominantly of Hispanos. Other Hispanos participate in many of the remaining groups as well.

The operation of the credit union, in which a member pays a specified amount from his paycheck each month, gradually building up savings upon which he earns interest and upon which he may borrow at low rates, is said to be peculiarly suited to the needs of the lower-income groups, provided they have some form of regular employment. Furthermore, the fact that debts contracted by a member are insured and "die with the debtor" is another factor which appeals to the less affluent. Although members may be sued for non-payment of debts, informants pointed out that the primary sanctions used to exact payment were often based upon friendship, kinship, and other personal ties. Thus, among local Hispanos, *compadres* are frequently co-signers, and priests and employers can exert pressure when necessary (Vincent 1966). The idea of "brother helping brother" is consciously utilized by the New Mexico Credit Union League when promoting credit unions among local Spanish-speaking groups.

The majority of credit union members in New Mexico are not Hispanos, however, and it is clear that this particular form of mutual-aid society is largely an Anglo institution in this state today. But it is of interest that the first such group in New Mexico was organized among Spanish-Americans. The structure of these societies seems closely related to many features of the previously existing Hispano social organization, and this compatibility has probably been a factor in their acceptance by this ethnic group. In the final analysis, however, here as elsewhere in the world, participation in such groups is probably best viewed as evidence of acculturation to a non-agricultural, urban type of existence.

Higher Education

There are at the present time eight state colleges and universities in New Mexico, as well as several private institutions of higher learning. Some of these have for some time had large percentages of Spanish-American students, most of whom have prepared themselves for a teaching career. Highlands University at Las Vegas was founded in 1909 with the chief purpose of training the Spanish-speaking youth to become rural school teachers. It was long known, both officially and unofficially, as the Spanish-American School (Burma and Williams 1962:1). Today it is a full-fledged university, offering curricula in a variety of fields, but it is still largely attended by Spanish-American, as well as Indian, students. Similarly, the College of Santa Fe (formerly St. Michael's College), founded by the Christian Brothers in

1859, has long been attended by the Spanish-speaking population of the state, as has the Northern New Mexico State School (formerly El Rito Normal School). Not all the institutions of the state have been equally well attended by this group.

In 1915 Cochrane was amazed to discover that at New Mexico State College (now New Mexico State University) in Las Cruces, only 18% of the students were Spanish-speaking, although their percentage of the state's population at that time was from 37 to 40% (Cochrane 1915:71). But research for the present study indicates that many of the students at that college in the early 1900's were in fact upper-class Mexicans sent to the United States especially for their college education.[4] This would make the percentage noted by Cochrane still lower and actually more consistent with what might have been expected for that school, considering the social position of the Spanish-American at that time. Actually, numerous writers comment upon the fact that until the end of World War II relatively few Hispanos were able to attend college, and many of the children of the wealthier classes were sent out of the state to the large eastern schools (Burma 1954:21; Calvin 1947:26; Senter 1945:39).

A survey of freshmen enrollment in nine New Mexico colleges and universities in 1958 showed a total of 4,173, of which 17.5%, or 732, were of Spanish-surname (Manuel 1965:60). Again, we can assume that some of these were citizens of various Latin-American countries, thus lowering the percentage of native Hispanos. In 1965–1966 the total enrollment at the University of New Mexico was 10,723, of which 1,026 had Spanish surnames. Of these, 146 were students from Latin America, excluding Brazil and Haiti. If we subtract the latter figure, 880, or roughly 8%, remain who might be considered native Americans of Spanish descent. This does not, of course, include students of Spanish descent whose names do not so identify them, and some of those included are American Indians unwilling to be classified with Spanish-Americans. Nevertheless, the figures suggest that a smaller percentage of those Hispanos attending college in New Mexico choose the larger state schools—the university in Albuquerque and the land-grant college in Las Cruces. Furthermore, it appears that this has been the case for some time. It was said that only 165 Hispanos out of a total 1,265 were enrolled at the University of New Mexico in 1933.[5] Furthermore, most of these were reportedly Albuquerque residents, although they may have been living with Albuquerque relatives simply for purposes of attending the university.

It is frequently assumed that a higher dropout rate is more characteristic of Hispano students than of Anglo students. However, if the figures for the University of New Mexico graduating class of 1965 are considered, one sees that 106 out of 1,368 students, or 7.75%, were of Spanish surname. It is not known how many of these were of foreign birth. This percentage is not significantly different from the percentage of Hispanos in the total enrollment during that year. A study of the dropout rate among members of minority groups at the University of New Mexico revealed the following information: in the academic year 1965–1966, Spanish-Americans made up 12.5% of the freshmen, 8.8% of the sophomores, 8.2% of the juniors, and 5.1% of the seniors. Of those receiving undergraduate degrees, 8.4% were Hispanos; and 6.2% of the graduate degrees were awarded to members of this ethnic group. The Spanish-surname group at the university includes not only local Hispanos and Latin Americans but also some Indians and persons of Spanish surname from other states. Some of the latter, as well as some New Mexicans, are not Spanish speakers, nor are they distinguishable from Anglos in anything but surname. They are hardly to be considered as members of the Spanish-American minority group.

The study corrected for these variables. It is possible that the dropout rate is higher among Hispanos who come from lower-class, less-privileged, or rural backgrounds, but this fact is obscured by lumping together all persons of Spanish surname. It is also possible that there is a selection factor involved, and that the group attending the University of New Mexico differs in some significant respects from those attending other New Mexican institutions of higher learning. Nothing is known of the dropout rate relative to ethnic background elsewhere.[6]

Regardless of how one reads the evidence, it does seem clear that larger numbers and a higher percentage of Spanish-Americans than ever before are today attending college. Although they still tend to prefer certain areas of study over others, they are also beginning to branch out into a variety of professions. Both of these facts can be seen from the information given in Table 2. Thus, it can be seen that in 1965 the two most popular colleges among Hispanos at the University of New Mexico were Arts and Sciences and Education. Many of those graduating in the College of Arts and Sciences were Spanish majors. This preference is again apparent at the post-graduate level from the high proportion of Spanish-surname students receiving the degree of Master of Arts in Teaching Spanish—a degree which combines both traditionally popular fields. But it should not be overlooked that three out of eight graduating in pharmacy were of Spanish descent, as were three out of 23 graduating as nurses.

The whole subject of higher education has more meaning when considered in relation to the lower levels of education which have preceded it, as well as the occupational demands and opportunities of the society involved. Barrett and Samora point out that "There appears to be a concensus of opinion among most observers, professional and non-professional alike, that the Spanish-speaking lack sufficient motivation to stay in school or obtain much

Table 2

FREQUENCY DISTRIBUTION OF CANDIDATES FOR DEGREES IN VARIOUS COLLEGES OF THE UNIVERSITY OF NEW MEXICO, JUNE 1965, BY PRESUMED ETHNIC ORIGIN, BASED UPON SURNAME

	Total Graduates	*Graduates with Spanish Surname*
Bachelor's Degrees		
College of Arts and Sciences	351	27
College of Engineering	147	6
College of Education	252	28
College of Fine Arts	87	9
College of Pharmacy	8	3
College of Business Administration	87	5
School of Law	17	1
College of Nursing	23	3
Total	972	82
Master's Degrees		
Master of Arts and Master of Science	275	16
Master of Industrial Administration	2	0
Master of Business Administration	9	0
Master of Music	5	0
Master of Music Education	4	1
Master of Education in Science	39	0
Master of Arts in Teaching Spanish	14	7
Total	348	24
Doctoral Degrees		
Ph.D.	33	0
Ed.D.	8	0
Total	41	0

education at all" (1963:13). Certainly, New Mexico has had a continuing problem since statehood and even earlier in educating the masses of its Spanish-American children. Not only have buildings, equipment, and teachers been lacking or inadequate, but even when basic opportunities have been provided, many children have failed to complete the minimum years required by law. Much has been written concerning the reasons for the Spanish-speaking child's inability to compete with Anglos in the school system; and it is today generally agreed that an inadequacy in handling the English language, plus an unfamiliarity with the Anglo world in general, and possibly poorer health, have contributed to this pattern.[7] The child becomes discouraged in the early years and never manages to close the cultural and intellectual gap between him and his Anglo peer. As Barrett and Samora have said, "In the process of gaining an elementary education the Spanish-speaking child internalizes attitudes of inferiority and futility" (1963:13).

However, some evidence indicates that today there are differences between the rural and the urban zones in this matter. In 1962 Burma and Williams, in discussing Rio Arriba and Taos counties in the northern part of the state, noted that in this area ". . . the number of children is increasing but the proportion the schools succeed in enrolling is smaller than ten years ago" (p. 67). Furthermore, "Over half of the area's children are handicapped permanently by failing to graduate from high school" (*ibid.,* p. 59). Those who do manage to graduate from high school find themselves ". . . at a serious disadvantage when trying to compete with high school graduates from other areas" (*ibid.*). The suggestion made previously that many of the college-bound Hispanos do not select the larger state institutions may very well be related to such patterns at the lower levels of schooling in the rural areas.

On the other hand, if materials from New Mexico—especially from Albuquerque—are compared with those from other states in reference to primary education among Spanish- or Mexican-Americans, we find some interesting points. Potts (1959:7), in a study of migrant laborers in Colorado, found that the rate of elementary school enrollment in New Mexico, as evidenced by the records of the New Mexican children contacted, was considerably better than that for similar groups in Texas and Arizona. Barrett and Samora found that the expected low rate of school participation among Spanish-speaking youths in the five southwestern states in general did not hold up for the elementary grades. But, "At the high school level only one-half to three-fourths of the age-eligible children in high-density Spanish neighborhoods are enrolled, *with the exception of Albuquerque,* where a higher percentage participates" (1963:13). Manuel also comments that for the Southwest as a whole, "In nearly every age bracket the percentage of Spanish-surname persons enrolled in school is less than the percentage of the total population enrolled in school. The percentages for the two groups are closest in New Mexico, where the Spanish-speaking population is a larger part of the total than in the other states" (1965:55).

It seems safe to conclude tentatively that the somewhat better performance of New Mexican Spanish-speaking children is a function of urban living and the type of acculturation which that entails in this state, and that the differences between Albuquerque and other southwestern cities may in part be attributed to Albuquerque's smaller size and peculiar ecology. Furthermore, the history of rural-to-urban migration within the state goes back at least 35 years, as outlined in the preceding chapter. Finally, the fact that persons of Spanish descent have always made up a larger percentage of the population of this state than in the other southwestern states, and that their problems as a minority group have been recognized for a longer time, seem to underlie their present somewhat better position in regard to educational status. The urban New Mexican Hispano has learned that a good education and complete fluency in English are necessary if he is to compete with Anglos in the business and social worlds. In the rural areas, still traditionally Spanish and isolated from the rest of the world, these skills have not in the past been of such clear value. Today, however, as the rural areas continue to decline economically and more people move into the cities, there seems to be a greater emphasis placed on learning English (frequently at the expense of Spanish) and staying in school. Some have felt that this trend indicates an anti-Hispanic attitude, but in the words of the educator, Joaquin Ortega, ". . . there is nothing anti-Hispanic in it: only an earnest desire of these citizens of Spanish extraction to free themselves from the taint of 'foreignism' and to enter fully into the life of the country which adopted them" (1941:3).

Representation in High-Status Professions

Any discussion of education should eventually get around to the question, Education for what? In a primarily agrarian society such as that found in New Mexico until a generation ago, formal education is frequently not highly valued by the masses and is usually common only among the upper classes, for whom it is more a validation of their status than useful in earning a living. In earlier times the wealthy Hispano frequently sent his sons east to study, primarily for the prestige and satisfaction to be gained from a liberal arts education. Rideling makes an interesting comment in regard to this pattern which may be symptomatic of the changes occurring at the time he was writing, in 1876. He says, ". . . because so few return, there is a decided prejudice against this custom" (1876:19). Apparently the opportunities available in the east, opportunities lacking in New Mexico, were even then attractive to many of these youths.

In the early days just after the American conquest of the territory, many wealthy Spanish went into business—frequently with an Anglo partner—and they found that a knowledge of the law helped not only in commerce but in gaining influence in the territory in general. Law provided an avenue to politics and to power, which in turn often led to increased riches. Indeed, in Albuquerque in 1870, two of the town's six lawyers were Spanish-American (Westphall 1947:38).

The fact that the *Albuquerque City Directory and Business Guide* for 1907 lists *no* Spanish-Americans in *any* profession is not completely understood by this writer. It is possible, although not likely, that any Hispanos in such positions might not have chosen to list themselves. It seems more probable, however, that this reflects the change in status which was to reach a climax in the 1930's. E. Fergusson said in 1928:

> The Mexican [i.e., Spanish-American] is not well represented in the learned professions and not at all in engineering or in science. There are Mexican lawyers, but in the entire history of the State only a few have attained first rank. Only two have been judges. Usually young men who study law come home and ask for political preferment, instead of struggling in obscurity as the young *gringo* does (1928:443).

Although the wording of this statement seems depreciating, it is probably an accurate reflection of the nature of the culture at that time. (See Chapter IV.)

With the increase in urbanization and acculturation after World War II, it seems reasonable to expect that the numbers of Hispanos as well as their percentage in relation to Anglos represented in the professions of medicine, dentistry, teaching, and law should increase. To determine whether this has occurred, a review was made of the 1964 telephone directories of the following New Mexico cities: Albuquerque, Carlsbad, Farmington, Gallup, Grants, Las Cruces, Las Vegas, Roswell, Santa Fe, Silver City, and Socorro (Table 3). All of these cities, with the exception of Socorro, had over 10,000 inhabitants in the 1960 U.S. Census. Other cities in this size category—Alamogordo, Artesia, Clovis, Hobbs, and Los Alamos—were excluded from the survey. This was done because Alamogordo and Los Alamos are largely dependent upon federal defense projects, and Artesia, Clovis, and Hobbs are located in the Little Texas eastern belt, which has a very low percentage of Spanish-American inhabitants and where prejudice and discrimination are so strong that more-educated Hispanos decline to live there. The majority of the Spanish-speaking who do live in this area are more recent migrants or descendants of migrants from Mexico and occupy the lowest rungs on the socioeconomic scale, mostly being employed as laborers. It was felt that the inclusion of Carlsbad and Roswell, both of which also lie in this area, would be sufficient to indicate the very low representation of persons with Spanish surnames in the professions there.

Quite clearly, Albuquerque and Santa Fe, the largest and the third-largest cities, show both the greatest numbers and the highest percentages of Hispano professionals. The conclusion seems warranted that this is related to urbanism, on the one hand, and to history, on the other. That is, it is precisely in the two largest cities of the *north,* always the stronghold of the Spanish population, that this phenomenon is observed. Roswell, the second largest city, has very few Spanish-surname professionals. This might be explained by the low percentage of Hispanos in that area, but Las Cruces, with a population of about 30,000 in 1960, about half of whom were of Spanish surname, also shows very

Table 3

NUMBERS OF ALL PERSONS AND THOSE WITH
SURNAMES IN SELECTED PROFESSIONS AS
TELEPHONE DIRECTORIES OF NINE MAJOR NEW
MEXICAN CITIES, 1966

City and Population *	Dentists	Physi-cians †	Chiro-practors	Optom-etrists	Lawyers
Albuquerque (201,189)					
Total	131	293	22	20	222
Spanish surname	14	8	0	1	32
Carlsbad (25,541)					
Total	11	24	2	2	22
Spanish surname	0	0	0	0	1
Farmington (23,786)					
Total	10	23	2	5	32
Spanish surname	0	0	0	0	1
Gallup (14,089)					
Total	4	7	3	3	13
Spanish surname	0	0	0	0	0
Grants (10,274)					
Total	2	7	0	1	3
Spanish surname	0	3	0	0	1
Las Cruces (29,367)					
Total	16	29	5	3	28
Spanish surname	0	0	0	1	1
Las Vegas (13,818)					
Total	3	11	3	1	8
Spanish surname	1	0	1	0	4
Roswell (39,593)					
Total	19	38	4	5	50
Spanish surname	0	0	0	0	0
Santa Fe (33,394)					
Total	29	54	4	4	82
Spanish surname	9	2	1	0	14

* U.S. Census, 1960
† Includes only M.D.'s

few professionals in this ethnic group. This would seem to be related to the lower status of Spanish-Americans or Mexican-Americans in Las Cruces, a situation also characteristic of Roswell, where their percentage in the population is smaller. On the other hand, Las Vegas, a medium-sized city in the very heart of the Hispano territory, also has few professionals with Spanish surnames. However, it is significant that Las Vegas has four Hispano lawyers out of a total of eight, which is the highest percentage for Spanish-American lawyers of any city in the state. This, too, is consistent with the former prestige of law as a profession in this population. Apparently Spanish-Americans who are upwardly mobile in the professional world seek the larger cities in those areas where they have traditionally been most successful; and, on the other hand, the higher percentages in these cities can also be viewed as a result of urbanization.

The professions relating to health (including osteopathic medicine, dentistry, optometry, pharmacy, and nursing) all seem to be increasingly attractive to Hispanos in New Mexico. This is clear from the number of persons in these professions in various cities, from the data concerning University of New Mexico graduates given in Table 2, and from other sources. With the recent opening of the School of Nursing (1956) and the School of Medicine (1964) at the University of New Mexico, this participation can be expected to increase.

It is interesting, in connection with this, to refer to D'Antonio and Samora's work on occupational stratification in four southwestern cities (1962). They found that within the health-services structure in Las Cruces, Spanish-surname persons were occupationally least mobile—that is, they were heavily represented in the more menial occupations and hardly at all in the highest levels. They also found that in the entire area under consideration persons with Spanish surnames were represented to a very low degree on hospital boards of directors, positions which they felt usually reflected a high status within the community at large. In Albuquerque in 1969 no Hispano was represented on any hospital board whatever, a finding which seems contradictory to what has so far been argued—that the social position of Hispanos has been steadily improving in this area since 1946. However, since many of the hospitals in Albuquerque are connected with Protestant churches and since most Hispanos are of the Roman Catholic faith, this may be an important factor to consider before adopting D'Antonio and Samora's assumption. There is only one Catholic hospital in Albuquerque (none in Las Cruces), and the fact that no Spanish-Americans are on its board as of 1969 may not be significant since the number of positions is limited, and we do not know the possible extent of Hispano participation in the past.

Another way of examining the position of Hispanos within the state through the years is to examine those compilations entitled "Who's Who in New Mexico." Admittedly, these lists are biased by the fact that the individual listed is often required to pay a fee, and that this, plus one's particular world view, may cause some worthy persons to be excluded. However, in Abousleman's edition of *Who's Who in New Mexico* in 1937, out of 1,101 persons listed in the state, only 37 were of Spanish surname. This amounts to 3.3%, a grossly low proportion in relation to the total population at that time. In Moore's *Who Is Who in New Mexico* in 1962, 72 out of 1,383, or 5.1%, had Spanish surnames. Since the percentage of Hispanos in the state decreased over that same period of time, this actually indicates an increase of more than the 1.8 percentage points that Moore's figures suggest. Of those persons listed, it is notable that 25 were in education, 15 in law and/or governmental positions, 9 in business, 7 in ranching, and the 16 remaining were scattered through a variety of professions. It should also be emphasized that there were no doctors, dentists, chiropractors, or others of the professions recorded above, with the exception of law. This shows that while the latter professional occupations may be roads to financial success and local prestige, other professions are of still greater importance in establishing or reflecting status on a broader level. It is also possible that persons in these categories, i.e., doctors, dentists, etc., are less anxious to have their names recorded in such volumes, even if invited. The reason the above professions have been used in this analysis is that they are occupations readily identifiable from listings in city and telephone directories.

Although at first glance it would appear from the percentages given that in recent years the position of Spanish-Americans in the wider society has come closer to that of the Anglos, we should be cautious in coming to this conclusion. To determine whether, in fact, the situation has really altered, it would be necessary to have accurate figures from each city showing the percentage increase in each profession as compared with the percentage distribution of Hispanos over the same period of time. The most that the present work can do, in the absence of such data, is to show that in most parts of the state, contrary to popular assumption, Hispanos are greatly under-represented in the professional fields. Only in Albuquerque and Santa Fe does the situation seem different. In Albuquerque, since it is a known fact that the total percentage of Hispanos is decreasing, the finding that the number of Hispano professionals is increasing indicates the probability of some sort of favorable change. The usual commentary on the state of affairs gives the impression that there has been a great deal of improvement. Here, as in college enrollments, there is probably some increasing participation, but Hispanos are still under-represented in comparison to their total proportion in the population.

In Santa Fe, which has continuously been the capital of the area during all of its changes in political status, and which is heavily dominated by Spanish-Americans even today, there is evidence that the situation is somewhat different from that found in Albuquerque. Santa Fe society is much more self-consciously "integrated" than elsewhere—in part due, perhaps, to its reputation as an art and cultural center. Nevertheless, one still finds cliques representing the different ethnic groups, and under the surface there is tension, even though individuals in the upper social strata seem to associate more often on the basis of class rather than ethnicity. It is also notable that of the 123 clubs, organizations, and associations listed by the Santa Fe Chamber of Commerce in 1965, 17 had presidents with Spanish surnames, a situation occurring nowhere else in the state. The organizations so headed included national service clubs, fraternal orders, charitable foundations, religious groups, and cultural or literary societies—in short, they ran the gamut of the usual types of voluntary associations found in United States society in general. The participation in these by Hispanos, and their acceptance to the point indicated by the number of presidents listed, would seem to confirm the generalization made above that Santa Fe presents a unique picture in the state as a whole. Persons with Spanish surnames are also apparently more highly represented here in the professions than elsewhere, as is apparent in Table 3.

At the same time, however, Santa Fe shows some of the same characteristics described for Albuquerque. Thus, there is an increasingly large lower-class made up almost entirely of Hispanos, a disturbing amount of juvenile delinquency among this group, problems stemming from linguistic and cultural barriers to achieving higher education, etc.[8] There is also an ever-expanding middle-class of Hispanos who come not only from Santa Fe but from rural areas all over the state—many of them to work in state offices. Local jargon refers to this group as "the Capitol crowd," which includes white-collar workers and professionals of both sexes. Most of these are highly upwardly mobile within the broader system, adopting English as their primary and sometimes only language, and they have usually had some education beyond high school. They are frequently highly skilled in their work, alert to the political maneuvering which takes place in the capital city, as well as throughout the state, and adept at moving within the system. Gossip is an important means by which this group keeps its fingers on the pulse of government and the sources of personal opportunity.

Yet it cannot be said that the members of this group, different as they are from their rural ancestors and contemporary older relatives, have become Anglicized. They are urban sophisticates but still highly visible as Hispanos, and proud of their heritage. Although most of the adults in this middle-class Santa Fe group still speak Spanish, few of their children do. Most of the younger parents are not fully aware of what this may reflect in terms of their children's futures. However, they are too preoccupied with the day-to-day business of living—and living better than their ancestors have lived for many generations—to be concerned about it. The atmosphere of Santa Fe is generally recognized by New Mexicans to be a very special one. Indeed, of all places in this Land of Enchantment, Santa Fe probably inspires the most romanticism. The Anglos who have adopted the city as their home are self-conscious about preserving its Hispanic charm, while the Spanish-Americans seem to accept the fact that change is inevitable, but that not all acculturation need be toward Anglicization. They are secure in their ethnicity—more secure than the Hispanos of Albuquerque, where the *agringado* is much more in evidence, or in Las Vegas, where recent changes have made many Spanish-Americans defensive about their background in a predominantly Hispano county.

Intermarriage with Anglos

According to Johnson, who studied marriage data for Bernalillo County in the late 1940's, "The amount of intermarriage into the dominant culture group and particularly the trends in the amount, is a good single index of degree and trends in assimilation" (1948:45). Zeleny also commented extensively on the subject and presented a set of figures regarding intermarriage with Anglos between the years 1924 and 1940 (1944:334).

It has been pointed out in a previous chapter that intermarriage between prominent Spanish families and Anglo trappers and traders occurred even before the American occupation and that several families today count their ancestry from Civil War soldiers who elected to stay in the territory after that war. Zeleny also documents a few cases in which other immigrant groups intermarried extensively with Hispanos (1944:332). However, intermarriage with Anglos seems to have declined after the turn of the century, if not before. Loomis (1943:23) says that mixed marriages were rare both in Taos and in Las Cruces in the 1930's. Johnson found in 1948 that the Anglo was not considered to be a suitable marriage partner by her informants from Bernalillo County, even though by that time intermarriage had begun again to increase, as shown by her own statistics (1948:33).

It is clear from accounts of early village life that most Hispanos not only preferred to marry Hispanos, but even Hispanos from their own village. Most Hispanos rarely came into contact with outsiders; even the men who engaged in migratory wage labor worked in specialized male occupations which seldom brought them into the company of women. The pool of potential mates for both sexes was almost exclusively limited to other members of *la raza,* so it is not surprising that intermarriage was rare, a social fact fully supported by a world view which disapproved of exogamy and called the product of such marriages "coyote." The process of urbanization brought large numbers of Hispanos into face-to-face contact with Anglos for the first time, and the inevitable result was both to increase and to diversify the pool of potential marriage partners.

Some figures concerning intermarriage in Bernalillo County are available in the unpublished manuscripts of Johnson (1948) and Zeleny (1944). To check, extend, and put these materials into context, a further study of marriages in this county was carried out in conjunction with the present research. Marriage license data were examined for every Monday in the years 1930, 1940, 1947, 1953, and 1964. These years were chosen in part to cross-check the reliability of the sampling method, since Zeleny also included 1930 and 1940; 1947 was chosen as the first post-World War II year; 1953 as the first post-Korean War year; and 1964 because it was the most recent year with complete statistics available at the time the survey was made. Marriages were considered to be between Spanish-Americans only if the surnames of both parties were Spanish and if both parties were born in the southwestern states of New Mexico, Colorado, Arizona, Texas, or California.[9] Persons of Spanish surname born in an Indian pueblo, in a foreign country, or in other states were excluded. All persons with non-Spanish surnames, regardless of place of birth, were considered to be Anglo. If marriage certificates were not recorded, the cases were excluded. The type of marriage ceremony was recorded by noting the status of the person who performed the wedding—i.e., Roman Catholic clergyman, Protestant clergyman, or Justice of the Peace. In a few cases the ceremony was performed by a U.S.A.F. chaplain, with denomination unspecified. These cases were included in a special list and classified in the religious-ceremony category as distinguished from the civil ceremony, but they were excluded in computations of Catholic versus Protestant marriage rituals. The raw data collected are presented in Tables 4 and 5.

Analyses were first carried out using the data from this study alone in order to determine whether there were any significant discernible trends. As is shown in Table 6, there was a significant increase in exogamous marriages relative to endogamous (including both Anglo endogamous and Spanish endogamous) over the sample period ($x^2 = 25.76$; $df. = p < .001$). Within the exoga-

Table 4

FREQUENCIES OF DIFFERENT TYPES OF CEREMONIES IN MARRIAGES INVOLVING HISPANOS RECORDED ON MONDAYS OF SELECTED YEARS IN BERNALILLO COUNTY, NEW MEXICO

	1930	1940	1947	1953	1964	Total
Roman Catholic						
Endogamous	24	15	54	57	63	213
Exogamous	1	5	4	8	22	40
Protestant						
Endogamous	0	3	6	3	7	19
Exogamous	0	1	0	3	8	12
Justice of the Peace						
Endogamous	21	14	31	22	40	128
Exogamous	4	3	3	13	21	44
Other						
Endogamous	0	1	0	0	0	1
Exogamous	0	0	0	1	2	3
Total	50	42	98	107	163	460

Table 5

FREQUENCIES OF ETHNIC ENDOGAMOUS AND MIXED
MARRIAGES RECORDED ON MONDAYS OF SELECTED
YEARS IN BERNALILLO COUNTY, NEW MEXICO

	1930	1940	1947	1953	1964
Hispano Endogamous	45	33	91	82	110
Anglo Endogamous	56	115	212	317	315
Hispano male, Anglo female	3	3	3	10	19
Hispano female, Anglo male	2	6	3	15	34
Total Mixed	(5)	(9)	(7)	(25)	(53)
Other combinations	2	5	16	23	8
Total	108	162	326	447	486

Table 6

FREQUENCIES OF ETHNIC ENDOGAMOUS AND
EXOGAMOUS MARRIAGES RECORDED ON MONDAYS OF
SELECTED YEARS IN BERNALILLO COUNTY, NEW
MEXICO

	1930	1940	1947	1953	1964	Total
Endogamous						
Observed	101	148	303	399	425	1376
Expected	(98.9)	(146.5)	(289.2)	(395.5)	(445.9)	
Exogamous						
Observed	5	9	7	25	53	99
Expected	(7.)	(10.5)	(20.8)	(28.5)	(32.1)	
Total	106	157	310	424	478	1475

mous marriage category there is no significant difference over
time between the types: Hispano male with Anglo female, and
Hispano female with Anglo male. The figures show a slight

predominance of the latter, but it is not statistically significant. This would appear to be consistent with Johnson's finding (1948:49); furthermore, when an x^2 test of significance is run on her data, the differences she suggests are seen to be well above chance expectations.

When data from 1930 and 1940, gathered during the present research, were compared with those of Zeleny—who presented complete data for those years—the results confirmed the reliability of the sampling technique the author of this study used. Because Johnson presented her findings in terms of mixed marriages as a percentage of all marriages involving Spanish-Americans, and Zeleny based hers on a percentage of the total marriages recorded, the two findings are not directly comparable. Furthermore, with the exception of 1936, none of Johnson's years coincides with any of Zeleny's, nor with those sampled in this study. Nevertheless, an effort was made to try to correct for the differences in methodology and achieve some basis for comparison in order to give a picture covering a fifty-year period from 1915 through 1964. The results may be seen in Table 7. Zeleny's figures have been used only for 1926 and 1936, Johnson's for 1915–1916 and 1945–1946, and the author's for 1953 and 1964, giving, roughly, ten-year intervals.

In general, there is a clear trend toward increasing intermarriage over the fifty-year period. It must be kept in mind that another consistent trend throughout this period has been population increase; this increase augmented the size of both Hispano and Anglo groups, but tended to increase the proportion of Anglos. Thus, the proportion of endogamous Hispano marriages has tended to decrease as a direct function of their decreasing percentage of the total population, as shown in Table 7, column 6. The same problem arises in connection with the figures in column 7 of the table—they are in part a function of the changing

Table 7

COMPARISON OF FIGURES CONCERNING
INTERMARRIAGE OF HISPANOS AND ANGLOS AT
ROUGHLY TEN-YEAR INTERVALS FROM 1915–1964

1	2	3	4	5	6	7	8
Time	Source	TM	TH	TH/TM %	HE/TM %	M/TM %	M/TH %
1915–16 *	Johnson	n.d.	108.5	—	—	—	14.3
1926	Zeleny	384	209	54.4	49.0	5.5	10.0
1936	Zeleny	684	313	45.8	37.6	8.5	17.9
1945–46 *	Johnson	n.d.	430.5	—	—	—	21.6
1953 †	González	2,235	535	25.2	18.3	5.6	23.4
1964	González	2,430	815	34.1	22.6	10.9	32.5

TM = Total marriages
TH = Total marriages involving Hispanos (Hispano endogamous plus mixed)
HE = Hispano endogamous
 M = Mixed marriages
  * = Half of two-year total
n.d. = no data
  † = Extrapolated figures: five times number of Monday certificates

composition of the population. Thus, the percentage of mixed marriages in relation to total marriages involving Hispanos (column 8) would seem to be more accurate a reflection of the true degree of intermarriage.

Some discrepancies in the data should be noted. Johnson's figures for 1915–1916 seem a little out of line in relation to the other years for which information is available. Thus, her total number of endogamous marriages seems very low, and her category "mixed" seems relatively high, resulting in a high rate of intermarriage. It is possible that the involvement of the United States in the Mexican border incident and indirectly in World

War I may have altered slightly the number of marriages occurring in those years, but it is difficult to accept an increase from 93 to 247 over an eight-year period from 1916–1924, which is what her figures show. These figures were not, therefore, included in the present study. Her figure for mixed marriages, although out of proportion in relation to the total marriages in those years, seems reasonable in relation to numbers of mixed marriages recorded from 1924 on. Therefore, it is possible that the figure referring to the total endogamous marriages was inaccurately recorded.

The 1947 figures recorded for this study also do not seem consistent with other materials. Thus, the figure for mixed marriages seems too low in relation to the figure for other years and in relation to the total number of marriages recorded. Again, it is possible that unusual circumstances prevailed during the first post-war year, but no explanatory hypothesis has been formed. The more likely explanation is error in the data. Nevertheless, over a long period of time the trend is clearly visible, whether 1947 was or was not an aberrant year.

Finally, it is important to note that the change has not been a gradual one, even though there has been a consistent trend. The biggest percentage-point change occurred between 1953 and 1964, which is what would be expected if in fact the trend were related to increasing urbanization and acculturation. Throughout this discussion it should be remembered that the whole subject of intermarriage will soon become almost impossible to study with the techniques applied in this research. It is obvious that there are many individuals with Spanish surname who, because their mothers have been Anglo, do not identify with the Hispano group. Yet if these persons marry Anglos, their marriages would be categorized as "mixed." Conversely, the person brought up by a Spanish-speaking mother is likely to speak that language and feel himself to be a part of *la raza,* even though his surname is Anglo. Yet if he marries an Hispano, again the marriage would be recorded as "mixed." Clearly, we do not yet know enough about the social characteristics of these mixed marriages in terms of how the children may be raised, with which group they identify, etc. Leonard said, "Intermarriage is rare, and when it occurs either the Spanish-American or the Anglo is taken into one of the groups and almost excluded from participation in the other" (1943:110). But we still do not know under what circumstances the couple will be taken into one group or another, or if, in fact, this pattern is still extant. Furthermore, as Hispanos themselves become more acculturated, it may soon be impossible to identify many individuals in terms of ethnic origin, at which point, of course, the whole question of how much intermarriage takes place will become meaningless. In 1915 Cochrane was able to record a very neat dichotomy between ethnic groups in Dona Ana County in reference to marriage. Of a total of 165 marriages occurring between January 1, 1914, and January 1, 1915, 100 were between Spanish-Americans, and 65 between Anglos (1915:42). This clearcut distinction has not been possible in Bernalillo County for a very long time, and will become increasingly more difficult to make in the future.

In conclusion, it is suggested that at the present time there still are two identifiable ethnic groups, that they are only partially distinguished by surname, that intermarriage is increasing, but that this increase will serve to compound the difficulties now apparent in trying to gather accurate statistics and make meaningful generalizations concerning the phenomenon of intermarriage.

Changes in Religious Behavior

There is a commonly held notion that the process of modernization among the Spanish-speaking involves, among other things, a switch from the Roman Catholic faith to one of the Protestant denominations. Madsen, in discussing Mexican-Americans of the lower Rio Grande Valley in Texas, has said that Protestantism is a common reaction of those who have attempted to adopt the Anglo value system (1961:16). Senter, speaking of New Mexicans, says much the same thing in his comment, "Some may even give up Catholicism in an attempt to 'pass over' (i.e., to adopt the Anglo ethnic group)" (1945:39). H. Ellis suggests that dropping of the old family religion and the weakening of family ties are aspects of the urbanization process in New Mexico (1948:7). F. C. Moore, in comparing information he gathered in Albuquerque in 1946 with that Waggoner obtained in the same locale in 1941, found that there had been a decrease in Catholicism of about 12 percentage points (from 84% to 72%) in that five-year period (1946:120).

There has been considerable Protestant missionary activity in the area since the American conquest in 1846, and in some towns the conversion rate has been quite high. For example, in the village of Chacon about half the population were Protestant in 1928 (Bohannan 1928:2). There are other small rural towns where a similar situation exists, but most writers agree that the majority of the Spanish-Americans of New Mexico has never altered their allegiance to Roman Catholicism. Leonard reported, "During the past half century some considerable converts have been made to the Protestant religions among the Spanish speaking people generally, with the exception of the strictly Spanish-American element" (1943:21). Zeleny, following Walter (1939), generally agrees with this opinion (1944:268). It seems clear from a general survey of the literature that the percentage of Roman Catholics among New Mexican Spanish-Americans is probably still close to 75% of their total number. Depending upon one's point of view, this could be considered evidence of strong retention of the religion or as a remarkable conversion rate, considering that these people were close to being 100% Catholic in 1846!

Other than conducting a survey among a random sample of Hispanos over the state, this writer knows of no way to ascertain the true figures regarding religious affiliation. However, there are some kinds of indirect, or circumstantial, evidence which may be presented in the absence of such data. A church directory, sponsored by the Albuquerque Ministerial Alliance listed 16 out of 213 churches in the city as giving sermons in Spanish in 1963. Five more churches were listed by informants which were not listed in that directory. This would bring the total number of churches conducting services in Spanish to 21. Of these, 18 were Protestant. Although the sizes of the congregations are unknown, one of the largest of the Protestant churches, for which there is information, can be taken as an example. The Second United Presbyterian Church was founded in Albuquerque in 1889 with 15 members. Through the years its congregation, almost exclusively Hispano, grew to a total of 303 members in 1963. Even if every other church listed had a congregation as large as this, there would still be only about 5,000 Hispano Protestants in the city of Albuquerque. Granting that many might regularly attend services without actually being members, these rough estimates still do not indicate any overwhelming Protestant movement among speakers of Spanish.

Another, perhaps more serious, source of error is that there is no way to identify and count the Hispanos who may attend English-language Protestant churches, and there is qualitative evidence to indicate that many do so. If, of course, Protestantism were indeed one aspect of a trend toward Anglicization, then it would follow that most acculturated individuals would seek churches where English is used. The above analysis, then, refers only to the possibility that Protestantism may be adopted while at the same time other Spanish cultural characteristics are retained. This does not seem to be a major trend.

To cast more light on this subject, one can examine the type of marriage ceremony chosen by persons of Spanish surname in Bernalillo County, assuming that this reflects to a considerable degree the social, if not the ideological, strength of the various sects. Not only can one compare the number of Catholic ceremonies with Protestant, but one can also compare the total number of religious and civil ceremonies as a rough index of secularization, a phenomenon which is usually considered to be a concomitant of urbanization in Western society in general.[10] Johnson found that in 1915–1916, 14.5% of the total of endogamous Hispano marriages were civil ceremonies. In 1945–1946, 34.5% in the same category were performed by Justices of the Peace. In both cases she found that a larger percentage of civil ceremonies was recorded for mixed marriages than for endogamous marriages. She concluded that there was more intermarriage with Anglos and less objection to it in Spanish-American families which were not Catholic (1948:70). However, she also concluded that the greatest change in Spanish-American marriage customs over the period studied was not in the religious denomination but in the great increase in civil ceremonies (*ibid.*, p. 43).

The present study also recorded information concerning type of marriage ceremony, as indicated. Taking the mixed marriages alone, there does not seem to be any kind of trend in the kind of ceremony chosen by these couples. The same is true of marriage ceremonies between Hispano partners. However, the Hispano couples chose Catholic ceremonies significantly more often than did those in which only one partner was Hispano ($x^2 = 12.22$; $df. = 2$; $p < .01$). This, then, would confirm Johnson's first conclusion, stated in the foregoing. However, her second conclusion that there has been a tremendous increase in the rate of civil, as contrasted with religious, ceremonies is not supported by the present study. Indeed, Johnson's own data, when submitted to a more rigorous statistical analysis, do not support her conclusion. There was a significant increase in civil marriages between the 1915–1916 and the 1925–1926 samples, but after that there is no significant trend whatever. When comparable figures for years covered in this research were placed in sequence with Johnson's figures, no significant patterns were apparent. If anything, the data indicate a possible reverse trend toward increasing numbers of religious ceremonies since 1945.

Thus, this evidence, plus that given above, suggests that the Spanish-Americans of New Mexico, unlike what has been reported for other areas, tend to cling to their traditional religious affiliation. Furthermore, the data concerning type of marriage do not indicate any increasing secularization over the years in Bernalillo County. This may or may not be significant in relation to urbanization. It would be valuable to have comparable information concerning types of marriage ceremonies in a predominantly rural county over a period of years to determine what effect, if any, urbanization may have upon this behavior. Neither can the author explain, on the basis of present evidence, the significant increase in civil ceremonies which took place between 1915–1916 and 1925–1926 in this county. Whatever the causative factors were, they apparently no longer operate at the present time.

Notes

1 Professor Morris Forslund of the Department of Sociology, University of New Mexico, supplied these figures from his own research materials. (Personal communication.)

2 The following list does not pretend to be exhaustive. It is included merely to

give an idea of the nature of the jargon used by Spanish-American gangs in Albuquerque. It will be clear to students of Mexican-American culture elsewhere that some words are shared with *Chicanos* everywhere, while others have a distinct local flavor. Translations given are not literal but are exactly as informants worded them to get their meaning across to the author.

Caballo—stupid person
Cargar el palo—to mess up the joint
Pendejo—a stupid person, a real ass
Voltear chanclas—to go dancing
Mayate—a Black (man)
Mayatera—a white woman who sleeps with Blacks
Mayata—a Black (woman)
No me dejas flate—Don't leave me flat.
Guete—gun (possibly from Sp. *cohete*)
Shante—house (possibly from Eng. *shanty*)
Refinar—to eat
Rifar—to be sent North (that is, to State Training School at Springer)
Jet—to cut out, leave in a hurry
Gain—hip, cool
I'm gain—I'm ready to fight.
Rumble—a gang fight
Blow—a gang fight
Chingaso—a fight, or a single blow (sexual reference)
Jodaso—a punch or blow (sexual reference)
Chingalo—Beat him up! (sexual reference)
Me tira al loco—She isn't paying any attention to me. She thinks I'm stupid.
No hay pedo—There is no reason for us to fight, no beef.
Frajo—cigarette
Leño—"stick" of marijuana
Hierba—marijuana
Una gorra—a "cap" of heroin
Un plomaso—a shot of heroin
Tecato—a mainliner, on heroin
Anda bien plomo—He's high on heroin.
Los vatos—"the guys," "the gang"

3 Pamphlet entitled, "Catholic Social Action Through the Parish Credit Union," Credit Union National Association, Madison, Wisconsin.

4 The writer perused old yearbooks from NMSC. Although information was not available for all years and was sometimes spotty and incomplete, personal data given for many of the students led to this conclusion.

5 The information for 1933 comes from the recorded minutes of a Regent's

Hearing on the so-called Racial Attitude Survey, which created quite a scandal in the state and resulted in the firing of a UNM Assistant Professor who had planned a research project on the topic of racial attitudes in New Mexico during this sensitive period. Zeleny (1944) refers briefly to the incident, but otherwise it has been suppressed and apparently forgotten. The minutes of the hearing have been partially preserved and are in the State Archives at Santa Fe, where they were read in the course of the present research. It is interesting to note that an Anglo student in 1933 estimated that there were from 50 to 60 Spanish-Americans on the UNM campus at the time. This gross underestimation may or may not be significant, but it seems consistent with the general Anglo attitude of simply ignoring this group whenever possible.

[6] The purpose of the study was to provide basic materials for an "enrichment program" for UNM undergraduates coming from minority-group backgrounds. This program was initiated in the fall of 1969 under the auspices of the Institute for Social Research and Development (ISRAD) at UNM under the direction of Dr. Richard Griego. The program will take into consideration the differences in socioeconomic level, national origin, and other cultural characteristics among incoming students of Spanish surname. The impetus for the program and the background study came from the Vice President for Research, Dr. George Springer.

[7] See especially Barela (1936:21); Burma (1949:136); Cochrane (1915:56); Edmonson (1957:25); Loar (1964:56); Sanchez (1940:18,31); Sanchez and Putnam (1959); Ulibarri (1958).

[8] This information is derived from interviews with Brother August Raymond of the Social Science Department of the College of Santa Fe. Brother Raymond, also active in O.E.O. activities, has been particularly interested in social disorganization in Santa Fe over the past years, and, together with his students, has conducted several surveys which suggest these conclusions. Unfortunately, none of their findings has been published.

[9] This differs from Johnson and Zeleny in that they included as Spanish-American only those persons born in New Mexico. Since the qualitative data resulting from the present study indicate that persons considering themselves to be Hispanos are frequently born outside the state, it was decided to include the larger area here.

[10] There is a large sociological and anthropological literature on this subject. For early, now classic, statements, see Becker (1950); Redfield (1934); and Wirth (1938).

Chapter VIII

THE CONTINUING SCENE:
ACTIVISM IN NEW MEXICO, 1966–1969

As the second edition of this book goes to press, in 1969, it seems appropriate to reconsider the conclusions drawn earlier in the light of the current situation. The earlier pages of this manuscript have been edited and updated in accordance with happenings over the two-year period since the manuscript was first completed. But an analysis of recent changes showed that more than this was necessary—that a new chapter had to be written embodying descriptive materials concerning major new trends, some of which were nonexistent or only beginning to bud at that time. And the rapidity with which activism has blossomed in New Mexico has been remarkable. A minority within the minority group of Hispanos has managed to make its voice heard in a variety of ways, and although some may fear the militancy of the new movements, others will welcome them as past-due harbingers of change.

Activism itself is not particularly new in New Mexico or anywhere else, if one means by this the attempts of some members of a depressed or underprivileged sector (or their sympathizers) to improve their status. Romano (1968) has emphasized this fact in a highly critical essay on works by Anglos on Spanish-American culture. Some of the older activist organizations in New Mexico among Spanish-Americans include *La Mano Negra, Las Gorras Blancas,* LULAC (League of United Latin American Citizens), the G. I. Forum, the American Legion, Veterans of Foreign Wars, and others mentioned in the preceding chapters. The first four of these organizations were founded specifically by Spanish-Americans in order to fight for better conditions for their group. The first two used extra-legal means, while the others worked within established channels. As previously discussed, the veterans' organizations in New Mexico also worked actively for similar causes, and have been said by some (Holmes 1967) to have been instrumental in illustrating the political power of the Hispanos as a group. Aside from these there have always been activists within the various church groups and even within the structure of welfare, as seen in the Life With Pride organization described in Chapter V.

The list could be extended considerably, but today when activism is mentioned it is not generally groups such as these which are meant. Indeed, all those mentioned, with the exception of *La Mano Negra* and *Las Gorras Blancas,* would most likely be considered by the newer activists as being hopelessly embroiled in and controlled by the Establishment and therefore incapable of improving the lot of those they claim to serve. Others might argue that these same groups in fact are out of touch with the lower-class elements of their particular minority or ethnic group and are for these reasons unable to accomplish the goal of improving the lot of those lowest on the social scale.

The Alianza

In tracing the development of the more militant activist organizations in New Mexico at the present time, one must once again return to a consideration of the Alianza described in Chapter V. It may truly be said that this organization was the first movement with civil rights implications to attract attention within the state of New Mexico. Before this there had been other groups such as the Mexican-American Political Association (MAPA) and others which had managed to make a small dent in areas such as Colorado, Texas, and California but which went largely unnoticed here. The plight of the migrant workers—particularly the grape pickers under Cesar Chavez—was considered to have only local (Californian) implications, and the kinship of their *Causa* with that of the Spanish-speaking in New Mexico was apparently not at first appreciated by most New Mexicans. The 1966 Delano Proclamation and its cry of *"huelga"* (strike) found sympathizers here, but there was no immediate action linking this with conditions in New Mexico.

After the incidents in June 1967 at Tierra Amarilla, the Alianza attracted the attention of the whole country. The national news media such as *Newsweek* carried stories of this "wild west show," as it was often presented, and an incredulous public was made to realize the fact that the poor farmers of Spanish descent in northern New Mexico had serious problems and needed to be heard.

However, the initial reaction, largely stimulated by the sensational aspects of the events which were highly dramatized in the press, was that law and order had broken down in New Mexico (if indeed they had ever existed) and that New Mexicans were witnessing a return to the simpler but more brutal code of the frontier. In a sense, there was an element of this involved; however, contrary to what most people thought, the Alianza saw itself as a citizens' group called upon to correct an injustice which the regularly constituted law enforcement bodies could not handle, in part because they themselves were involved in bringing about the infringement of rights. Some members of the Alianza had been arrested and imprisoned for unlawful assembly after they had been forbidden by the state's attorney to gather. Their brethren then attempted to free them and at the same time make a citizen's arrest of the responsible party. The rest is history, but it is important to repeat that a jury found Reies Tijerina, the leader, not guilty of the state's three most serious charges stemming from this incident.

At first there seems to have been no direct connection between the Alianza and other activist organizations in existence outside the state of New Mexico. However, after Tierra Amarilla many of these groups made offers of assistance in order to bring the Alianza into the ranks of the Spanish-American and other radical civil rights movements.

Many of the people deeply involved in the Alianza took part in the Poor People's March on Washington in 1967, and here again national publicity was achieved. By this time many persons from outside the state had come to work with the Alianza and it appears that there were some attempts at reorganization or restructuring of the group at this time. There seem to have been efforts to model it after more radical civil rights movements elsewhere, but these efforts did not have complete success.

In addition to the Alianza, several other new activist-type organizations have appeared only recently on the New Mexican scene; they will be described very briefly, including what seem to this author to be the interrelationships among them and offering an interpretation of the relationships between this new activism and the rest of the New Mexican sociocultural system. Among the groups which will be considered are the Alianza itself, the Brown Berets, the United-Mexican American Students (UMAS), and two youth groups called *Los Caballeros de Nueva*

España and *Los Comancheros del Norte*. Finally, the development of an underground Chicano press, represented by eighteen newspapers which have recently popped up all over the Southwest,[1] will be examined.

In the analysis of the Alianza as a nativistic, revivalistic cult movement presented in Chapter V, the author noted that many of the demands of the group were unrealistic and impractical and that survival might depend upon the group's willingness to modify some of its claims and doctrine and, at the same time, align itself more closely with other civil rights movements in the nation. As Frances Swadesh (1968) and Joseph Love (1969) have shown recently, the Alianza to an increasing extent has taken on many of the characteristics of true civil rights movements. Along with Love, but contrary to Swadesh, the author feels that the Alianza is still better understood as a nativistic cult than as a civil rights movement, in spite of the fact that it has tended to move in the latter direction over the past two years.

Tijerina, the leader of the Alianza, remains a charismatic figure and has become a symbol of the plight of the underdog Spanish-American in New Mexico. Yet he steadfastly refuses to modify many elements in his doctrine and his behavior which might bring his cult more fully in line with the broader New Left movements. He has been strongly criticized by non-Hispano spokesmen of the radical New Left, precisely on the basis of the charismatic and cultlike flavor of the movement (Kennedy 1968). As such, the Alianza remains something unique within New Mexico and among the Spanish-speaking everywhere. It is still largely rural in its membership; it is still almost exclusively dependent upon its leader for guidance and formation of doctrine; and it frequently comes into philosophical collision with representatives of other American minority groups such as Blacks, Jews, and White radicals. It is noteworthy that Cesar Chavez and his grape pickers union have not been particularly brotherly. Relations are cordial but not overly close between the two leaders. Chavez heads a union and a civil rights movement, not a revivalistic or nativistic cult.

It is perhaps significant to note the differences in the terminology used by the Alianza and the Californian and Texas activist movements. The Alianza stresses the mestizo blood of its members and places great value on being brown, a result of having sprung from a union between Indian and Spanish. In this respect, the activist movements share the ideology of the Mexican-American who also prides himself on being a mestizo. However, the term Mexican-American, which is so broadly accepted outside the state of New Mexico, is still not used by the Alianza itself. The Alianza prefers the term *"Indo-Hispano,"* and although the members frequently refer to themselves as *Mexicanos,* there is still no real identification with the term "Mexican-American."

The insistence upon use of *Indo-Hispano* has the effect of clouding the issue of Spanish theft of land belonging to the American Indians. This issue is one of the really weak spots in the peculiar logic of the Alianza. When Indians question the right of the Hispano to the lands as granted by the King of Spain, the answer, usually considered inadequate by Indian observers, is that the Alianza represents the interests of both Indians and the descendants of the early Hispano settlers. In fact, it is true that they represent the mixed-blood descendants of the Hispanicized Indians, but hardly of the Indians who have retained their ethnic identity and purity of race.

In the fall of 1968 the Alianza made its first venture into organized politics in the state of New Mexico. Tijerina ran for governor as a candidate of the Peoples Constitutionalist Party (the Alianza party) until his name was removed from the ballot at a very late point in the campaign on the grounds that he had been convicted of several charges in regard to the 1966 sit-in in the Echo Amphitheater incident. Since his case had been appealed before the District Circuit Court it was decided, after some dispute, that he really was not eligible to run for office. Therefore, the man chosen to run as his lieutenant governor (interestingly enough, an Indian, Jose Alfredo Maestas) ran in his stead. Only 1,540 votes were secured for the positions of governor and lieutenant governor.

The voting record probably reflects several related facts—first, the generally short campaign period, since the Alianza determined to run candidates at a fairly late date; second, the possibility that some votes were improperly counted (this possibility always exists in New Mexico, and there were many rumors to this effect in the fall of 1968); third, the probable decline in organization membership (recognized by Tijerina himself, who felt that by running he might be able to reawaken fervor among some of his former adherents); fourth, the very real and certain fact that Tijerina is a charismatic leader whose followers are not all likely to vote for a substitute even though endorsed by the leader himself. Other candidates of the Peoples Constitutionalist Party had varying success in gathering votes, although none won an office. Those who obtained the highest number of votes were well-known names in the community, often for reasons other than their association with the Alianza.

In assessing the present position of the Alianza the author would predict that it will continue to make itself heard and may have some success in stimulating social change. The fact that it is already having some impact is shown by the bombings of the Alianza headquarters and of the homes and property of its officers. There have been at the time of this writing four such bombings, the latest occurring on March 15, 1969. So far no one has been injured, and the bombings have been, in a sense, tokens of the resentment and fear that the Alianza awakens among some sectors of the New Mexican population. Another kind of evidence that the Alianza may be having some effect is the recent suggestion by Representative Gonzales from Texas that Congress investigate the land claims issue.

The Brown Berets

This group, modeled after the black berets of the Black Panther movement, has only recently appeared in New Mexico. It seems likely that the local organization sprang from contacts made by some New Mexicans in Washington for the Poor People's March. The Brown Beret idea apparently originated in California, and now there are local chapters in many southwestern cities. Unlike the Alianza, it is not only urban-based but has a much broader coverage. It includes primarily young people, which also sets it apart from the Alianza in which older persons predominate.

In Albuquerque the Brown Berets first burst upon the scene with demands for police reform following the killing of a young Spanish-speaking man by a police officer in the summer of 1968. It is reported that at the present time the organization has reached fifteen of the lower-class Spanish-American *barrios* in Albuquerque and that each of these is represented by three individuals whose names are kept secret for their personal protection. One of their spokesmen, whose name has been frequently in the local news in relation to Mexican-American civil rights, has also been associated with the Alianza, even though he has never been a member. During the recent school board election this spokesman ran as a candidate of the Peoples Constitutionalist Party. He and his running partner lost, although another person of Spanish surname garnered more votes than any other candidate in history.

The Brown Berets reject individuals such as the latter who

cooperate with the Establishment. This includes persons who work for the Office of Economic Opportunity, Model Cities, and other governmental or governmentally funded agencies. Such persons are referred to as *vendidos* (sell-outs), *Tio Tomases, Espanglos, Lulacks,* and, most recently, "Oreo Cookies" (brown on the outside and white on the inside).

This terminology reflects the increasing polarization among persons of Spanish heritage in New Mexico, as well as elsewhere. The group seems to be dividing along the politically defined lines of extreme Right on the one hand and extreme Left on the other. These differences are certainly linked to increasing radicalism in a broader political sense in the United States as a whole. There are clear linkages on the Right with the John Birch Society and other such groups. Similarly, there are linkages on the Left with non-Hispano groups such as the Students for a Democratic Society (SDS), the Third World Liberation Front, and others. The increasing differences between the poles is also symbolized by the terms Chicano and Hispano. Neither is a new term, but their more subtle meanings have changed.

Chicano has always had a bit of defiance in it and has also been used, at least in New Mexico, to indicate a clever person, one with the ability to outwit the unsuspecting Anglo. There has also been a certain amount of derogation in its usage, even by the Spanish themselves. However, it has only been recently that it has also come to include a sense of militancy. Today the youthful Spanish-Americans are using Chicano more and more, and as it becomes more fashionable it also becomes less derogatory.

On the other hand, the term Hispano is still preferred by many, especially the older persons and the less militant. In view of these linguistic distinctions, in the succeeding pages the term Chicano will be used when referring to the newer activist movements or ideology, and Hispano will be retained for the older type of activity, including what may be referred to as the Establishment "activism."

However, at this point some note should be made of the increasing usage of the term "Mexican-American" in New Mexico. Although, as has been pointed out several times, this term has for many years been resented by the local Spanish-speaking community, in the past two years there has been an increasing pride in making this self-identification—again largely among the more youthful militant activists. The author attributes this new usage to the greater linkages between local and Texan and Californian groups. It should be emphasized, however, that those who use the term "Mexican-American" are still probably a minority in New Mexico, and most of the persons preferring this term live in or south of Albuquerque.

There is some evidence that this newer terminology is becoming fashionable even among some middle-class Hispanos. One informant told of a recent incident at a LULAC meeting where the members were asking each other what term they preferred to use for themselves. The informant stated that most of the people replied "Mexican-American." This would hardly have been the case two years ago and would still not likely be true in the northern areas. Bodine (1968) has made this point in reference to Taos where he recently did field work.

The newer activism is found among youth ranging from high school through college and among the younger elements who are not necessarily highly educated at all. Thus, there is a group known as *Los Caballeros de Nueva España* (The Gentlemen of New Spain) which was formed in Albuquerque in the fall of 1968. They welcome members between the ages of 10 and 24, but most of them appear to be high school students or dropouts. The group claims to have about 150 members, and they are primarily interested in furthering educational policies which will be more beneficial for children of Spanish heritage.

Other Groups

Another group of youth, but with a rural rather than an urban base, is called *Los Comancheros del Norte*. This group appears to be centered in Tierra Amarilla, with members from the entire northern New Mexican area. It is important to note that both the Comancheros and the Caballeros have stated principles and goals which support the Alianza. In referring to themselves they use, at least in print, the term Indo-Hispano which is a self-conscious term used only by the Alianza.

In addition to an interest in improving the educational system, both of these youth groups emphasize the return of the land-grants and specifically mention the Alianza in this regard. Neither group expresses the militancy of the Brown Berets, although it is possible that they might become more militant in the future. One young Chicano was quoted in the newspaper, *El Grito del Norte* (January 11, 1969), as follows:

> Let's not fight among ourselves. Let's get organized and fight the gringo who controls everything. Let's not fight in the bars, let's not hit our wives. Let's not have one barrio fighting the other. Let's organize, vatos!

At the University of New Mexico a branch of the United Mexican-American Students (UMAS) was formed late in 1968. Like so many other organizations, this one's structure does not conform to the usual organizational form. As one young member said, "Whenever two or three Chicanos are gathered together we have a meeting." The group has so far restricted itself to protesting the Anglo students' domination of a spring campus event known as "Fiesta." The group claims that the Fiesta activities in past years have tended to emphasize the "cowboy" aspect of New Mexican culture to the exclusion of its Mexican or Spanish heritage. They wish to have included *Mariachis,* Mexican-type *Charro* events, Spanish or Mexican food at the barbecues, etc.

Although this kind of activity would seem to be merely the playful antics of college students, most observers feel that this again is only a symbol of general discontent of UMAS members and that their activities will become more serious in the future. The group declines to give names of its members, and it is at this time almost impossible to find out how many there may be. They claim a potential strength of 1,500, but this seems a little high. At meetings during the spring of 1969 on the campus of the University of New Mexico they sometimes drew up to 200, but some of these were sympathizers or curiosity seekers and not potential members.

UMAS is sufficiently well organized to publish a mimeographed bulletin entitled *Plumas de Umas* (Pens of the United Mexican-American Students), written partly in Spanish and partly in English. One of their goals is to create a Mexican-American Studies program at the University of New Mexico, preferably under the control of Chicanos. In line with this, they are beginning to agitate for the hiring of more Chicano professors. (There were thirty-nine professors, instructors, and graduate assistants of Spanish surname at the University of New Mexico in the spring of 1969, but most of these were considered "oreo cookies" by the Chicano students.)

UMAS has probable linkages with the Denver Crusade for Justice, which sponsored what it called the "Chicano Youth Liberation Conference" in March of 1969. Delegates from New Mexico as well as from other southwestern states attended this meeting and exchanged views and techniques which will undoubtedly give a still greater homogeneity to the activities of these youth groups throughout the Southwest.

In summarizing these budding Chicano organizations, it should be noted that each one serves a somewhat different segment of the total deprived population, and although there is no overall formal organization among them there are nevertheless clear linkages through the network of individual contacts. Thus some members of UMAS may also be Brown Berets, and all look to the Alianza and its activities as somehow being symbolic of their cause as well. On the other hand, the Alianza itself seems more closely tied in with the two high school youth groups mentioned previously and may even have been instrumental in their formation. At the same time, as the individual young members of the high school groups grow up they will probably unite with the Brown Berets or UMAS, or both.

The goals of these groups are not easy to define specifically, although in general they are concerned with the lack of power of the Spanish-surname or Spanish-speaking segment of the population in this country. They feel that organized agencies in the past have not been successful in relieving the plight of the poor, and they now preach more revolutionary tactics in achieving a better way of life. Certainly there have been many instances of appalling injustice for persons of Spanish surname in New Mexico, as elsewhere. But since here most of the persons in the lowest social classes are of this ethnic group, it is sometimes tempting to suggest that they are in this position because they have been discriminated against. The author would reverse this and argue that they are discriminated against because they are in the lower class, but that being of Spanish-American origin is related to the fact that they are in the lower class. In trying to account for this, the position is sometimes advanced that they are genetically inferior and therefore doomed to perpetual poverty and low status. This is clearly a bigoted, uninformed viewpoint. On the other hand, the suggestion that these people are in this position because they have been and are being discriminated against also seems to the author to derive from an uninformed point of view.

The problem has to do with social structure and the values supporting it rather than with personal relationships, in this writer's opinion. What is meant by this is that the dominant society is structured in such a way that certain kinds of behavior are better rewarded than others. The author would thoroughly agree with the opinion that the lower-class Spanish-American's lack of ability in his second language, English, has often hindered his progress in achieving material well-being. This is most often a result of his inability to compete in schools at the lower level, and his feeling of inferiority when he recognizes that he is not being rewarded as are his Anglo schoolmates. Although there are undoubtedly some teachers who dislike or even despise their Spanish-American wards for their differences, there are also many who feel anguished by what they perceive to be a lower level of performance among these children. They are unable to advance these students according to the same set of criteria as those they use for the Anglo children, and having no other guidelines they fail the Spanish-speaking child.[2] This position is now quite well recognized by educators in general, and it is becoming a particular issue in the Southwest. The Southwestern Cooperative Educational Laboratory, Inc. (SWCEL), a private, nonprofit educational, research and development facility, is currently conducting research and constructing programs to deal with the problem of bilingualism and teaching English as a second language in New Mexico public schools.[3]

Given this lower level of performance in grade school, the system continues to work against the individual with this background. But at this point these individuals share more with the poverty-stricken across the nation than they do with the majority of the Hispanos in New Mexico. That is, when it comes to getting jobs, the less well educated are the ones who suffer. Without jobs, material well-being is difficult or impossible. The structure of welfare is one which prevents starvation, but welfare does nothing to improve the individual's feeling of dignity and worth. Once on welfare the individual has, in effect, "two strikes" against him socially, and it is very difficult for him to go on to anything else.

One informant, himself an Hispano with a Master's degree from the University of New Mexico, told of interviewing an eight-year-old boy—a dropout from the second grade. He asked the boy what he thought he might do when he grew up. The child replied, "Well, there's always welfare." Welfare as a way of life can clearly become a pattern which is passed on from generation to generation, and it is one of the most damning indictments against the welfare system that this should be so.

However, the alternative to poverty and low status is not necessarily complete assimilation or "anglicization," as many of the Chicanos seem to believe. There are thousands of persons of Spanish heritage in New Mexico today who live comfortably, who are able to move in any social circle they desire without fear of prejudice or discrimination, and who at the same time have preserved their sense of identity with *la raza*. Many of these speak Spanish poorly or not at all, but this is in part a function of our educational system and not necessarily because they themselves have desired to give up all that is Spanish in their background. Furthermore, many of these middle-class Hispanos retain some of the values of the traditional culture in relation to such things as family structure, religion, and everything else which forms part of the Spanish-American mystique. Social scientists have not yet investigated thoroughly and do not understand the process of acculturation, either in terms of sociocultural systems or in terms of an individual's adaptations to systems other than the one he first learns. Whatever occurs, it is not a matter of clearcut and total change in way of life and world view. One must pose further questions, such as What are the criteria by which acculturation may be evaluated? Which factors operate as independent variables and which co-vary as interdependent units?

The concept of pluralism is one with which many people are concerned today. The position that several cultures may coexist within the same society—equal in terms of material welfare, self-determination, and role in government, but each retaining its individuality and self-pride—is for some a dream and for others a very possible reality.

New Mexico, with all its faults, with all its poverty, nevertheless comes closer to the pluralistic dream of society than does any other area in the nation. It is to be hoped that current events do not further polarize the positions within the Spanish-American ethnic group to the point that some deny *la raza* altogether while others attempt to overthrow the entire system which has so far permitted and reinforced the Spanish traditions in the struggle for survival. At the same time, thousands of Hispanos have achieved positions in life which they appreciate and value— positions which they feel are dignified, free from harassment, and well remunerated. These individuals, understandably enough, resent what they see as racist militancy. Called *vendidos* themselves, many of them feel it is the militants who are "selling out" *la raza* by bringing the issue of ethnicity into what should be a war on poverty.

New Mexico needs to revamp some of its worst features. This will be difficult, because New Mexico is a part of the structure of the nation itself and as such is subject to the same pressures as are the other states. But the unique history and the pride of heritage found here among the Hispano people could be the raw materials for a true pluralism in the future—a pluralism which encompasses not just one ethnic minority but all variations on the theme of Hispanic America, as well as those non-Spanish groups which have also been involved in building the unique society of New Mexico.

Notes

1 Members, Chicano Press Association

Carta Editorial
P.O. Box 54624
Terminal Annex
Los Angeles, Calif. 90054

El Chicano
San Bernardino, Calif.

Chicano Student Movement
P.O. Box 31322
Los Angeles, Calif. 90031

Compass
1209 Egypt St.
Houston, Texas 77009

El Gallo
1265 Cherokee St.
Denver, Colo. 80204

El Grito del norte
Route 2, Box 5
Espanola, N.M.

La Hormiga
1560 34th Ave.
Oakland, Calif. 94601

Inferno
321 Frio City Road
San Antonio, Texas 78207

Inside Eastside
P.O. Box 63273
Los Angeles, Calif. 90063

Lado
1306 N. Western Ave.
Chicago, Ill. 60622

El Machete
206 Oakland Ave.
San Jose, Calif. 95116

El Malcriado
P.O. Box 130
Delano, Calif. 63215

El Paisano
UFWOC Box 155
Tolleson, Ariz. 85353

El Papel
P.O. Box 7167
Albuquerque, N.M. 87104

La Raza
2445 Gates St.
Los Angeles, Calif. 90031

La Voz
2820 Whittier Blvd.
Los Angeles, Calif.

La Verdad
3717 University Ave.
San Diego, Calif. 92105

La Voz Mexicana
P.O. Box 101
Wautoma, Wis. 54982

Source: *La RAZA Yearbook*, September 1968, p. 60

[2] A. M. Padilla and K. K. Long, graduate students of psychology at the University of New Mexico, carried out a study in which they ". . . sought to identify factors which could be used to differentiate successful from unsuccessful students of Spanish-American backgrounds.

"The unsuccessful population consisted of students who had failed to complete a four year course of studies at the University of New Mexico. Successful students were defined as those who had completed studies for an advanced degree. A 101-item questionnaire was completed by students from both populations (N = 50). Items related to: family history, early and later school adjustment, interpersonal relations, and vocational attitudes. Analyses indicated that both groups did not differ significantly on items relating to family history (e.g., number of siblings, father's educational level, etc.); however, successful students were shown to be both highly competitive and more achievement-motivated than the unsuccessful students. In addition, successful students were better able to adjust to university regulations" (personal communication).

The results of this study will be published in the future.

[3] The focus of SWCEL in general is the improvement of early educational opportunities for culturally divergent children of the Southwest. Its principal source of funds is the U.S. Office of Education, although it also welcomes donations from private sources. The Lab began operations in June, 1966, under the direction of Dr. Paul Petty, then Dean of the School of Education, University of New Mexico.

Chapter IX

SUMMARY AND CONCLUSIONS

It is now recognized that Americans of Spanish descent form one of the largest and most neglected minority groups in the country. Even though the total number of Mexican-Americans or Spanish-Americans is exceeded elsewhere, no state has such a high percentage of its total population claiming this ancestry as New Mexico. Whether the problems faced by these people in New Mexico are truly comparable to those found in other southwestern states is, however, not entirely clear. It is of importance to know to what extent or in what manner the Hispanos form a distinctly recognizable social group, distinguishable not only from non-Hispanos, but from other segments of the U.S. population of Spanish descent. In order to provide information upon which a judgment can be made, a review of the social history of this state has been made, emphasizing particularly those events which seem to loom large as factors helping to mold the present-day sociocultural configuration.

During the early period of occupation in this area, the Spanish Colonial culture was profoundly modified by that of the Pueblo Indians. The latter had been successful exploiters of this semi-arid environment for hundreds of years, and the Spanish found the

Indian foods, agricultural techniques, house styles, pottery, and many other items to be of great value. However, the tie with the homeland, via Mexico, although attenuated, was never broken; and the early European inhabitants of the northern river valleys remained peasants—relatively isolated, but ultimately dependent upon the larger society.

This dependence—economic, political, and ideological—was intensified during the Mexican period lasting from 1821, when Mexico declared its independence from Spain, until the United States conquest in 1846. New settlers from Mexico arrived, claiming new lands; and trade with the south as well as with the east and west increased. Sheep became ever more important in the total economy, and the destruction of the land cover, already underway, continued at a greater rate of speed.

When Kearny's forces marched into Las Vegas and later into Santa Fe, a chain of events was begun which irrevocably changed the face of the land and the fate of its inhabitants. The primary early effects of United States ownership were (a) to open new areas of the state for settlement, partially through new capital and modern technology and partially through the final subjugation of the nomadic Indians; and (b) to provide new opportunities for wage labor in agriculture, ranching, and industry, thus increasing the standard of living and making it possible for larger numbers of persons to maintain a valued rural existence. Seasonal migration to work on the railroads, as cowboys, sheepherders, miners, and in various agricultural enterprises soon became an integral part of the Hispano way of life. Inevitably, some left their villages permanently for the cities, thus starting a trend toward urbanization which continues to the present day.

The depression of the 1930's hit New Mexico hard, for the wage labor opportunities virtually disappeared at that time, and the land which had been so misused for a century or more was incapable of supporting the population in the rural areas. The various types of federal aid and work programs initiated by President Franklin D. Roosevelt became the mainstay of the people until World War II again brought prosperity to the national economy. Many Hispanos then left the state to work in defense projects in California and elsewhere, and many thousands joined the armed forces. Those who remained struggled with the land and their livestock, taking advantage of agricultural extension assistance, but most still depended upon remittances from absent relatives with wage-paying jobs. Many others simply deserted their holdings and took up a new way of life in the cities.

The period since World War II has brought about the greatest changes in the Hispano way of life because the returning veterans, partly as a result of their experiences in the service, sought further technical and academic educational levels and went into jobs requiring skills they had never had before. The continuing federal commitment to defense projects in New Mexico has helped to sustain an economy which is still not highly industrialized. Larger numbers of Hispanos are entering the colleges and universities, as well as the technical schools, and many have left the state for better opportunities elsewhere. Intermarriage with Anglos has steadily increased, and many of the values and life goals usually associated with Anglo culture have been adopted by Hispanos.

From an evolutionary point of view, the result of this train of events has been progress for the state as a whole, measured in terms of numbers of people who can be supported by the local resources through more efficient utilization of those resources and increased interdependence with the rest of the nation and the world. However, from the point of view of the Hispano population, the effects have not been uniformly advantageous. Indeed, many claim just the opposite—that is, that the Hispanos as a class have been increasingly dispossessed of their land, their rights, and their cultural heritage.

One of the primary questions to which this work has been addressed has been, Is New Mexico comparable to the other southwestern states in terms of the problems of the Spanish-American minority group? This writer, after reviewing the evidence available, feels that the answer cannot be given in an unequivocal Yes or No. Certainly it is clear that in New Mexico there is much poverty, juvenile delinquency, crime, illiteracy, poor health, and dependence upon public assistance, all of which tend to be largely concentrated among Spanish-Americans, who form the bulk of the lower class. The relations between Spanish-Americans and Anglos include distrust, even hostility, prejudice, and discrimination, but this operates in both directions. Furthermore, in terms of particular culture traits and types of social organizations, the Spanish-Americans of this state cannot be said to be too different from those hundreds of thousands calling themselves Mexican-Americans. The stamp of their Spanish heritage is still clearly evident on both groups, as is their debt to the American-Indian cultures from which the Spanish borrowed so much and to which they contributed heavily as well.

The Spanish-speaking in the United States today are largely an urban population, but they have only recently become so. Whether their origins were the small isolated farming communities of northern New Mexico or the peasant villages of Mexico, many of the problems they have faced in adapting to the United States cities have been the same. They have had to overcome linguistic and cultural barriers in competing for jobs, and in doing so they have become at least partially acculturated to the Anglo middle-class way of life. They have had to make the transition from a folk to an urban existence, and this has involved much social disorganization—breakdown of the extended family, and even of the nuclear family through divorce or desertion, crime, delinquency, drug addiction, etc. There has been an increasing emphasis on economic advancement as a major goal in life (Samora 1953), and this has led to higher educational levels, greater use of English with concomitant loss of Spanish as the mother-tongue, and adoption of a world view in which people are more often classified on the basis of economic success. In New Mexico, as well as in California and Texas, there has been an increasing amount of intermarriage with Anglos (Mittelbach, *et al.,* 1966), movement into Anglo neighborhoods, and joining of predominantly Anglo voluntary associations.

These changes are sometimes viewed as part of the process of Anglicization, and in a sense they are. Yet it should also be emphasized that some of these changes seem to be associated with urbanization, wherever that may occur. Some of the recent literature concerning urbanization in Latin America, for example, indicates that similar responses have occurred there.[1] It might be said that the process by which rural immigrants become adjusted to urban life always includes a certain amount of acculturation to the way of life of the dominant ethnic group in the country in question. Thus, in Mexico, Guatemala, or Peru, where many migrants are Indians, they must learn Spanish (and in the process their children fail to learn the native Indian dialects), acquire skills necessary for securing jobs, and gradually take on the way of life of the mestizo—usually quite different from that of the native Indian. It is difficult or impossible to separate, even for purposes of analysis, the phenomena of urbanization and acculturation when they take place simultaneously.

Another similarity between New Mexico and the other states with large numbers of Spanish-speaking inhabitants in the Southwest is the recent interest on the part of these people themselves in their position vis-à-vis the Anglo majority group. Although

New Mexico has been a bit behind California and Texas in this development, there is evidence of some activity in this direction, as shown in Chapter VIII. The various Spanish-language newspapers constantly remind their readers of their heritage and of their responsibilities for maintaining it on the one hand and for improving their present position on the other. A prominent Californian of Mexican descent commented that ten years ago in that state persons of his social class tended to avoid movements which he termed "pro-Mexican." Now, however, it has become not only acceptable but fashionable to become involved. The Spanish-American community in New Mexico has not yet reached that point, although there is some indication that they are currently moving further in that direction.

Yet in spite of all these similarities, it must also be concluded that New Mexico is, as its citizens insist, quite different in many respects from the other states in question. The difference, however, seems to lie not so much within the Spanish-speaking population per se. Certainly it has nothing to do with genetic differences between this group and any other—even though this is sometimes said to be the case. Neither is it simple to describe the differences by tabulating variations in cultural components. It seems rather, to this writer, that the major differences between the Spanish-Americans of New Mexico and the Mexican-Americans of other states are in the ways in which each of these groups is articulated into the larger society within which it lives. This could also be stated in terms of group status, or position, relative to Anglos and other minority groups, but the term "articulate" seems to imply a more dynamic relationship and is therefore used.

The strong emotional attachment to the term Spanish-American and the disdain for Mexican which prevail at the present time are symbolic of the jealousy with which the New Mexican of

Spanish descent guards his place in the social structure. It was apparently not until the mid-1920's that the term Spanish-American generally replaced Mexican. E. Fergusson, writing in 1928, said, " 'Mexican' was the term universally applied to them within the memory of most of us. Suddenly, nobody knows just when or why, it became politic to use the hybrid term, 'Spanish-American' " (p. 437). Austin further pins the time down to the period just following World War I (1931:143). The evidence suggests that during the early decades after the conquest by the United States there was little prejudice or discrimination against the natives of the area on the basis of their ethnic differences. However, there is also evidence that this situation began to change after the turn of the century. Certainly, by the mid-1930's ethnic intolerance had become rife, even though, as Zeleny has shown, it was never openly admitted. The following passage illustrates the point:

> . . . although observation shows that prejudice clearly exists, any mention of it in writings or in public or official discussion is strictly taboo, according to the local code . . . the reflection of this pattern is found in the lack of clear emphasis on inter-ethnic clashes in the writings of New Mexican historians, who sometimes even refer to the Spanish Americans in an indirect manner as the 'non-English speaking population.' Interviews made by the writer in New Mexico brought out the strength of the taboo on mention of intergroup relationships. . . . One social worker, surrounded by Spanish-speaking clients, made the ridiculous assertion she could not tell the difference between an Anglo and a Spanish-American. Several people interviewed in New Mexico indicated that such a study as this thesis could not be undertaken by anyone whose future lay in New Mexico, either as a member of the faculty of the state institutions or in other prominent walks of life, without seriously jeopardizing his position. Individuals living in the state hesitate to publish studies of this kind after they are made (1944:339).

Hidden away in the State Archives at Santa Fe is the un-published record of an incident occurring at the University of New Mexico in 1933 which cost a young assistant professor his position and threatened the stature of a few others in even higher positions. Reading the materials today, it becomes clear that the professor, in all innocence, touched upon the weakest spot in New Mexican society at that time—a sore which was still festering when Zeleny did her research and was only healed by changes and prosperity brought by World War II.

The explanation for the lowering of the status of the Spanish-speaking population in New Mexico during the 1920's, 1930's, and 1940's seems to be related to population migrations which occurred roughly during the same period. The first was the influx of Texans and other southerners who settled primarily in the eastern plains area of the state, engaging in dry farming and in cattle raising. Vogt (1955) and others have pointed out that Texans tend to lump Spanish-Americans and Indians together with Negroes and assign an inferior status to all. The second migration was the entrance of large numbers of Mexican nationals in the twenty years following the 1910 revolution in Mexico.[2] Many of these were lower-class, largely illiterate peasants. Those who did not continue their migration to the northern industrial areas became agricultural laborers throughout the Southwest. As such, they were often in direct economic competition with the rural New Mexican who had depended at least partially upon migratory wage labor to eke out his subsistence agriculture since before the turn of the century. Furthermore, Anglos tended to make no distinctions in assigning inferior status to both natives and newcomers engaged in these lower-class occupations.

The change in status of the Spanish-speaking population of New Mexico, brought about by the changed composition of the state's population as a whole, seems to have led to the origin of the myth, now become a legend, of cultural differences between New Mexico and Mexico. This myth functions in a fairly clearcut manner as an attempted means of preserving the dignity, the worth, and the prestige of the New Mexican Spanish cultural patterns, while at the same time countering discriminatory behavior based upon perceived differences between Anglo and Mexican culture patterns. In effect, the New Mexican, perceiving himself in danger of being pushed down or swallowed up completely, fought back by making scapegoats of his foreign cousins. Thus, it could be said, "You don't like Mexicans, and we don't like them either, but we are different. We are Spanish-American, not Mexican." This writer was told by a local Spanish-surnamed social worker that even today the poverty-stricken illiterate, "problem" persons in the population were Mexican, not Spanish, and that this explained their lower-class position.

There are two other general patterns by which discrimination has been countered in New Mexico. One has been to take on as fully as possible the Anglo way of life. This appears to be most typical of the middle economic classes, most of whose members have risen from the lower class. But, as has been pointed out, it does not necessarily include all persons who have achieved a comfortable way of life. The second general pattern involves primarily the lower class and tends to group together all Spanish and Mexicans. These people are frequently openly antagonistic to Anglos as a class, as well as to the *agringado* members of *la raza*. This group may prefer to call itself *mexicano* or even Mexican-American and turns a sympathetic eye to problems of the Mexican-Americans of south Texas and of the Californian grape pickers. This group, represented most dramatically by the *Alianza de Pueblos Libres,* is potentially somewhat militant, and confuses feelings of ethnic inferiority with frustrations encountered in making a decent living. Persons in this category are supersensitive when it comes to discrimination and are likely to blame any felt slight upon the prejudice of those around them, rather than upon personal inadequacy.

On the other side of the coin is the fact that this group often is discriminated against. They are highly visible since they tend to dress more poorly, speak English ungrammatically and with an accent, have few employable skills or social graces, and are often of a somewhat darker skin color than the more successful Hispano. As D'Antonio and Samora have said, "The factor of skin color is hard to assess, but . . . nevertheless, it seems certain . . . that as one descends the occupational ladder, the skin color gets darker" (1962:24). There can be no doubt whatever that all of these factors are involved in the prejudice felt against these people, and it is also significant in relation to this discussion that these same characteristics are typical of the immigrants from Mexico—a fact which makes the Mexicans themselves feel more at home, but which also serve as a thorn in the flesh of the Hispano who is proud of his United States citizenship and is trying to better his standard of living and position in society. As long ago as 1930, the Mexican anthropologist, Gamio, said, "The Spanish-Americans are generally farmers owning their own land. They get on well with these Mexicans with whom they come into contact, through a similarity of language and tradition, but evidently resent being confused with them, as is so often done by Anglo-Americans" (1930:209).

But in New Mexico, perhaps more than elsewhere, being of Spanish descent is not an impermeable barrier, as several writers have recognized.[3] Indeed, in the higher-status context the Spanish name may carry a prestige value (Broom and Shevky 1952:154). The individual tends to be accepted on the basis of his apparent class position, quite apart from either name or color. More than one darker-skinned informant for the present study told of having met prejudice and overt hostility in former years, but that with increasing education and sophistication, plus evidence of affluence, these have disappeared. This state of affairs has two sides, of course. On the one hand, there does seem to be less prejudice shown today, in part probably because of the emphasis by the federal government upon civil rights, the rise of citizens' movements for equal opportunities, etc. It is no longer either legal or in good taste to show one's prejudice in the former usual ways.

Burma said in 1954, "The Hispano in New Mexico may go to any school, be served at any cafe, stay at any hotel, ride anywhere in the streetcars or get a haircut at any barbershop" (1954:29). Yet informants say that the situation was different in the 1930's, and there are some reports that in the southeastern part of the state especially, there are still some barbershops and restaurants where the Spanish-American is not welcome.[4] Schools there, too, are sometimes segregated along ethnic lines with the excuse that the linguistic inadequacy of the Spanish-speaking child will hold back the Anglo. In 1930, however, segregation of children was sometimes made on the basis of the fear that Anglo children would "catch diseases" from Mexican children who came from unhygienic homes (Bogardus 1930:79). Burma went on to list some other evidences of social discrimination which because of their very nature are more difficult to evaluate. Thus he continues "He (i.e., the Hispano) likely will not be accepted socially, will have difficulty in securing employment commensurate with his ability, and may lose his turn to an Anglo when standing in line" (*ibid.*).

What does it mean to say that one is not accepted socially? It would seem to mean that an individual may be excluded from certain types of social groups or gatherings on the basis of his ethnic background alone. As indicated in the preceding chapters, this does not any longer seem to be the case in New Mexico. Lower-class Hispanos may not be invited to join the Junior League, but neither are lower-class Anglos. The Hispanos can always blame it upon ethnic or racial prejudice, and the Anglos can call it class snobbery.

The matter of employment is similarly difficult to assess. If an individual is passed over either in obtaining a job or in being advanced to a higher position, do the reasons involve ethnicity, or religion, or color, or sex, or bad breath—or perhaps plain inefficiency or lack of proper skills? Sociologists know that all these factors and others may be involved, and in any given case any one factor or a combination of factors may have been active. However, the New Mexico District Office of the Internal Revenue Service recently had a seminar for its management personnel on the subject of equal employment opportunities.[5] It is interesting to note that during the two-day study conference, the conclusion was drawn that in New Mexico the two minority groups who were not adequately represented in the IRS were Indians and Negroes. They found that Hispanos were already employed in about one-third of all positions, many of them at the higher-ranking levels. There continue to be accusations now and then against specific agencies or companies concerning discrimination in employment; but without accurate statistics, such as those noted in the IRS, it is impossible to say whether these are complaints of a few disgruntled individuals or whether they represent actual inequalities. Talbert found that persons of Spanish surname in New Mexico had a somewhat higher status as evidenced by occupational patterns than was true for Spanish-speaking workers in the other four southwestern states (1955:69).

And the final point made by Burma—that an Hispano may lose his turn to an Anglo when standing in line—seems not to be typical at all. No informant in Albuquerque had ever had such an experience, nor did any of them think it likely that such a thing would happen here. A few surmised that it might occur in Little Texas or in the extreme south of the state, but that entire area has different characteristics, as has been described.

In general, the situation for most of New Mexico seems to be more like that described for the Negro in Latin America—the Hispano can rise to the top of the social scale and be accepted anywhere by accumulation of wealth, education, and the other symbols of upper-class status.[6] However, it is harder for him to succeed than it would be for a lighter-skinned person with an Anglo name.

It is important to keep in mind that the legend of cultural differences and the insistence upon use of the terms "Hispano" or "Spanish-American" in distinction to "Mexican" are strongest among the members of the middle and upper classes who have not been willing to give up their cultural heritage, but who at the same time wish to be accepted as full members of the larger society. These people wish to dissociate themselves from poverty, dependence upon public assistance, juvenile delinquency, crime, etc., which they perceive to be characteristic of the lower classes who also happen to be made up predominantly of their own ethnic group. Through word magic and the legend of cultural differences, the members of the upper classes may identify the less admirable members of their own ethnic group as Mexican. The term, then, has come to mean lower-class, and is, in fact, meaningless in any other context today. It refers to cultural differences only insofar as it suggests subcultural class differences within the ethnic group. It does not necessarily imply Mexican citizenship, or even that one's parents or grandparents came from Mexico. In fact, second- and third-generation descendants of Mexican immigrants who have succeeded in achieving middle- or upper-class status are careful to designate themselves as

Spanish-American. Although the legend probably originated in an attempt to distinguish the native New Mexican from the lower-class foreigner, this is obviously not its primary function today, when there are only about 900 Mexican citizens in Bernalillo County as a whole.

Finally, it should also be emphasized that the status of the middle- and upper-class Spanish-speaking groups appears to be considerably higher in New Mexico than in other areas of the United States, such as California and Texas. It has not always been so, as Zeleny illustrated in 1944. These groups have had to fight to retain the position assured them by the Treaty of Guadalupe Hidalgo and the state constitution. They have overcome much, and they have kept their heads high. They may have accomplished much more than they realize in preserving for posterity much of their heritage.

It is both amusing and revealing to examine statements made through the years by a series of observers in New Mexico as to the status of the Spanish-American culture. In spite of the fears voiced at intervals that the old culture is "breaking down" or "disappearing," [7] some of the most recent investigators have emphasized the fact that it is remarkably resistant to change. Zeleny stated, "The changes which have occurred are chiefly in the material realm, however, and the basic elements of the old culture continue to survive" (1944:313). Saunders also made the pertinent observation, ". . . even the most fully acculturated of the Spanish-speaking group retain some residual elements of the 'Spanish' cultural heritage and even the least acculturated Spanish-American or Mexican-American has already taken on some Anglo characteristics" (1954:59).

But the sociocultural system in New Mexico goes further even than this. It is also true that many Anglos—perhaps even a majority of those living in the northern area—are not only sympathetic to the Spanish and Indian heritage but are even proud of the unique flavor it gives to the state. Saunders and Samora have pointed out that the acculturation process has been two-way, that Spanish-Americans and Anglos, like the Spaniards and Indians 400 years ago, have "swapped" many traits (1955: 383). Although agreeing with Shannon that "assimilation implies more than the mere borrowing of certain cultural traits" (1965:25), nevertheless, the material traits themselves do symbolize something deeper—a world view, a conception of self. In New Mexico nearly everyone, regardless of descent, eats green chili and hangs strings of red peppers outdoors as a decorative symbol of the harvest. Pinto beans, tacos and enchiladas are regularly served on the Albuquerque Public School lunch program. At Christmastime the votive-type candles inserted in paper bags (that are weighted down with an inch or so of sand), known as *luminarias,* flicker on the rooftops and pathways of commercial buildings, hospitals, Protestant churches, and the homes of any and all who wish them. Squaw dresses and turquoise jewelry are worn more by local New Mexicans of all ethnic backgrounds than most tourists would believe. Adobe houses, corner fireplaces, carved furniture, Navajo and Chimayo blankets, and carved statues and *retablos* of Catholic saints are the property or exclusive symbols of no particular group.

If one attends the festival in honor of the patron saint at any Indian pueblo or Spanish-American town, he will find there representatives of all three ethnic groups. Some, to be sure, may be tourists—others may be thrillseekers or members of the "artsy-craftsy" set, and still others may be anthropologists, but there are also many ordinary New Mexicans—ranchers, lawyers, secretaries, salesmen, maintenance men—who attend the festival because they enjoy it, which is to say that they have internalized some of the values of the group sponsoring the festival. Probably the meaning is not the same for all of these, but the fact that they may go year in, year out to witness these and other ceremonies is behavior not customary elsewhere in the United States where different ethnic groups co-reside. There are many persons, Anglos and Hispanos, who travel from 30 to 50 miles or farther on Christmas Eve and stay up all night, shivering with cold, to attend services in a Spanish-designed Catholic church in an Indian pueblo.

New Mexico history books do not start with 1846, but with 1598 or before; and the story of the Spanish conquest, as well as the glories of the Indian cultures revealed by archaeology, are taught all school children. There are many Anglos, even today, who would echo the sentiments of Governor Lane (1852–1853) who wrote of the people of New Mexico:

> I do not advise them to change any of their beneficial or praise-worthy customs, nor do I advise them to forget their parent stock, and the proud recollections that cluster around Castilian history. I do not advise them to disuse their beautiful language, to lay aside their dignified manners and punctilious attention to the proprieties of social life, and I sincerely hope the profound deference that is now paid to age by the young will undergo no change. . . . True it is that the Mexican people have been always noted for their distinguished manners and Christian customs. It is only to be regretted to see that some of their good usages are disappearing little by little before what is called progress in our day (quoted by Horn 1963:43–44).

There have been changes since then, and there will be more changes in the future. But to the extent that the Spanish-American heritage has become the New Mexican heritage, it will be preserved by Hispanos and Anglos alike. It may fairly be said that in this sense, the New Mexican situation is different from that in other areas, but the primary differences seem to be in the social behavior relating the various classes and ethnic groups to each other and to the whole. No wonder that the New Mexican Hispano exhibits little of the deference, the obsequious behavior, the deprecation of his own background so often reported among Mexican-Americans of other states when dealing with Anglos. The New Mexican Hispano's heritage of pride is not only recognized but validated by the participation of the Anglos themselves.

Notes

[1] See, for example, Breese (1966); Butterworth (1962); Fried (1959); Hammel (1964); Hauser (1961); Lewis (1961); Mangin (1959).

[2] See Grebler (1966).

[3] Barrett and Samora (1963:18); Broom and Shevky (1952:154); D'Antonio and Samora (1962:24–25); among others.

[4] Zunser (1935:141) says, "Mexicans are underpaid, discriminated against, not admitted into restaurants and barber shops." She, too, felt that this was one reason for the local preference for the term "Spanish-American." See also Judah (1949 and 1961); Chambers (1949).

[5] Equal Opportunity Seminar, January 19–20, 1967, Albuquerque, New Mexico. Sponsored by Internal Revenue Service.

[6] Logan (1940:33); Tannenbaum (1947).

[7] Many writers have asserted this. For some of the most recent, see Edmonson (1957:21); McWilliams (1943:141); Reeve (1946:18). And for the opposite point of view, see Marden and Meyer (1962:138); Saunders (1954:59–60); Watson and Samora (1954:414).

BIBLIOGRAPHY

Abousleman, Michel D. (comp.)
  1937 *Who's Who in New Mexico*, Vol. 1. Albuquerque: Abousle-
        man Co.
Adams, Eleanor B. (ed.)
  1954 *Bishop Tamaron's Visitation of New Mexico, 1760*. Historical
        Society of New Mexico, Publications in History, No. 15.
Adams, Eleanor B., and Fray Angelico Chavez
  1956 *The Missions of New Mexico, 1776*. Albuquerque: University
        of New Mexico Press.
Adams, Richard N.
  1957 *Cultural Surveys of Panama, Nicaragua, Guatemala, El
        Salvador, Honduras*. Pan American Union Scientific Pub-
        lication, No. 33.
Agenda
  1966 Washington, D.C.: Industrial Union Department, AFL-CIO.
Aitkin, B. (Freire-Mareco)
  1930 "Temperament in Native American Religion," *Journal of
        the Royal Anthropological Institute* 60:363–387.
The Albuquerque City Directory and Business Guide, 1907. Albu-
        querque: Citizen Publishing Company.
Albuquerque Industrial Development Service, Inc.
  1964 Albuquerque—Population Characteristics.
Alianza
        Published by Alianza, a Fraternal Organization. Tucson,
        Arizona.

Anderson, Arnold M.
   1909 "The Native New Mexican," *Great Southwest,* Sept. 1909: 156–158.
Armstrong, Patricia Cadigan
   1959 *A Portrait of Bronson Cutting through His Papers, 1910–1927.* Albuquerque: Division of Government Research, University of New Mexico, Publ. No. 57.
Arsdale, Jonathan Van
   1937 "Railroads in New Mexico," *Research* 2(1):3–16.
Atencio, Tomas C.
   1964 "The Human Dimensions in Land Use and Land Displacement in Northern New Mexico Villages," in *Indian and Spanish American Adjustments to Arid and Semiarid Environments* (ed. by Clark S. Knowlton). Lubbock: Texas Technological College.
Austin, Mary
   1931 "Mexicans and New Mexico," *Survey* 66:141–144,187–190.
Bailey, Jessie Bromilow
   1940 *Diego de Vargas and the Reconquest of New Mexico.* Albuquerque: University of New Mexico Press.
Bancroft, Hubert Howe
   1889 *The Works of Hubert Howe Bancroft,* Vol. XVII. (*History of Arizona and New Mexico 1530–1888.*) San Francisco: The History Company.
   1962 *History of Arizona and New Mexico 1530–1888.* (50th Anniversary Facsimile of 1889 ed.) Albuquerque: Horn and Wallace.
Barela, Fred
   1936 "The Relation Between Scholastic Achievement and Economic Status as Shown by Parental Occupation." Unpublished Master's thesis, University of New Mexico.
Barker, Ruth Laughlin
   1931 *Caballeros.* New York: D. Appleton and Company.
Barrett, Donald N., and Julian Samora
   1963 *The Movement of Spanish Youth from Rural to Urban Settings.* Washington, D.C.: National Committee for Children and Youth (mimeo.).

Becker, Howard
   1950   "Sacred and Secular Societies," *Social Forces* 28:361.
Bergere, A. M.
   n.d.   *Early History of the Estancia Valley.* Pamphlet, New Mexico
          Archives, Santa Fe.
Bernstein, Harry
   1938   "Spanish Influence in the United States: Economic Aspects,"
          Hispanic American Historical Review 18:43–65.
Blackmar, Frank W.
   1891   *Spanish Institutions of the Southwest.* Baltimore: Johns
          Hopkins Press.
Bloom, Maude E. McFie
   1903   "A History of Mesilla Valley." Unpublished B.A. thesis,
          New Mexico State University, Las Cruces.
Bodine, John J.
   1968   "A Tri-ethnic Trap: the Spanish-Americans in Taos," *Pro-
          ceedings* of the 1968 Annual Spring Meeting, American
          Ethnological Society, Seattle, pp. 145–153.
Bogardus, Emory S.
   1930   "The Mexican Immigrant and Segregation," *American
          Journal of Sociology* 36:74–80.
Bohannan, C. D.
   1928   *Report on Survey of Chacon, New Mexico Community.*
          Auspices of the Presbyterian Church in the U.S.A. (mimeo.).
Breese, Gerald
   1966   *Urbanization in Newly Developing Countries.* Englewood
          Cliffs, N.J.: Prentice-Hall.
Broadbent, Elizabeth
   1941   "Mexican Population in the Southwestern United States,"
          Texas Geographic Magazine 5:16–24.
Broom, Leonard, and Eshref Shevky
   1952   "Mexicans in the United States: a Problem in Social Differ-
          entiation," *Sociology and Social Research* 36:150–158.
Brown, F. J.
   1945   "Spanish Americans," in *One America* (ed. by F. J. Brown
          and Joseph S. Roucek). New York: Prentice-Hall.
Bunting, Bainbridge
   1964   *Taos Adobes.* Santa Fe: Museum of New Mexico Press.

Burma, John H.
   1949   "Present Status of the Spanish-Americans of New Mexico,"
          Social Forces 28:133–138.
   1954   *Spanish-speaking Groups in the United States.* Durham:
          Duke University.
Burma, John H. and David E. Williams
   1962   "An Economic, Social, and Educational Survey of Rio Arriba
          and Taos Counties." El Rito, New Mexico: Northern New
          Mexico State College (mimeo.).
Butterworth, D. S.
   1962   "A Study of the Urbanization Process Among Mixtec Mi-
          grants from Tilantongo in Mexico City," *América Indígena*
          22:257–274.
Callon, Milton W.
   1962   *Las Vegas, New Mexico—The Town That Wouldn't Gam-
          ble.* Las Vegas: Las Vegas Publishing Company.
Carter, Genevieve Wiley
   1936   "Juvenile Delinquency in Bernalillo County," *Research*
          1:45–69.
Cassel, Virginia
   1956   "Cultural Change Among Spanish-American Aid-to-De-
          pendent-Children Clients." Unpublished Master's thesis,
          University of New Mexico.
Castañeda, Pedro de
   1904   *The Journey of Coronado 1540–1542* (trans. and ed. by
          George Parker Winship). New York: A. S. Barnes and Com-
          pany.
Chambers, R. L.
   1949   "The New Mexico Pattern," *Common Ground* 9:20–27.
Charles, Ralph
   1940   "Development of the Partido System in the New Mexico
          Sheep Industry." Unpublished Master's thesis, University of
          New Mexico.
Chavez, Fray Angelico
   1954   *Origins of New Mexico Families.* Santa Fe: Historical So-
          ciety of New Mexico.
Cochrane, Leon John
   1915   "A Social Survey of Dona Ana County." Unpublished
          Master's thesis, New Mexico State University, Las Cruces.

Cocklin, H. W., and A. F. Geiger
1965 "Dormant Energy Awakens in the Four Corners," *New Mexico Business* 18(12):5–10.

Community Survey Committee
1965 Report of the Community Survey Committee: Health, Welfare, Education. Albuquerque.

Cordova, Alfred G., and Charles Judah
1952 *Octaviano Ambrosio Larrazolo, the Prophet of Transition in New Mexico, an Analysis of his Political Life.* Albuquerque: Division of Government Research, University of New Mexico, Publ. No. 32.

Cottrell, Fred
1955 *Energy and Society.* New York: McGraw-Hill Book Company.

Culbert, James
1943 "Distribution of Spanish-American Population in New Mexico," *Economic Geography* 19:171–176.

D'Antonio, William V., and Julian Samora
1962 "Occupational Stratifications in Four Southwestern Communities," *Social Forces* 41:18–25.

De Onis, Frederico
1942 "Spain and the Southwest," in *Cultural Bases of Hemispheric Understanding,* papers read at a Conference on Latin-American Culture. Austin: Institute of Latin American Studies, University of Texas.

Dickerson, R. E.
1919 "Some Suggestive Problems in the Americanization of Mexicans," *Pedagogical Seminary* 26(3):288–297.

Dickey, Roland F.
1949 *New Mexico Village Arts.* Albuquerque: University of New Mexico Press.

Donnelly, Thomas C. (ed.)
1940 *Rocky Mountain Politics.* Albuquerque: University of New Mexico Press.

Dozier, Edward P.
1961 "The Rio Grande Pueblos," in *Perspectives in American Indian Culture Change* (ed. by Edward H. Spicer). Chicago: University of Chicago Press.

1966   "Factionalism at Santa Clara Pueblo," *Ethnology* 5(2):172–185.

Edmonson, Munro S.

1957   *Los Manitos: a Study of Institutional Values.* New Orleans: Middle American Research Institute, Tulane University.

Ellis, Florence Hawley

1955   "Tome and Father J.B.R.," *New Mexico Historical Review* 30(2):89–114; (3):195–220.

Ellis, Helen H.

1948   *Public Welfare Problems in New Mexico.* Albuquerque: Division of Government Research, University of New Mexico, Publ. No. 18.

Embudo Report

See under *Pilot Planning.*

Fergusson, Erna

1928   "New Mexico's Mexicans," *Century* 116:437–444.

1935   "Tearing Down the West," *Yale Review,* n.s., 25:331–343.

1940   *Our Southwest.* New York: Alfred Knopf.

Fergusson, Harvey

1925   "Out Where the Bureaucracy Begins," *Nation* 121:112–114.

1933   *Rio Grande.* New York: Alfred Knopf.

Fierman, Floyd S.

1964   "The Spiegelbergs of New Mexico, Merchants and Bankers, 1844–1893," *Southwestern Studies* 1(4):3–48.

Foscue, E. J.

1931   "The Mesilla Valley of New Mexico, A Study in Aridity and Irrigation," *Economic Geography* 7:1–21.

Foster, George M.

1953a "Relations Between Spanish and Spanish-American Folk Medicine," *Journal of American Folklore* 66:201–218.

1953b "What is Folk Culture?" *American Anthropologist* 55(2):159–173.

Francis, E. K.

1956   "Multiple Intergroup Relations in the Upper Rio Grande Region," *American Sociological Review* 21:84–87.

Fried, Jacob

1959   "Acculturation and Mental Health among Migrants in Peru," in *Culture and Mental Health* (ed. by Marvin Opler). New York: Macmillan Co.

Gamio, Manuel

1930 *Mexican Immigration to the United States: A Study of Human Migration and Adjustment.* Chicago: University of Chicago Press.

Gans, Herbert

1959 *The Urban Villagers.* Boston: Center for Community Studies.

Gilbert, Fabiola Cabeza de Baca

1954 *We Fed Them Cactus.* Albuquerque: University of New Mexico Press.

Gleason, H. A.

1961 *An Introduction to Descriptive Linguistics,* rev. ed. New York: Holt, Rinehart and Winston.

Goldschmidt, Walter

1947 *As You Sow.* New York: Harcourt, Brace and Co.

González, Nancie Solien de

1961 "Family Organization in Five Types of Migratory Wage Labor," *American Anthropologist* 63(6):1264–1280.

1966 "A Nativistic Movement in New Mexico." Paper delivered at the 37th International Congress of Americanists, Argentina, Sept., 1966.

Gordon, B. L., and J. L. McConville

1965 *Human Ecology of the Upper Rio Grande Basin.* Ms. in possession of authors.

Grebler, Leo

1966 *Mexican Immigration to the United States: the Record and Its Implications.* ("Mexican-American Study Project.") Los Angeles: Graduate School of Business Administration, University of California, Advance Report 2.

Greer, Richard R.

1942 "Origins of the Foreign-born Population of New Mexico During the Territorial Period," *New Mexico Historical Review* 17:281–287.

Hamilton, David

1957–58 "New Mexico's New Industrial Revolution," *New Mexico Quarterly* 27(4):322–326.

Hammel, Eugene A.

1964 "Some Characteristics of Rural Village and Urban Slum

Populations on the Coast of Peru," *Southwestern Journal of Anthropology* 20(4):346–358.

Harper, Allen G., A. R. Codova, and Kalervo Oberg
  1943   *Man and Resources in the Middle Rio Grande Valley.* Albuquerque: University of New Mexico Press.

Hauser, Philip M. (ed.)
  1961   *Urbanization in Latin America.* New York: International Documents Service, Columbia University Press.

Hawkins, Lina J.
  1966   "The AEC in New Mexico," *New Mexico Business* 19(4):5–10.

Hawley, Florence, and D. Senter
  1946   "Group-Designed Behavior Patterns in Two Acculturating Groups," *Southwestern Journal of Anthropology* 2(2):133–151.

Heller, Celia S.
  1966   *Mexican American Youth: Forgotten Youth at the Crossroads.* New York: Random House.

Hill, Gladwin
  1965   "The Political Role of Mexican-Americans," in *Minority Problems* (ed. by Arnold M. Rose and Caroline B. Rose). New York: Harper and Row.

Holmes, Jack Ellsworth
  1967   *Politics in New Mexico.* Albuquerque: University of New Mexico Press.

Horn, Calvin
  1963   *New Mexico's Troubled Years, The Story of the Early Territorial Governors.* Albuquerque: Horn and Wallace.

Hurt, Wesley Robert, Jr.
  1941   "Manzano: a Study of Community Disorganization." Unpublished Master's thesis, University of New Mexico.

Irion, F. C.
  1959   *New Mexico and Its Natural Resources, 1900–2000.* Albuquerque: University of New Mexico Press.

Jaramillo, Cleofas M.
  1941   *Shadows of the Past.* Santa Fe: Seton Village Press.

Johansen, Sigurd Arthur
  1941a   *Recent Population Changes in New Mexico.* Las Cruces:

New Mexico Agricultural Experimental Station, New Mexico State University, Press Bull. 931.

1941b "Rural Social Organization in a Spanish-American Culture Area." Unpublished Ph.D. dissertation, University of Wisconsin, Madison.

1942 "The Social Organization of Spanish-American Villages," *Southwestern Social Science Quarterly* 23:151–159.

1943 "Family Organization in a Spanish-American Culture Area," *Society and Social Research* 28:123–131.

1948 *Rural Social Organization in a Spanish American Culture Area.* Albuquerque: University of New Mexico Press, University of New Mexico Publications in Social Sciences and Philosophy, No. 1.

Johnson, Irma Y.

1948 "A Study of Certain Changes in the Spanish-American Family in Bernalillo County, 1915–1946." Unpublished Master's thesis, University of New Mexico.

Jones, Hester

1932 "Uses of Wood by the Spanish Colonists in New Mexico," *New Mexico Historical Review* 18:273–291.

Judah, Charles B.

1961 *Recruitment of Candidates from the Northern and Eastern Counties to the New Mexico House of Representatives, 1956.* Albuquerque: Division of Government Research, University of New Mexico, Publ. No. 59.

Keleher, William A.

1929 "Law of the New Mexico Land Grant," *New Mexico Historical Review* 12(4):350–371.

1945 *The Fabulous Frontier.* Santa Fe: Rydal Press.

1957 *Violence in Lincoln County 1869–1881.* Albuquerque: University of New Mexico Press.

Kluckhohn, Clyde, and Dorothea Leighton

1951 *The Navaho.* Cambridge, Mass.: Harvard University Press.

Kluckhohn, Florence R., and Fred L. Strodtbeck

1961 *Variations in Value Orientations.* Evanston: Row, Peterson and Co.

Knowlton, Clark S.

1961 "The Spanish Americans in New Mexico," *Sociology and Social Research* 45(4):448–454.

1967 "Land-Grant Problems among the State's Spanish-Americans," *New Mexico Business* 20(6):1–13.

Kroeber, A. L.

1917 "Zuni Kin and Clan," *Anthropological Papers of the American Museum of Natural History* 18:ii,39–204.

Kutsche, Paul

1968 "The Anglo Side of Acculturation," *Proceedings* of the 1968 Annual Spring Meeting, American Ethnological Society, Seattle, pp. 178–195.

Lahart, Edward

1958 *The Career of Dennis Chavez as a Member of Congress 1930–1934.* Albuquerque: University of New Mexico Press.

LaLonde, Peter J.

1966 "A Preliminary Report on New Mexico's Economy in 1965," *New Mexico Business* 19(1):1–7.

Larson, Olaf L.

1937 *Beet Workers on Relief in Weld County, Colorado.* Fort Collins: Colorado State Experimental Station, Rural Section, Division of Social Research, WPA.

Laughlin, Ruth

1940 "Coronado's Country and Its People," *Survey Graphic* 29:277–282.

Leonard, O. E.

1943 *The Role of the Land Grant in the Social Organization and Social Processes of a Spanish-American Village in New Mexico.* Ann Arbor: Edwards Brothers.

Leonard, Olen, and C. P. Loomis

1941 *Culture of a Contemporary Rural Community: El Cerrito, New Mexico.* Washington, D.C.: U.S. Bureau of Agriculture Economics Rural Life Studies: 1.

Lewis, Oscar

1961 *The Children of Sanchez.* New York: Random House.

Linder, Robert L.

1939 "Life Span of Business in Albuquerque, New Mexico," *New Mexico Business Review* 8:31–35.

Loar, Robert L.

1964 "Bilingualism and Verbal Comprehension." Unpublished Master's thesis, New Mexico State University.

Logan, Rayford W.
  1940 "The Negro in Spanish America," in *The Negro in the Americas*. Washington, D.C.: Published Lectures of the Division of the Social Sciences of the Graduate School, Howard University, Vol. I:24–35.

Loomis, Charles P.
  1941 "Informal Groupings in a Spanish-American Village," *Sociometry* 4(1):36–51.

  1942 "Wartime Migrations from Rural Spanish-Speaking Villages of New Mexico," *Rural Sociology* 7:384–395.

  1943 "Ethnic Cleavages in the Southwest as Reflected in Two High Schools," *Sociometry* 6(1):7–26.

  1958 "El Cerrito, New Mexico: A Changing Village," *New Mexico Historical Review* 33:53–75.

Loomis, Charles P., and Glen Grisham
  1943 "Spanish Americans: The New Mexico Experiment in Village Rehabilitation," *Applied Anthropology* 2(3):13–37.

Loomis, Charles P., and Olen E. Leonard
  1938 *Standards of Living in an Indian-Mexican Village*. Washington, D.C.: United States Department of Agriculture, Social Research Report No. 14.

Love, Joseph P.
  1969 "La Raza: Mexican Americans in Rebellion," *Trans-Action,* Feb.:35–1.

Loyola, Sister Mary
  1939 "The American Occupation of New Mexico, 1821–1852," *New Mexico Historical Review* 14:34–75; 230–286.

Lummis, Charles F.
  1893 *The Land of Poco Tiempo*. New York: Scribner's. (Reprinted 1969. Albuquerque: University of New Mexico Press.)

McWilliams, Carey
  1943 *Brothers Under the Skin*. Boston: Little Brown.

Madsen, William
  1961 *Society and Health in the Lower Rio Grande Valley*. Austin: The Hogg Foundation for Mental Health.

Maes, Ernest E.
  1935 "The Labor Movement in New Mexico," *New Mexico Business Review* 4:137–140.

1941   "The World and the People of Cundiyo," *Land Policy Review* 4:8–14.

Maloney, Thomas J.
1964   "Recent Demographic and Economic Changes in Northern New Mexico," *New Mexico Business* 17(9):2,4–14.

Mangin, William
1959   "The Role of Regional Associations in the Adaptation of Rural Population in Peru," *Sociologus* 9:21–36.

Manuel, Herschel T.
1965   *Spanish Speaking Children of the Southwest.* Austin: University of Texas Press.

Marden, Charles F., and G. Meyer
1962   *Minorities in American Society.* New York: American Book Company.

Martinez, Antonio Jose
n.d.   Pamphlet in Huntington Library, Ritch Collection Memo Book No. 4. (Microfilm), San Marino, Calif.

Maxwell, Grant
1938   "New Mexico Grows," *New Mexico Magazine* 16:13–15,47.

Mayfield, Thomas, Jr.
1938   "Education in New Mexico During the Spanish and Mexican Periods," *Research* 2(3):99–106.

Meaders, Margaret
1958   "Copper Chronicle: the Story of New Mexico 'Red Gold,'" *New Mexico Business* 11(5):2–9; (6):2–9.

Minge, Ward A.
1965   "Frontier Problems in New Mexico Preceding the Mexican War, 1840–1846." Unpublished Ph.D. dissertation, University of New Mexico.

Mittelbach, Frank G., Joan W. Moore, and Ronald McDaniel
1966   *Intermarriage of Mexican-Americans.* ("Mexican-American Study Project.") Los Angeles: Graduate School of Business Administration, University of California, Advance Report No. 6.

Moore, Frank C.
1947   "San Jose, 1946, a Study in Urbanization." Unpublished Master's thesis, University of New Mexico.

Moore, Joan W., and Ralph Guzman
 1966 "New Wind from the Southwest," *The Nation,* May 30, 1966:645–648.
Moore, John M. (ed.)
 1962 *Who Is Who in New Mexico.* Albuquerque: privately printed.
Murbarbarger, Nell
 1964 *Ghosts of the Adobe Walls.* Los Angeles: Westernlore Press.
Neal, Helen Davis
 1951 "A Study of Some of the Characteristics of the Broken Homes of Aid to Dependent Children Recipients in San Miguel and Mora Counties, New Mexico." Unpublished Master's thesis, New Mexico State University, Las Cruces.
New Mexico Rural Council Study
 n.d. *San Geronimo.* San Miguel County, New Mexico.
Oberg, Kalervo
 1940 "Cultural Factors and Land-use Planning in Cuba Valley, New Mexico," *Rural Sociology* 5:438–448.
Officer, James E.
 1964 "Sodalities and Systematic Linkage: The Joining Habits of Urban Mexican-Americans." Unpublished Ph.D. dissertation, University of Arizona.
Oppenheimer, Alan James
 1957 "An Ethnological Study of Tortugas, New Mexico." Unpublished Master's thesis, University of New Mexico.
Ortega, Joaquin
 1941 *The Compulsory Teaching of Spanish in the Grade Schools of New Mexico: an Expression of Opinion.* Albuquerque: University of New Mexico Press.
Pearce, T. M. (ed.)
 1965 *New Mexico Place Names.* Albuquerque: University of New Mexico Press.
Perrigo, Lynn I.
 1960 *Texas and Our Spanish Southwest.* Dallas: Banks Upshaw and Company.
Pilot Planning (Embudo Report)
 1961 A Pilot Planning Project for the Embudo Watershed of New Mexico. By the Interagency Council for Area Develop-

ment Planning and New Mexico State Planning Office, Santa Fe.

Potts, Alfred M.

1959   *A Social Profile of Agricultural Migratory People in Colorado.* ("Migrant Education Research Project," Resource Report E-1.) Denver Office of Instructional Services, Colorado State Department of Education.

Rahm, Father Harold J.

1958   *Office in the Alley.* Austin: University of Texas Press.

Ramsay, Dwight M., Jr.

1951   "A Statistical Survey of Voting Behavior in New Mexico." Unpublished Master's thesis, University of New Mexico.

Redfield, Robert

1934   *The Folk Culture of Yucatan.* Chicago: The Free Press.

1953   *The Primitive World and Its Transformations.* Ithaca: Cornell University Press.

Reeve, Frank Driver

1946   *New Mexico: Yesterday and Today.* Albuquerque: Division of Government Research, University of New Mexico, Publ. No. 5.

Rendon, Gabino

1953   *Hand on My Shoulder.* New York: Board of National Missions, The United Presbyterian Church in the U.S.A.

Rideling, William H.

1876   "A Trail in the Far Southwest," *Harper's New Monthly Magazine* 53:15–24.

Romano, Octavio

1968   "The Anthropology and Sociology of the Mexican Americans: the Distortion of Mexican American History," *El Grito,* fall 1968:13–26.

Rusinow, Irving

1938   "Spanish Americans in New Mexico," *Survey Graphic* 27:95–99.

Rubel, Arthur J.

1965   "The Mexican American Palomilla," *Anthropological Linguistics* 7(4):92,97. Also: University of Texas Institute of Latin-American Studies Offprint No. 16.

1966   *Across the Tracks: Mexican Americans in a Texas City.* Austin: University of Texas Press.

Russell, John C.
  1938 "Racial Groups in the New Mexico Legislature." *Annals* of the American Academy of Political and Social Science 195:62–71.

Samora, Julian
  1953 "Minority Leadership in a Bi-cultural Community." Unpublished Ph.D. dissertation, Washington University, St. Louis.
  1963 "The Educational Status of a Minority," in *Theory into Practice* 2:144–150.

Samora, J. (ed.)
  1968 *La Raza: Forgotten Americans.* Notre Dame: University of Notre Dame.

Sanchez, George I.
  1940 *Forgotten People: A Study of New Mexicans.* Albuquerque: University of New Mexico Press.

Sanchez, George Isidore, and Howard Putnam (eds.)
  1959 *Materials Relating to the Education of Spanish-speaking People in the United States; an Annotated Bibliography.* Austin: University of Texas Press.

Saunders, Lyle
  1950 "The Social History of Spanish-speaking People in the Southwestern United States Since 1846." *Proceedings* of the First Congress of Historians from Mexico and the United States, Monterrey, Sept. 4–9. *Editorial Culture, Mexico, 1950:* 152–165.
  1954 *Cultural Difference and Medical Care; the Case of the Spanish-speaking People of the Southwest.* New York: Russell Sage Foundation.

Saunders, L., and J. Samora
  1955 "A Medical Care Program in Colorado County," in *Health, Culture, and Community: Case Studies of Public Reactions to Health Programs* (ed. by B. D. Paul). New York: Russell Sage Foundation.

Scotford, John Ryland
  1953 *Within These Borders, Spanish-speaking Peoples in the U.S.A.* New York: Friendship Press.

Senter, Donovan
  1945 "Acculturation among New Mexican Villagers in Compari-

son to Adjustment Patterns of other Spanish-Speaking Americans," *Rural Sociology* 10(1):31–47.

Shannon, Lyle W.

1965   "Economic Absorption and Cultural Integration of the Urban Newcomer," in *Emerging Problems in Housing and Urban Redevelopment.* Iowa City: Institute of Public Affairs, University of Iowa, pp. 24–46.

Sharp, Harry, and Morris Axelrod

1956   "Mutual Aid Among Relatives in an Urban Population," in *Principles of Sociology,* rev. ed. (by Ronald Freedman, *et al.,* New York: Holt.

Shinkle, James D.

1964   *Fifty Years of Roswell History—1867–1917.* Roswell: Hall-Poorbaugh Press.

Sifuentes, Fernando

1940   "A Comparative Study of New Mexican and Mexican Popular Songs." Unpublished Master's thesis, University of New Mexico.

Simmons, Marc

1965   "Spanish Government in New Mexico at the End of the Colonial Period." Unpublished Ph.D. dissertation, University of New Mexico. (Published 1968—*Spanish Government in New Mexico.* Albuquerque: University of New Mexico Press.)

Sjoberg, Gideon

1947   "Cultural Change and Its Influence upon the Family as Revealed by a Study of Relief Clients in a Suburban New Mexico Community." Unpublished Master's thesis, University of New Mexico.

Smith, Joel, William Form, and Gregory Stone

1954   "Local Intimacy in a Middle-Sized City," *American Journal of Sociology* 60:276–284.

Smith, M. W.

1959   "Towards a Classification of Cult Movements," *Man* 59:8–12.

Spicer, Edward B.

1954   "Spanish Indian Acculturation in the Southwest," *American Anthropologist* 56(4):663–678.

Stevens, Rev. J. Paul
  1964 "Changes in Land Tenure and Usage among the Indians and Spanish Americans in Northern New Mexico," in *Indian and Spanish American Adjustments to Arid and Semiarid Environments* (ed. by Clark S. Knowlton). Lubbock: Texas Technological College.

Stevenson, Philip
  1936 "Deporting Jesus," *The Nation* 143:67–69.

Stowell, Jay S.
  1920 *A Study of Mexicans and Spanish Americans in the United States.* New York: Home Missions Council.

Swadesh, Frances L.
  1964a *Kin, Residential and Community Units of Tri-Ethnic Community Hispanos and Their Ancestors, A Population Study in Time Depth.* Boulder: Research Report No. 43, Tri-Ethnic Research Project, University of Colorado (mimeo.).
  1964b *Property and Kinship in Northern New Mexico.* Boulder: Research Report No. 44, Tri-Ethnic Research Project, University of Colorado (mimeo.).
  1966 *Hispanic Americans of the Ute Frontier from the Chama Valley to the San Juan Basin 1694–1960.* Boulder: Research Report No. 50, Tri-Ethnic Research Project, University of Colorado.
  1968 "The Alianza Movement: Catalyst for Social Change in New Mexico," *Proceedings* of the 1968 Annual Spring Meeting, American Ethnological Society, Seattle, pp. 162–177.

Swayne, James B.
  1936 "A Survey of the Economic, Political, and Legal Aspects of the Labor Problem in New Mexico." Unpublished Master's thesis, University of New Mexico.

Talbert, Robert Harris
  1955 *Spanish-name People in the Southwest and West; Socioeconomic Characteristics of White Persons of Spanish Surname in Texas, Arizona, California, Colorado, and New Mexico.* (Prepared for Texas Good Neighbor Foundation, Fort Worth.) Fort Worth: Leo Patishman Foundation, Texas Christian University.

Tannenbaum, Frank
   1947   *Slave and Citizen, The Negro in the Americas.* New York:
          Alfred Knopf.
Tireman, L. S.
   1930   "Reading in the Elementary Schools of New Mexico,"
          Elementary School Journal 30:621–626.
Twitchell, Ralph Emerson
   1914   *The Spanish Archives of New Mexico; Annotated and
          Chronologically Arranged with Historical, Geneaological,
          Geographical and Other Annotations* . . . (2 vols.). Cedar
          Rapids: Torch Press.
Ulibarri, Horacio
   1958   *The Effect of Cultural Difference in Education of Spanish
          Americans.* Albuquerque: University of New Mexico, Col-
          lege of Education.
U.S. Department of Commerce, Bureau of the Census
   1963   Census of Population: 1960, *Subject Reports, Persons of
          Spanish Surname* (Final Report PC(2)-1B.) Washington,
          D.C.: U.S. Government Printing Office.
U.S. Dept. of Agriculture, Forest Service
   1964   *National Forest Areas.* Washington, D.C.: U.S. Government
          Printing Office.
U.S. Dept. of Agriculture, Soil Conservation Service
   1935a *Preliminary Report on Concho.* Reg. Bull. No. 29, Cons.
          Economics Series No. 2.
   1935b *Rural Rehabilitation in New Mexico.* Reg. Bull. No. 50,
          Cons. Economics Series No. 23.
   1937a *A Report on the Cuba Valley.* Reg. Bull. No. 36, Cons.
          Economics Series No. 9.
   1937b *Tenant Herding in the Cuba Valley.* Reg. Bull. No. 37,
          Cons. Economics Series No. 10.
   1937c *Destruction of Villages as San Marcial.* Reg. Bull. No. 38,
          Cons. Economics Series No. 11.
   1937d *Population of the Upper Rio Grande Watershed.* Reg. Bull.
          No. 43, Cons. Economics Series No. 16.
   1937e *Village Livelihood in the Upper Rio Grande Area and A
          Note on the Level of Village Livelihood in the Upper Rio*

Grande Area. Reg. Bull. No. 44, Cons. Economics Series No. 17.

1937f Village Dependence on Migratory Labor in the Upper Rio Grande Area. Reg. Bull. No. 47, Cons. Economics Series No. 20.

1937g Notes on Community-owned Land Grants in New Mexico. Reg. Bull. No. 48, Cons. Economics Series No. 2.

University of New Mexico

1935 Biennial Reports, 1933–1935.

Van Dresser, Peter

1964 "The Bio-Economic Community: Reflections on a Development Philosophy for a Semiarid Environment," in Indian and Spanish American Adjustments to Arid and Semiarid Environments (ed. by Clark S. Knowlton). Lubbock: Texas Technological College.

Vincent, Maria

1966 "Ritual Kinship in an Urban Setting: Martineztown, New Mexico." Unpublished Master's thesis, University of New Mexico.

Vogt, Evon Z.

1955 Modern Homesteaders: The Life of a Twentieth Century Frontier Community. Cambridge, Mass.: Belknap Press.

Waggoner, Laura

1941 "San Jose, A Study in Urbanization." Unpublished Master's thesis, University of New Mexico.

Walker, E. S. Johnny

1966 "The Scope of Federal Defense-Related Activity in New Mexico," New Mexico Business 19(4)1–5.

Wallace, A. C.

1956 "Revitalization Movements," American Anthropologist 58:264–281.

Walter, Paul A., Jr.

1938 "A Study of Isolation and Social Change in Three Spanish-Speaking Villages of New Mexico." Unpublished Ph.D. dissertation, Stanford University.

1939 "The Spanish-speaking Community in New Mexico," Sociology and Social Research 24:150–157.

1947 "Population Trends in New Mexico," in The Population of

New Mexico. Albuquerque: Division of Government Research, University of New Mexico, Publ. No. 10.

1952   *Race and Cultural Relations*. New York: McGraw-Hill.

Watson, James B., and Julian Samora

1954   "Subordinate Leadership in a Bicultural Community," *American Sociological Review* 19(4):413–421.

Weaver, Thomas

1965   "Social Structure, Change and Conflict in a New Mexico Village." Unpublished Ph.D. dissertation, University of California.

Weeks, Douglas

1929   "The L.U.L.A.C.," *Southwestern Political and Social Science Quarterly* 10(3):257–278.

Welch, Vernon E.

1950   "Las Vegas and the Adjacent Area During the Mexican Period." Las Vegas, N.Mex.: Ms. on file at Highlands University Library.

Westphall, Victor

1947   "History of Albuquerque 1870–1880." Unpublished Master's thesis, University of New Mexico.

Whiteman, Laura M.

1941   "Economic and Social Status of Wards in State Welfare Home for Girls." Unpublished Master's thesis, University of New Mexico.

Whyte, William Foote

1955   *Street-Corner Society: The Social Structure of an Italian Slum*. Chicago: University of Chicago Press.

Winnie, Wm. W., Jr.

1955   "The Hispanic People of New Mexico." Unpublished Master's thesis, University of Florida.

1960   "The Spanish Surname Criterion for Identifying Hispanos in the Southwestern United States: A Preliminary Evaluation," *Social Forces* 38:363–366.

Wirth, Louis

1938   "Urbanism as a Way of Life," *American Journal of Sociology* 44:1–24.

Wolff, Kurt H.
  1950 "Culture Change in Loma: a Preliminary Research Report,"
        Ohio Journal of Science 50:53–59.
Woodward, Dorothy
  1935 "The Penitentes of New Mexico." Unpublished Ph.D. dis-
        sertation, Yale University.
Young, Michael, and Peter Willmott
  1957 *Family and Kinship in East London*. London: Routledge
        and Kegan Paul, Ltd.
Zeleny, Carolyn
  1944 "Relations Between the Spanish-Americans and Anglo-
        Americans in New Mexico. A Study of Conflict and Accom-
        modation in a Dual-Ethnic Relationship." Unpublished Ph.D.
        dissertation, Yale University.
Zunser, H.
  1935 "A New Mexican Village," *Journal of American Family*
        48:125–178.

INDEX

Abiquiu, 26, 42

Abousleman, Michel D., 161

Acculturation, 83, 136, 155, 157, 164, 194, 200, 211

Adams, Eleanor, 87

AFL-CIO, 93

Agriculture, 5, 9, 11, 121; dry farming, 8, 10, 50, 125, 204; irrigated farms, 10, 11, 120; small farmers, 39, 44, 76, 121, 122

Agringado, 77, 82, 164, 205

Aid to Dependent Children (ADC), 91, 129, 130

Alamogordo, 11, 133, 158

Albuquerque, 5, 11, 13, 33, 38, 61, 87, 92, 108, 114, 125, 132, 134, 137, 139, 140, 142, 143, 144, 145, 147, 148, 155, 158, 161, 162, 163, 164, 173, 174, 186, 188; population, 12, 132

Albuquerque City Directory and Business Guide, 1907, 157

Albuquerque Civic Symphony, 110

Albuquerque Journal, xii, 18

Albuquerque Ministerial Alliance, 174

Albuquerque Symphony Women's Association, 109

Alianza (*Alianza Federal de Mercedes,* Federal Alliance of Land Grants, *Alianza de los Pueblos,* Alliance of Free City-States), 82, 94, 95, 97, 98, 99, 100, 101, 102, 103, 104, 105, 106, 107, 114, 181, 182, 183, 184, 185, 186, 189, 191, 205; constitution, 100; goals, 95–96, 97; membership, 97; protest march, 98

Alianza (magazine), 88, 89

Alianza Hispano-Americana, 88–89

Americanizado, 77

American Legion, 80, 107, 180

Anglos, x, xiii, xiv, 8, 9, 10, 11, 12, 18, 21, 24, 25, 28, 49, 50, 62, 72, 73, 74, 78, 81, 83, 118, 127, 128, 133, 164, 180, 187, 201, 202, 203, 204, 209, 210, 211, 212, 213

Arcabuceros, 34

Arizona, 36, 95, 155, 166

Armstrong, Patricia Cadigan, 80, 107

Arsdale, Jonathan Van, 119, 120

237

Artesia, 158
Association of Mexican-American Educators, 92
Atchison, Topeka and Santa Fe Railroad, 119
Atencio, Tomas C., 61, 63
Atrisco, 6, 131
Austin, Mary, 34, 80, 203
Axelrod, Morris, 137

Baca Grant, 79, 117
Bailey, Jessie Bromilow, 35, 37
Bancroft, Hubert H., 7, 26, 43
Bandera Americana, 18
Barca, Madame Calderon de la, 88
Barela, Fred, 17
Barker, Ruth Laughlin, xi, 18. *See also* Laughlin, Ruth
Barrett, Donald N., 17, 126, 129, 131, 136, 152, 154, 155
Barrios, 70, 186, 189
Belen, 6, 26, 42
Bergere, A. M., 79, 117
Bernalillo, 5, 36
Bernalillo County, 23, 40, 130, 210
Bernalillo County Juvenile Detention Home (Juvenile Detention Home), 145, 146
Bilingualism, xii, 18, 21, 22, 192
Billy the Kid, xiii, 49
Blackmar, Frank W., 39
Black Panthers, 186
Bodine, John J., 188
Bogardus, Emory S., 207
Bohannan, C. D., 173
Boys' Club of America, 144; Albuquerque branch, 144–45
Braceros, 120
Brown Berets, 182, 186, 189, 191
Brown, F. J., 89
Bunting, Bainbridge, 33

Burma, John H., 17, 52, 96, 122, 124, 130, 131, 149, 150, 154, 207, 208

Los Caballeros de Labor, 92
Los Caballeros de Nueva España, 182–83, 188
California, 72, 82, 83, 95, 106, 119, 120, 124, 166, 181, 186, 201, 202, 210; immigration to, 125, 199
Callon, Milton W., 117
Campesino, 43
Carlsbad, 24, 158
Carson National Forest, 52
Carter, Genevieve Wiley, 138
Cassel, Virginia, 60, 130
Castañeda, Pedro de, 6
Catholics, 59, 74, 88, 96, 103, 161, 173, 174, 175; the church, 41, 118, 148, 166, 167; Pueblo converts, 75; Pueblo missions, 87, 212
Cattle. *See* Livestock industry
Causa, 181
Cebolleta, 42
Chacon, 173
Chacon, Sen. Mathias, xii
Chamber of Commerce, 109
Chamuscado, x
Charles, Ralph, 45, 47, 48, 66
Charro, 190
Chavez, Cesar, 181, 183, 184
Chavez, Fray Angelico, 26, 33, 87, 88, 118
Chavez, Sen. Dennis, 16, 21
Chavez, Sen. Tibo, xii
Chicano, 187, 189, 190, 191, 193
Chicanos, 141
"Chicano Youth Liberation Conference," 190
Chihuahua, Mexico, 37
Chimayo, 35

Civilian Conservation Corps (CCC), 123

Civil rights, 181, 182, 183

Civil War, 25, 36, 118, 165

Class conflicts: lower class, 16, 30, 45, 51, 59, 76, 77, 78, 79, 81, 82, 99, 102, 163, 191, 192, 200, 205, 208, 209; middle class, 74, 76, 77, 78, 81, 83, 111, 138–39, 163, 164, 193, 205, 210; upper class, 29–30, 35, 36, 37, 46, 59, 61, 75, 76, 79, 81, 83, 102, 138–39, 156, 209, 210

Clovis, 158

Cochrane, Leon John, 89, 113, 150, 172

Cocklin, H. W., 9

Cofradía, 41, 87

Colfax County, 90, 92

College of Santa Fe (St. Michael's College), 149–50

Colorado, 40, 88, 95, 109, 120, 121, 124, 127, 155, 166, 181

Los Comancheros del Norte, 183, 189

Commission on Civil Rights, 103

Community Council, 90

Community ties, 63, 64, 65, 66, 128, 131, 137

Compadrazgo, 41, 63, 131, 137

Compadres, 109, 148

La conducta, 29, 41

La Confraternidad de Nuestro Padre Jesus Nazareno, 87

Confraternidades, 87

Confraternity of the Blessed Sacrament, 87

Confraternity of Our Lady of Light, 87

Confraternity of the Poor Souls, 87

Confraternity of the Rosary, 87

Constitución Nacional de la Alianza Federal de Mercedes, 100

El cordon, 29

Cordova, Alfred G., 80, 119

Coronado, x; expedition, 6

Cottrell, Fred, 122

"Coyote," 166

Crusade for Justice, 190

Cruz, Pedro de la, 35

Cuba Valley, 44, 124

Culbert, James, 40

Cultural heritage, ix, x, xii, xiii, xiv, 28, 29, 30, 78, 164, 209, 210–11, 212, 213

Cutting, Sen. Bronson, 107

D'Antonio, William V., 160, 161, 206

Dawson, 120

Delano Proclamation, 181

Deming, 119

Democrats, 59, 74

Depression of the 1930's, 124, 125, 198

Dickey, Roland F., 34, 35, 40, 89, 117

Disabled Veterans, 107

Discrimination, ethnic, 73, 78, 80, 81, 82, 90, 93, 96, 100, 108, 111, 158, 191, 192, 193, 200, 203, 204, 205, 206, 207, 208

Ditch Association, 89

Dominguez, Juan, 87

Dona Ana County, 60, 172

Douglas, Ariz., 36

Dozier, Edward P., 28

Durango, Mexico, 37

Echo Amphitheater, 185

Eddy County, 92

Edmonson, Munro, S., 16, 27, 29, 54, 61, 68, 69, 82

Education, 16, 17; elementary, 101, 102, 152, 154, 155, 192; institutions of higher learning, xiii, xiv, 13, 149, 150, 152, 153, 163, 164; dropouts, 151, 152, 154, 193. *See also* colleges and universities by individual names
El Cerrito, 46, 63, 126, 130, 132
Elephant Butte Reservoir (Dam), 11, 51, 121, 122
Elks Club, 108, 110, 111
Ellis, Helen H., 173
El Paso, Texas, x, 5, 113, 144
Embudo Report, 126
Employment: in defense projects, 11, 93, 125, 199; on farms, 52, 93, 124; government jobs, 67; in industry, 132; in livestock industry, 119; as laborers, 8, 11, 24, 93; migratory labor, 124, 155, 181, 198; part-time, 10, 120; wage labor, 10, 11, 20, 54, 55, 120, 123, 125, 198, 199; women wage earners, 129
English-speaking Spanish-Americans, xii, 15, 16, 17, 18, 19, 20, 21, 101, 156, 164, 192, 201
Espanglos, 187
Espanola Valley, 12
Espejo, x
Esperanza, 146
The Establishment, 180, 187, 188
Estancia, 43; Estancia Valley, 6, 43, 79, 117

Familia, 59
Family solidarity, 42, 43, 58, 59, 60, 61, 62, 63, 65, 70, 129, 137; breakdown of, 55, 60, 129, 130, 137, 138, 144, 200–01
Farmington, 11, 158
Farm Security Administration, 90

FBI, 103
Fergusson, Erna, 7, 42, 44, 157, 203
Fergusson, Harvey, 36
F. M. Vigil land grant, 52
Folkways, xi, xiii, xiv, 13, 29, 41, 128, 175, 211, 212
Foods, xi, 28, 29, 43, 79, 102, 198
Ford Foundation, 72
"Forgotten people," 13
Foster, George M., 38
Fraternal Aid Union, 89

Gadsden Purchase, 117
Gallup, 23, 158
Gamio, Manuel, 107, 206
Gans, Herbert, 137
Gavaches, 141, 142
Gavillas, 90
Geiger, A. F., 9
Genizaros, 26, 75, 88
G. I. Forum, 91, 92, 180
Gilbert, Fabiola Cabeza de Baca, 45, 46, 50
Girls Welfare Home (State Welfare Home), 138
Gonzales, Don Jose's family, 46
Gonzales, Henry, 186
Good American Association, 91
Gordon, B. L., 12
Las Gorras Blancas (The White Caps), 90, 180
Grant County, 92
Grants, 158
Greek letter societies, 108, 111, 112, 113
Greer, Richard R., 23
Griego, Juan, 35
Gringos, 10, 189
Grisham, Glen, 90
El Grito del Norte, 189
Guadalupe County, 11

Hamilton, David, 12, 13
Harper, Allen G., 119
Heller, Celia S., 22, 25, 29, 141, 146, 147
Herrera, Marcos de, 35
Highlands University (Spanish-American School), 149
Hispano, 187
El Hispano, 19, 105
Hobbs, 158
Hollywood, Calif., 49
Holmes, Jack Ellsworth, 10, 68, 69, 92, 124, 180
Hondo River, 8
Horn, Calvin, 119
Huelga, 181
Hurt, Wesley Robert, Jr., 41, 61, 89

El Independiente, 18
Indians, x, xi, xii, xiii, 2, 6, 7, 28, 96, 100, 111, 151, 184, 204, 208, 211; arts, xiii; conquered, 44, 119, 198; culture, xiv, 27, 28, 29, 200, 211; Apache, xiii, 6, 34, 119; Comanche, 6; Mexican, 5; Navajo, xiii, 6, 9, 34, 119; Plains, 26; Pueblo, xiii, 6, 7, 26, 27, 28, 29, 37, 58–59, 75, 87, 197, 210, 211; Ute, 6
"Indo-Hispano," 184, 189
Industry, 125, 132; atomic energy, 12; cotton, 24, 121; forest products, 13, 120; government defense projects, 11, 93; handcrafts, xiii, 117; manufacturing, 13, 54; mining, 8, 9, 10, 13, 92, 93, 120; natural gas, 9; petroleum, 8, 9; tourism, xiii, 12, 13. *See also* Agriculture, Livestock industry
Inglesado, 77
Intermarriage: with Anglos, 24, 25,

80, 118, 133, 169, 170, 171, 176, 199, 201; study on, 165, 166, 167, 168, 172, 175; secular service in, 166, 175, 176; with Indians, 7, 26
Internal Revenue Service, N.M. District Office, 208

Jaramillo, Cleofas M., 29, 90
Jemez Springs, 43
Johansen, Sigurd Arthur, 11, 16, 27, 51, 60, 121
John Birch Society, 187
Johnson, Irma Y., 165, 166, 169, 175, 176
Jornada del Muerto (Journey of Death), 5
Judah, Charles B., 68, 80, 124
Junior League, 109, 208
Junior Service League, 108
Juveniles: delinquency of, 137, 138, 163; gangs of, 139, 140, 141, 142, 143, 144, 145, 146, 147

Kansas City, Mo., 8
Kearny, Gen. Stephen W., 117, 198
Keleher, William A., 8, 49
Kiwanis Club, 109
Kluckhohn, Florence R., 42, 61, 62, 128, 131
Knowlton, Clark S., 7, 17, 36, 37, 52, 122, 124, 126
Kroeber, A. L., 58

Labor unions, 92–93
LaLonde, Peter J., 9
Lamy, Bishop Jean B., 118
Land: early division of, 39, 40; family holdings, 63, 64; grazing restrictions on, 52, 53, 122; loss of,

10, 50, 51, 52–53, 61, 124, 184; overuse of, 10, 44, 51, 121, 198

Land grants, 45, 82, 96, 98, 101, 103; to individual, 45, 52, 76, 79, 117

The Land of Enchantment, xi, 164

Lane, Gov. William C., 213

Larrazolo, Octaviano A., 80

Las Cruces, 24, 158, 160, 161, 165

Las Trampas, 126; Las Trampas land grant, 52

Las Vegas (Town of Las Vegas), 6, 7, 43, 46, 125, 127, 132, 143, 158, 160, 164, 198

Latin America, influence on state, xi, xii, 29, 63, 110

Latin American Educational Foundation, 92

Latin American Research and Service Association ("LA RASA"), 72, 92

Latin Americans, 68, 150, 151, 201

Laughlin, Ruth, 122. *See also* Barker, Ruth Laughlin

Law of the Indies, 27, 95

League of United Latin American Citizens (LULAC), 91, 180, 188

Leonard, Olen E., 24, 38, 39, 40, 46, 48, 63, 64, 67, 76, 126, 132, 173

Life with Pride, 91, 180

Liga Obrera de Habla Espanol (League of Spanish-Speaking Workers), 93

Lincoln County ward, 8, 49

Linder, Robert L., 12

Little Texas, 8, 49–50, 158, 209

Livestock industry, 9, 10, 13, 43, 44, 118; cattle, 8, 10, 11, 43, 46, 49, 50, 54, 118, 119; sheep, 7, 8, 43, 44, 45, 46, 48, 54, 55, 117, 119, 122, 123, 198

Llano Estacado. See Staked Plains

Loar, Robert L., 17

Loomis, Charles P., 33, 38, 46, 60, 63, 65, 66, 67, 90, 123, 125, 126, 130, 132, 165

Los Alamos (the Atomic Energy City), 11, 132–33, 158

Love, Joseph, 183

Loyola, Sister Mary, 121

Lujan, Miguel, 35

Lulacks, 187

Luminarias, 211

McConville, J. L., 12

McKinley County, 92

McWilliams, Carey, 33

Madrid, 120

Madsen, William, 77, 173

Maes, Ernest E., 40, 92, 93

Maestas, Jose Alfredo, 185

Maloney, Thomas J., 11, 127, 128

La Mano Negra (The Black Hand), 90, 180

Manuel, Herschel T., 16, 17, 155

Manzano, 43; Water Commission, 89

Marden, Charles F., 72, 83

Mariachis, 190

Marijuana, 140, 141

Martinez, Antonio Jose, 90, 92

Martineztown, Albq., 131

Meaders, Margaret, 9

Mesilla Valley, 6, 8, 11, 51, 79, 121

Mestizo, 27, 30, 70, 75, 111, 184, 201

"Mexican-American," 184, 188

Mexican-American Political Association (MAPA), 92, 181

Mexican-American Project, 23

Mexicanos, 82, 184

Mexican period, 1821–1846, 8, 11, 43, 45, 79, 116, 117, 121, 198

Mexicans, 19, 24, 26, 119, 150, 210;

ancestry, 26; immigrants, 9, 11, 29, 82, 113, 204, 206, 209; laborers, 23, 24, 78

Mexico, x, xii, xiii, 7, 8, 9, 23, 29, 42, 75, 82, 95, 116, 117, 140, 198; allegiance to, 51, 79, 117, 118; Mexico City, 79; Valley of Mexico, 5

Meyer, G., 72, 83

Miami, 16, 23

Middle Rio Grande Conservancy District Project, 52

Minority groups, 183, 197, 200. *See also* Indians; Negroes; Spanish surnames, people with

Mittelbach, Frank G., 201

Moore, Frank C., 60, 129, 173

Moore, John M., 161

Mora, 6

Mora County, 90, 130

Mora land grant, 52

Murbarbarger, Nell, 36

Mutual-aid societies, 86, 89, 90, 91; credit unions, 137, 147, 148, 149

National forests, 52, 53, 122; claimed by Alianza, 98

National Youth Administration (NYA), 123

Neal, Helen Davis, 130

Negroes, xiii, 26, 96, 99, 103, 111, 142, 204, 208, 209

The New Mexican, 18–19; *The Sunday New Mexican,* 19

New Mexico Credit Union League, 148, 149

"The New Mexico legend," x

New Mexico State University (New Mexico State College), 150, 151

Newsweek, 181

New York, N.Y., 18, 23

Northern New Mexico State School (El Rito Normal School), 150

El Nuevo Mexicano, 18, 19

Oberg, Kalervo, 119, 124

Office of Economic Opportunity, 90, 187

Officer, James E., 109

Oklahoma, 8, 119

Oñate, Don Juan de, x, 5, 33

Oppenheimer, Alan James, 16

Orden Hijos de America (Sons of America), 91

"Oreo Cookies," 187

Ortega, Joaquin, 156

Palomilla, 146

Pan American Round Table, 110

Partidario, 119

Partido, 46, 47, 48

Patron, 45, 48

Patronship, 41, 45, 46, 48, 63, 65, 66, 67, 68, 69, 70, 86, 129

Peace Corps, 90

Pechucos, 141

Pecos River, 12, 40

Penitentes (Penitente Brotherhood), 41, 87–88, 104, 118

Peoples Constitutionalist Party, 184, 185, 186

Petroleum Club, 109

Phoenix, Ariz., 61

Phrateres, 108

Pinos Altos Mountains, 88

La Plaza de Missouri, 8

Plumas de Umas (Pens of the United Mexican-American Students), 190

Politics, 67, 68, 69, 157
Poor People's March, 182, 186
Population, 12, 23, 125, 127, 132.
    See also U.S. Census of Popula-
    tion
Porticos, 42
Potts, Alfred M., 155
President of the United States, 98
Primos hermanos, 59
Professions, 137, 152, 157, 158, 160,
    161, 162
La propia lengua, 129
Protestants, 59, 74, 77, 95, 161, 166,
    167, 173, 174, 175
PTA meetings, 114
Pueblo Revolt of 1680, x, 33
Puerto Ricans, 19–20, 23, 145

Racial ancestry, x, xi, 7, 8, 26, 27,
    45, 71, 78, 95–96, 112, 184, 197,
    207, 210
Rahm, Fr. Harold J., 113, 114, 144
Railroads, 10, 44, 52, 119, 120
Ramsay, Dwight M., Jr., 69
La raza, 70, 71, 72, 73, 74, 75, 83,
    107, 166, 172, 194, 205
Reclamation, 11, 52, 121, 122
Reconquest of 1692, x
Redfield, Robert, 38
Religion, xi, 41, 137, 173. See also
    Catholics, Protestants
Rendon, Gabino, 8
Republicans, 59, 74
Retablos, 39, 211
Revolt of 1847, 79, 117, 118
Ricos, 46, 79, 118
Rideling, William H., 17, 156
Rio Arriba County, 154
Rio Chama, 5, 6
Rio Grande, 5, 6, 8, 37, 40, 79, 121;

Rio Grande Valley, 5, 12, 36, 38,
    117, 122
Rodriguez, x
Romano, Octavio, 179
Roosevelt, Franklin D., 199
Roswell, 8, 158, 160
Rotary Club, 108, 109
Rubel, Arthur J., 59, 73, 146, 147
Rural communities: agricultural, 10,
    12, 13, 41, 45; described, 35, 36,
    39, 40, 41, 42, 120; deserted, 126,
    198; family-controlled, 59, 61, 63,
    64, 65, 113, 130; isolated, 16, 28,
    38; poverty of, 122, 123, 124, 127

St. Joseph, Mo., 8
Samora, Julian, 16, 90, 93, 109, 126,
    129, 136, 152, 154, 155, 160, 161,
    201, 206
Sanchez, George, 13, 83
Sandoval County, 43
San Geronimo (New Mexico Rural
    Council Study), 126
La Sangrelidad, 64
San Jose, Albq., 62, 129
San Juan, 5
San Juan Basin, 9
San Luis Valley, Colo., 6, 8
San Marcial, 122
San Miguel County, 11, 38, 46, 90,
    124, 127, 130
Santa Barbara land grant, 52
Santa Cruz de la Canada, 87
Santa Fe, 6, 38, 40, 87, 110, 125, 127,
    158, 162, 163, 164, 198; "the Capi-
    tol crowd," 164; Chamber of
    Commerce, 163; detention home,
    138; Opera, 110; State Archives,
    204
Santa Fe National Forest (Pecos
    River Forest), 52

Santa Fe Trail, 8, 116
Santa Rita, 9
Saunders, Lyle, 90, 128, 210, 211
Scotford, J. R., 12, 132
Senter, Donovan, 76, 150, 173
Shannon, Lyle W., 211
Sharp, Harry, 137
Sheep. *See* Livestock industry
Shinkle, James D., 8
Silver City, 8, 23, 158
Simmons, Marc, 37
Sjoberg, Gideon, 17, 62, 128 129
Smith, Joel, 137
Sociedad Cervantes, 89
Sociedad Espanola de Beneficiencia Mutua, 89
Socorro, 6, 18, 36, 79, 158
Sonora, Mexico, 37
Southern Pacific Railroad, 119
Southwest Council of La Raza, 72
Spain, 7, 116, 198
Spaniards, 5, 6, 7, 8, 9, 20, 211, 212
Spanish *conquistadores,* x, xi, 81
Spanish language, xi, xii, 15, 16, 17, 18, 19, 20, 21, 71, 101, 102, 105, 193, 201
Spanish settlements, described, x, 5, 6, 7, 8, 33, 34, 35, 36, 37, 38, 39, 40, 41, 42, 46, 105
Spanish surnames, people with, ix, xii, 22, 23, 24, 71, 72, 78, 93, 110, 112, 151, 158, 160, 163, 166, 191, 208, 210
Spicer, Edward B., 75
Staked Plains (*Llano Estacado*), 7, 12
State Training School, 138
Stevens, Rev. J. Paul, 122
Stevenson, Philip, 93
Stock Association, 53
Stowell, Jay S., 18

Street Corner Offense Reduction Experiment (SCORE), 145
Strodtbeck, Fred L., 42, 128, 131
Students for a Democratic Society (SDS), 187
Swadesh, Frances L., 25, 42, 106, 183
Swayne, James B., 93

Talbert, Robert Harris, 208
Taos, 165, 188
Taos County, 90, 154
Taylor Grazing Act, 53
Texas, 8, 18, 72, 73, 82, 83, 95, 96, 106, 119, 124, 155, 166, 173, 181, 202, 210
Tewa Basin Study (U.S. Dept. of Agriculture Report 135c), 38, 123
Third Order of Saint Francis, 87
Third World Liberation Front, 187
Tierra Amarilla insurrection, 98, 122, 181, 182, 189
Tijerina, Reies, 94, 95, 97, 98, 99, 100, 103, 104, 182, 183, 185; doctrines of, 95–96, 106, 183
Tio Tomases, 187
Tireman, L. S., 17
Tome, 26
Torreon, 34
Trade, 8, 10, 116, 117, 120, 198
Treaty of Guadalupe Hidalgo, 96, 210
Twitchell, Ralph Emerson, 9

Union County, 8
United Mexican-American Students (UMAS), 182, 189, 190, 191
United Nations, 22
United States, x, xi, 12, 21, 23, 24, 27, 28, 29, 68, 82, 116, 117, 187,

210, 212; army, 44; Constitution, 96; laws, 50; territory, 117

U.S. Census of Population: 1930, 26; 1960, ix, 23, 24, 26, 124, 158

U.S. Conquest of 1846, ix, x, 9, 10, 11, 13, 44, 50, 68, 79, 117, 121, 157, 173; opposition to, 79, 117, 118, 198, 203

U.S. Dept. of Agriculture Reports: 1937, 10, 44, 47, 119, 120, 122, 123; 1963, 124

University of New Mexico, 19, 91, 102, 108, 109, 110, 111, 112, 113, 150, 151, 152, 153, 160, 189, 190, 193, 204

Upper Pecos watershed, 40, 43

Urban communities: advantages of, 128, 156, 157, 158, 160, 164, 166; changing traditional culture, 130, 173; growth of, 13, 20, 28, 126, 198; kinship-controlled, 59, 60, 61, 63, 65, 131, 137; living standards in, 17, 83, 124, 125, 126, 127, 132, 133

Utah, 127

Van Dresser, Peter, 12, 13

Vargas, Diego de, 33

Vendidos, 187, 194

Veterans of Foreign Wars, 107, 180

Vincent, Maria, 60, 63, 131, 149

Vista, 91

Vogt, Evan Z., 204

Waggoner, Laura, 173

Walter, Paul A., 24, 27, 28, 124, 128, 173

Washington, D.C., 182, 186

Water Supply Association, 89

Watson, James B., 93

Weaver, Thomas, 34, 60, 62, 63, 64, 65, 69, 89, 90, 122, 126, 127, 129

Westphall, Victor, 118

Wheatley, Sen. W. C., xii

Whiteman, Laura M., 138

White Sands, 5, 11

Who Is Who in New Mexico, 161

Who's Who in New Mexico, 161

Williams, David E., 149, 154

Wolff, Kurt H., 53, 69, 122

Woodward, Dorothy, 33

Willmott, Peter, 137

Winnie, Wm. W., Jr., 12, 22, 126, 131

Works Project Administration (WPA), 123

World War I: 24, 80, 107, 125, 170–71, 203

World War II, 13, 25, 93, 114, 125, 150, 199, 204

Young, Michael, 137

Zeleny, Carolyn, 8, 10, 27, 43, 45, 79, 83, 108, 117, 143, 165, 166, 169, 173, 203, 204, 210